Authoress, sitting with her father & mother, after her first newspaper review –

*Enid Bagnold's
Autobiography*

Also by ENID BAGNOLD

PROSE:

A Diary Without Dates
The Happy Foreigner
Serena Blandish: or the Difficulty of Getting Married
Alice and Thomas and Jane
National Velvet
The Squire
The Loved and Envied
The Girl's Journey (reprint)

PLAYS:

Lottie Dundass
National Velvet
Poor Judas
Gertie
The Chalk Garden
The Last Joke
The Chinese Prime Minister
Call Me Jacky
Four Plays (*The Chalk Garden*, *The Last Joke*, *The Chinese Prime Minister* and *Call Me Jacky* in one volume)

POETRY:

Sailing Ships

TRANSLATION:

Alexander of Asia (*Alexandre Asiatique* by Princesse Marthe Bibesco)

Enid Bagnold's Autobiography
(from 1889)

*

HEINEMANN : LONDON

William Heinemann Ltd
LONDON MELBOURNE TORONTO
JOHANNESBURG AUCKLAND

First published 1969
© Enid Bagnold 1969
434 04303 6

It may not be out of place to say that the Heinemann Windmill Colophon was originally drawn by William Nicholson in 1897 from the windows of the same Burne-Jones house from which Enid Bagnold writes. It was done at the request of William Heinemann ('for my new publishing firm') when both were guests at the house

Printed in Great Britain by
Cox & Wyman Ltd,
London, Fakenham and Reading

*To my two eldest granddaughters
Annabel and Hattie**

* Annabel Jones and Harriet d'Harcourt

Contents

Chapter One	Officers' quarters. 'Young Mrs Bagnold's little girl is very spoilt.' But not by her grandmother.	1
Two	Nine years old. My father's command in Jamaica. We return. – 'Find her a school on sandy soil.' So I go to school with the Huxleys.	13
Three	Marburg, Lausanne, Paris. Finished and burnished, but where are the men? I determine not to marry. . . . 'In between going for walks and plans to be seduced I take my bicycle to pieces.'	33
Four	The general's daughter and the colonel's daughter go to London in search of adventure.	60
Five	I return home and enter high society through the garden hedge. – Antoine Bibesco. Horrors of the telephone when used for love.	100
Six	My first book. H. G. Wells makes a small pass but a bigger friendship. I begin, after all, to get engaged to people. I meet Roderick who insists on marriage. I become Lady Jones.	128
Seven	*Grandeurs et Misères* of Lady Jones. Laurian is born. Timothy is born. Roderick buys the London house. – Riches and writing. – Can it be done?	146
Eight	Roderick buys the Rottingdean house. Richard is born. Tucker is born. The groom comes. And the horses. I write *National Velvet* and throw my tax claims away.	163
Nine	Albrecht Bernstorff makes our social life lighter in texture. At last, at last, Roderick and I like the same people. Ribbentrop dines and Hoesch dies.	178

Ten	Dogs. Kipling. Desmond MacCarthy. The last and tawdry goodbye to Antoine.	193
Eleven	Maurice Baring. Diana. Roderick comes home. I write my first play, which runs five months in London: and my second, which is a first-night failure in New York. – 'We would never have put it on,' they said, 'if we had known it was a comedy.' Back in England I finish *The Chalk Garden*. Binkie refuses it. Irene takes it for Broadway. 'But first I must work with the author.' An account of terrible battles.	209
Twelve	After two years we stand together. Casting – rehearsals – tour. The theatres of New Haven, Boston and Philadelphia grow emptier and emptier. – Triumph in New York. Triumph in London. We run twenty-three months. I have a face lift. Charles Laughton comes into my life and stirs the next play with the wrong spoon.	227
Thirteen	*The Last Joke* and the rattle of its failure. I start *The Chinese Prime Minister*. – Roderick dies, the end of my marriage. I try to save myself.	242
Fourteen	I go on with *The Chinese Prime Minister*. A New York director who 'loves the play' comes to London. We work together and discuss casting. I go to stay with the Lunts. – Ina Claire. Margaret Leighton. The running battle into the first night. The scene at Sardi's.	252
Fifteen	*The Chinese Prime Minister* in London. Nothing to be said.	266
Sixteen	The past swims up and floats on the present. Another play, another failure. I am lame, I am eighty. But to be buffeted is as new as travelling, a change of country. – The Animal Kingdom. – The water-lizard, the eremurus, the woman-companion. – The last party. Family love. The last cliff. I jump.	273
Index		289

Illustrations

Photographs

	facing page
My mother	6
My father and mother (with me)	6
Me. Aged three	6
E.B. on Queenie	7
Cold Spring House, Jamaica	7
My mother	22
Enid, nine; Ralph, three	22
Colonel Arthur Henry Bagnold, C.B., C.M.G.	23
Head by Gaudier-Brzeska	86
E.B. at about twenty	86
Walter Sickert	87
Ralph Hodgson	87
Frank Harris	87
Ralph on leave from Ypres	102
Just before I married	103
E.B. in the business man's coat and skirt	103
Roderick and I	166
Myself with Timothy, Tucker, Richard and Laurian	167
Timothy	182
Laurian	182
Richard	183
Dominick (Tucker)	183
The Library at Rottingdean	262
From Old Hall into New Hall	262
Roderick about 1951	263
Roderick with Zoë and Edward	263
Charles Laughton	278

Alan Webb and Margaret Leighton in *The Chinese Prime Minister*	278
Lucy	279

Line drawings

	page
'A curious phenomenon' (from my great-uncle's diary, 1804)	44
Two self-portraits by Lovat Fraser, 1911 and in the trenches	71
E.B. by Walter Sickert, 1913 (*originally re-produced in* The New Age)	74
'The truer, sterner, kinder friend', Lovat Fraser	76
Letter from Walter Sickert	78
Letter from W. H. Davies, 12 October 1916	81
Ralph Hodgson's dogs	82
Letter from Ralph Hodgson	84
'The Best Talker in London, with one of his best listeners', by Max Beerbohm (*by kind permission of the Trustee to the Estate of the late Max Beerbohm*)	98
One of E.B.'s drawings on publication of *A Diary Without Dates*	129
'Your servant, Madam', H. G. Wells	131
H. G. Wells and the Pursuit	133
'Lionetta', by Desmond MacCarthy, 19 May 1918	201
Endpapers by the author – drawn on the day of publication of *A Diary Without Dates, 1918*	

Chapter One

*

'You must write your autobiography.'
   'Why?'
   'You have known so many interesting people.'
'Psha!'
'Why?'
'Because I can't waste the end of my life telling you anecdotes about interesting people. I can only write about myself.'
(But oneself is so unknown. Myself has no outline.)

            *   *   *

'Things must have been different in your day.'
'The door handles were different. We used the words "scullery", "pantry" and "fingerbowl". It was known how to build a coal fire with paper and sticks. The water closet was enclosed in mahogany. The fears were the same.'
'How old are you?'
'I was born with the first motor cars, and I never thought I should die. Death is so unnatural.'
'Stop whining about death. What was your life?'
'But one doesn't want to pass on those few things, those thin facts that one remembers. My father when he was very old shrank from telling me... facts. My husband too, when he was old, had the same unwish. A life, which has steamed like manure, doesn't like to look thin.'
'Go on. Why do you stop?'
'Because there has to be an art form. Nothing can make you live again one single day, except art. Telling won't do it.

Memory isn't enough. Every day has leaked like a sieve ever since the beginning. The extraordinary thing about life is that it is made of single days – each one killed at nightfall. And the limit of looking forward is twenty-four hours. And that has made a necklace.'

*   *   *

I must be read from where I am – backwards. Otherwise it's just a story. If I don't make it work like that we are not looking out of the same window.

The Time is 1967. The Place is the house. I am alone in it. There are old nurseries, old rocking horses, damp books, tea-boxes of broken trains, iron boxes of cartridges, seven baskets of vanished dogs, the skeletons of rooks that have got down the chimneys, twenty empty loose-boxes, and I have become a woman I can't describe. I can see what I was but I have no idea what I am.

*   *   *

In 1888 my father met my mother. He was stationed at Plymouth, a major of Royal Engineers; thirty-four. She was twenty-two and a beauty, with golden hair and violet eyes. Her waist was eighteen inches.

On April 9th she wrote in her diary: 'To the Pell's Musical At Home. I sang. (*The Last Rose.*) Major Bagnoll introduced to me.'

(Below that)

'Well-made broad man, good height, brown hair tinged with red, a kind of auburn. Long fierce moustache, blue eyes.'

July 28th. 'Major Bagnold. Pleasant man.'

August 7th. 'Sprained my ankle jumping over a gate with Major Bagnold.'

September 8th. 'We went for a ride. Arthur's horse bolted twice.'

September 17th. 'Lady John Hay's Ball. I did not go as Arthur did not wish me to go without him.'

They were married on December the 10th, and went to Nice and Monte Carlo.

I was born in October of the following year, at Borstal Cottage, Rochester.

Chatham: 1894.
Parties – five-year-olds – officers' children.
'Nuts and May' – 'Oranges and Lemons' – 'Chop off her head!'. Running processions and music.
'I want to be first! I want to be liked!'
(You can't get one and keep the other.)
But elbowing, thrusting, dressed in frills, I thought you could.

* * *

'Young Mrs Bagnold's little girl is very spoilt.'
Grannie heard it and rubbed it in. That too was her opinion. If I had heard it myself I would have put out my tongue. Young Mrs Bagnold was my shield and my adored. When I was with her I don't remember thinking: only talking. 'That child has a diarrhoea of conversation!' (My father.) But Mummie listened as though it was a spell. You'd have thought I was the Infant Jesus. She gave me so much attention that I could read at four. I stood up in the train shouting out advertisements that stood on boards in the meadows going up to Charing Cross.
'Peeds Seeds', and 'The Pickwick, the Owl, and the Waverly Pen'. But I didn't want to read books. I wanted a horse. I prayed for a horse. Not to God. I didn't trust Him to do a straightforward thing. It was to my father, on my knees, in Staff Quarters.
My father was a clever man. If I asked some questions he would answer. If I asked too many he told me to stop. He knew the difference between curiosity and trying for attention. I asked him, 'What's the world?' He got it over to me that I lived on the surface of a rolling ball, glued down by gravity.
'Who rolls it?'
'Ask your mother.'
'She'll say it's God. Might I roll off?'
'No. Take it from me. That's enough now. I'm busy.'
He was the rooftree and knew everything. He knew why one was ill; and the cure. Tapeworm, ringworm, the taking out of thorns, the laying down of drains (privies were once the basic business of the Royal Engineers).
With doctors he was firm. He wouldn't touch a medicine

unless he knew the ingredients, and he had a chemist's Encyclopaedia which I was forbidden to look at in case I got fanciful. Once, before I was born, or when I was a baby, he had asked for his bill and the doctor had replied, 'We never charge our medical brethren.' This had confirmed him that he had a medical bent. He never painted his throat with glycerine and tanin bought at the chemist's. It had to be *fresh*. He mixed it himself on the gas ring in a special mortar, jacketed by a saucepan of boiling water.

He would look up from his newspaper at breakfast and catch my mother putting salt in her egg.

'You'll be sorry for it.' As she still continued to sneak the salt in, he one day left the room, purposefully but not angrily, and was ten minutes gone.

He came back with a small phial of his own blood. I don't know how he got it out.

'Watch me add the salt,' he said; and holding the phial under the simmering gas mantle he added it. The blood changed into sharp particles, daggers of future pain.

'And you wonder you have rheumatism!'

She murmured, radiant, 'How clever Daddy is. . . .' But she went on doing it. She loved salt in her egg.

No one corrected me except Daddy (I must call him what I called him), and though he whipped me three times I knew he thought I was a miracle. He was severe. I didn't get to know him. He wouldn't have minded that. He wanted obedience.

The first whipping was at Brompton Barracks after church when I was five. He was a major then, instructing Y.Os.; but all my life I knew him as a colonel.

We had a batman and a soldier-groom, a horse and a wagonette. On Sundays there was belt-cleaning before Church Parade. The officers wore scarlet, with gold epaulets, and narrow trousers, fastened inside their boots under their feet with elastic. After church little girls who had sat too long yelped and banged each other and boasted. I had a friend called Molly Main. I dared her to run under the belly of the horse as it stood harnessed to the wagonette by the front door after church. The groom was having his tea in the kitchen. The price I would pay, I said, was every flower in the garden. She ran under the horse.

I rushed up one stiff border and down the other, tearing up geraniums potted out between lobelias, and threw them at her. Daddy whipped me with a ruler on my bottom for putting her life in danger – still wearing his silver helmet with white cocks' feathers.

The second whipping was for telling my first lie. He said if you caught the first lie, hard, you could stop the others.

The third whipping was in Jamaica.

At that age I was full of jealousy and misery when laid in bed. Most children are not tired enough and bed was so early. If there were guests I howled, and most especially if Mummie sang to them after dinner. Finally one night Daddy came out of the drawing-room and took off his shoe. Mummie crouched on the stairs and cried out, 'Oh, Arthur, *don't*!' Daddy came up all the same but as he raised his hand with the shoe I gave a long sigh and fell asleep. He told the story often because it had upset him.

Grannie, who was staying with us, thought it would have served me right. She knew I was spoilt. Mummie tried to bridge it over but it wouldn't do. If I shook Mummie's shoulders and roared at her, which I often did, Grannie had the impudence to interfere – like coming between lovers.

I roared at Mummie for special reasons. One was that she said she was old. That was stupid. And of course it teased me with the idea of death, though I wouldn't say so. Another was that she wouldn't admit her looks.

'You're *beautiful*.' She shook her head.

'Yes you are!' I shook her. She laughed at that: I suppose I was small: she would put up with anything. Not because she was meek but because she had everything she wanted. (Daddy and me.) She wasn't ambitious. She never got cross. The only thing I ever knew to worry her was the newspapers. She worried about the Balkans. You see how things work out. There aren't any Balkans. If she had had the hydrogen bomb to think of she couldn't have worried more. If Daddy was cross with her (very seldom) she looked tragic but recovered at once.

When Grannie got into the house on a visit the values went wrong. I was perfectly accepted, when she wasn't there, as a rough little girl. If a boy is what mothers want then the first child is all but born a boy. But Grannie didn't admire me. She said I was 'a pity'. I despised little boys and girls; grown-ups too; and said so. I had thought despising people was splendid. I got it from my father but I got it wrong.

He didn't despise people but he disliked what he called hobnobbing. He allowed my mother to give dinner parties because she was young and beautiful – though shy. But she knew he thought the fuss never worth it. When Grannie got there this idea began to seem wrong. She didn't like people but she loved hobnobbing on a grand scale (a butler and an épergne). I became aware what 'class' was, as seen by Grannie. When people were invited in, as they were when she was there, it was plain that mice weren't rats and dogs weren't cats and nobody thought they were. People, she indicated with little h'ms and smiles, were born on shelves and very nice if you were near the top one. She had been pretty. Was pretty still, only children never think so. Her waist was tiny, her elegant dress of black ruched silk glittered with jet on rare occasions. At ordinary times she was engine-turned with fine braid. Her ornaments were strictly gold. Diamonds (and she had them) were loud, except for a big party. She was well turned out, like a charming horse. She had a total belief in Society.

The first Grannie-battle was when I was three. I threw a saucer on the floor.

'Pick it up, darling,' said Mummie.

'I won't.'

I wouldn't, because I wanted to show Grannie that Mummie and I had a relationship quite other than she understood. This sounds elaborate but I know it was true.

It went on with I-won't-I-will till Mummie had tears in her eyes which I knew were caused by Grannie and not by me. She went out of the room and Grannie caught me to her. I could feel the temper in her hand. She pointed out that I was hurting '*her* little girl'. I screamed with possessive, jealous rage: 'She's MINE! – Not yours!'

Grannie and Grandpa Alger were rich. Or he was. Not Onassis – not Fuad-rich, but well-to-do. The family owned the Cattedown Wharves. But as they had five children, and as Grandpa was Mayor of Plymouth three times, the money that came down to the next generation was a good deal less. She dragged him every winter to what she called the Reveera.

My mother

My father and mother (with me) at Manor House, Stoke Davenport, my grandmother's house after Wiley Court, 1891

Me. Aged three

E.B. on Queenie, Jamaica. I sat far back on Queenie's rump as the Negroes did

Cold Spring House, Jamaica

For him it was every year a gamble because he wanted to die in his own bed.

Grandpa had been brought up a Plymouth Brother; but with searing doubts and pain he had moved away from a belief in God. It was about the Gosse period in Plymouth.

Grannie was always name-dropping about God. You'd have thought He was an earl. My grandfather's deep God-trouble annoyed her. She went to church. He didn't. It was humiliating to attend St Andrew's without one's husband.

He saw her into her carriage with two horses (from The Manor House, Devonport), and she wore a dainty look of sorrow as though she was leaving him in hell.

The Manor House was rich and wonderful. A long glass corridor led in from the street and there were pots of blue cineraria along the side. In the hall beyond were two statues of Negroes and a standing bear with a silver tray for cards. Outside the dining-room was a veranda with dangling passion fruit, and beyond again the garden dropped away in terraces with flower beds and boys brushing chip gravel. At the bottom were the stables, a coach house, and the coachman's cottage. But above all things (so now-desired) there was a domed and very-heated conservatory opening from the library. At once you were in the tropics, with spiny ogres of cacti, red flowers like meat-eruptions, water bubbling through black hairpin-stalks of maidenhair, in a scented, damp heat.

The drawing-room, upstairs, looked golden when you walked into it. Everything was yellow brocade. It was furnished from the Great Exhibition. Satinwood and tulipwood and bog-oak and ebony shone, polished, under complicated chandeliers. But chiefly there were two Chinese cabinets, not the same, with a life of fantasy up and down their frontage. Cliff fronts were scaled by men in ivory, and chasms crossed by bridges. Shopkeepers with pigtails came out of nooks and doorlets.

Who got those cabinets in the end? Or were they sold in that indifferent way families have who have lived with furniture for a lifetime?

I often saw the dining-room downstairs dressed up for parties, the épergne in the centre, tufted with glass-grown carnations, and silver dishes fastened by special hooks from top to bottom for sweets and almonds. Smilax was round its base, and stretched to the four corners of the cloth. Name-cards lay ready on the sideboard on a tray. Menus stood in holders, and above the handwritten list (vulgar to type or print) of eight or nine courses was an ornament of fish or fruit embossed with chips of mother-of-pearl.

We had breakfast in the dining-room. My grandfather had a special kind of bread and milk. I had it too. Stale bread, cut up, was handed to him, dry, in a bowl. The boiling milk, in a silver jug, he poured over the bread himself. The point being that the bread be eaten so quickly that it was both hard and soft. Thick yellow cream, served as it had set, in ridges, was heaped on top. But what was basic to breakfast – underneath kidneys or eggs and bacon – was chopped (not mashed) buttered potato, frizzled across the top. Nobody spoke of liver trouble, but my grandmother kept Andrew's Salts by her plate.

I stayed often at the Manor House. I knew every corner of it. It was there when I was six that my brother Ralph* was born. Of course there had been mystery. I had thought it was a bicycle. I was led into the room and told to walk on tiptoe and there lay the baby – a disappointment. He was to become an explorer, a Fellow of the Royal Society, and the greatest living expert on the flow of sand (by wind to form sand dunes and by water in rivers and under the sea),† but oh I would have exchanged him that day for a bicycle.

As Mummie lay in bed with the baby I went about much more with Grannie. She was kind but she didn't worship me. I was one of the values I thought she got wrong. I went to church with her on Sundays, behind the horses, and in the church, kneeling or standing, I stole glances at her holy acting. I was sharp at six and I saved it up for Mummie. I acted her acting. I should have been scolded but I wasn't. Grannie couldn't sing in tune. (Neither can I but I don't try.) When the hymn came she stood up in a noble kind of way, lowered her lashes on to her cheek and mewed on a single note.

* Brigadier Ralph Bagnold, O.B.E., F.R.S. Author of *Libyan Sands; The Physics of Blown Sands and Desert Dunes;* originator of the Long Range Desert Group (Second World War); and in 1969 awarded the G. K. Warren Prize by the United States Academy of Sciences 'for his outstanding contribution to fluvial geology'.

† The dynamics of two-phase flow.

Although I talk like this I didn't hate her. She was my grandmother. I never hated a relation. They were like my own clothes.

But I was a clown trying things out on a risible nerve, and the nerve was Mummie's. The monstrous things I said made her laugh. She had a weakness of laughter: like being incontinent. Though she wanted to be shocked, I could get away with murder if I could make her laugh.

(Roderick, my husband, had another technique. 'I may be laughing but I'm just as angry as I was before.')

Sometimes I think I learned to write this way. It was only by the right word that I could 'work' what I said. If it went lame and lost its point Mummie was able to be angry.

All around us in church were sub-relations who were never asked to lunch. They spoke to us in the porch – with what I thought ignoble respect. Why did they accept this? Why did they so much want to speak to us? Was it that Grannie had married 'up'? There was her own brother there, who took round the plate and wore black gloves. Why was he never asked to lunch? I was shocked. Not at Grannie but at them. I vowed I would never accept to be of such inconsequence.

These sub-relations of Grannie's spoke with a clipped ee.ee, hard to describe. I met it again when I knew General Smuts.

After church we called on Grannie's father and mother. They were called Wills (tobacco or not – I should think not). They were ninety and had given up spectacles at sixty. I was taken so that I might know them but I never knew more than that. Ten minutes, a quarter of an hour, and on we went to Great Aunt Mary Grace and Great Aunt Lizzie. Great Aunt Mary Grace gave me shortcake. In an inner room trembled Great Aunt Lizzie with her neck broken. Her head had lain flat on her shoulder since she had fallen from a swing as a child, and the face that trembled was still pretty. On to Great Aunt Bertha Snell who had a lot of money that went to Missions. They all died over ninety. Taking a child to see very old people leaves nothing at all, except a sad, sad impression of inhumanity. They all seemed to be made of a different material. My eyes met those old eyes, my head got those trembling pats. They might have been (but not as good as) animals. It's enough just remembering them, and in self-defence, to make me write my own autobiography.

In the afternoons I went 'calling'; and if it was in the victoria with one horse I sat on the floor, and under the shelter of Grannie's skirts I slipped one foot down past the iron step and scuffed it on the road. In the lanes we were often blocked by hay carts; the hay came off on the hedges like hair and the horse snatched strands in spite of the coachman. Grannie sat upright with a silver card-case in her hand. She sent in the cards with the corners turned down by the footman (who was really the gardener's boy) as the coachman couldn't leave the horse.

When Grannie went to the Earl of Mount-Edgcumbe (once a year) she carried the cards to the door herself. She wasn't a climbing snob in the sense that she wanted to know him better. She was content with her position. But she simply venerated his.

Provincial social position was different then. People stayed put much more, and the respect they had they kept.

In the early summers of my life Grannie took houses on Dartmoor. They were ancient, fragile and grand; dropping away even then. Prince Hall, near Princetown, had stabling for hunting and its own tumbling river. Archeton, beyond Two Bridges had half a mile of tree'd avenue leading to the front door. It had a heronry (I was told to say 'hernery'). The smell of Dartmoor went to my head. I used to pick up my shoes and smell the soles.

When Grannie stayed with us she had the *Western Morning News* forwarded on. She crackled the paper at breakfast as though she was looking for the general news. But she was not. She was looking for the Social Column. When she found it the murmur began. She read it through not quite aloud and not quite to herself. It drove my father mad. If she read anything about God or earls her voice broke and quavered. She had this Earl of Mount Edgcumbe. If there was something about him in the paper there was this quaver. Or if she drove by a cemetery it came again. 'Go . . . od's Acre.' 'If you say that again,' I said when she took me to Rome and I was nineteen, 'I'll get out at the next station!' (There had been masses of cemeteries all the way from Calais.)

I got a rough intimacy with poor Grannie on that journey,

and we were nearer to being friends than we had ever managed before. I bullied her and she slipped back into what she had been with my grandfather, a pretty little person not meant to command.

As the years went by she was less a menace but always a trouble. (I am speaking of much later.)

'Can't you get your mother to have her breakfast in bed?'
No. Mummie couldn't.

When I was twelve and Daddy bought Warren Wood . . . (this is out of sequence but it finishes off my grandmother) . . . she still came to stay: but bit by bit she got Mummie to go to her instead, and Mummie took Ralph with her. That left Daddy and me alone together – at meals, and every evening – a thing that had never happened before.

When Mummie was there we had a relationship of three which worked beautifully. My mother laughed, I chattered. My father kept us in a light harness with sometimes the flick of a whip. But alone with him he couldn't have this driver-character. I became willing and amiable with responsibility. There was nothing to drive. He would have liked so much to have been in his study after tea and after dinner with his drawing board and compass, but he sat with me.

What should I talk to him about?

I was aware of his sacrifice, but he had a kind of kinglike relationship over my head with my mother. What should we say to each other? He was impatient of subjects like puppies, which was all I had in my head. We neither of us read. There were not many readable books. We were not a reading household. Mummie had a short shelf by her side of their bed with her girlhood's books, with *Lorna Doone, Marcus Aurelius,* Carlyle's *French Revolution,* and a red leather case with the little works of Shakespeare.

My father, then, was too difficult for me to understand. As the years went by he peeled away a little towards me. But it took an endless time. He died at ninety. And even when I understood a little more it didn't bring communication; but I wish he knew that I look back on him with so much respect. There were people who thought he was eccentric. But he wasn't eccentric at all. He just did what he liked. He disregarded other people's opinions. (Except for his astonishing attitude when I wrote *Serena Blandish*. Innocently I sent him the typescript before it was printed. He absolutely forbade publication. He said he couldn't go into his club in London if it was known that his daughter had written it. 'I should feel,' he said flatly to my husband, 'as if she'd been raped under a hedge by a sergeant.' This was why it was published under a pseudonym.)

His remarks return to me, little drops of advice, little chips of practical living – I hear them pass, through my children to theirs. How to tie a parcel – how to find a right angle – a pint of water weighs a pound and a quarter – always grease a screw before you screw it in.

He had also the remains of very annoying dictums. 'No woman can wind a clock,' was one. 'Never have more than one dog,' was another. I fought against this one long and hard, bringing puppies back that had to be returned. And if you 'never had more than one dog' – it was *his* dog! It went with him all day to the office. Old Nell, knowing what he felt, buried her puppies and they were dead in the morning. But Togo, a small fox terrier who bit the office messenger, was left at home. I played with him endlessly. The dining-room table was long; and large books, such as atlases and encyclopaedias, could be propped open along its length to make a tunnel. Down this I threw a ball. Togo, passionately trembling at the other end, would, if the ball stuck, dash in and heave the books on the floor. Nobody minded when the backs were broken. I should have minded now.

But this was when I was twelve.

Before I was nine we had been quartered all over the south of England. We 'moved' with mule-trunks, numbered in white paint, that Daddy had had in Egypt and South Africa before he married.

Each time we moved there were mountains of newspaper, and things to be wrapped like the silver biscuit-box and the lemon squeezer. I waded, swishing and crackling in the paper.

'That child . . .'

I sank on my knees.

'If I am good for ever will you give me a horse?'

'Tell her,' he said to Mummie, and walked away.

It was that he had a Command in Jamaica.

Chapter Two

*

When I was nine and Ralph was three, my father sailed ahead to prepare a house. We followed – my mother, the baby, Miss Evans and I – in an old fruit ship called the *Don*. It rolled like a whale.

Miss Evans was to be my governess. I was in the Manor House drawing-room when she was interviewed by Mummie and Grannie.

Having been told to go out of the room, I lingered behind an armchair, fascinated by the awkward shyness of my mother and the pursiness of my grandmother towards the stranger. Then I was seen and sharply told again to go away. I took against Miss Evans from that moment.

The storm in the *Don* was a hurricane. It has frightened me of the sea ever since. I was in an upper berth above an old lady, and my mother and Ralph were next door. Water came in from a broken pipe and the trunks got loose and swam about the floor. The old lady cried out again and again that she was dying. I was too sick to care. The stewardess came in with two men carrying a stretcher. 'She's making so much noise, dear, we're putting her in another cabin.' She was making no noise then. She was dead.

I wasn't allowed to land at Barbados – query smallpox. A very young doctor, a slight fever, and the crochet-lace of my sleeve had pocked my arm. We sailed on. The voyage had taken eighteen days. And now a spit of land lay beside the ship.

The engines hardly turned: we floated – on a sea still and oily after so long a voyage. How often I have arrived at ports like this – Table Bay particularly – when the cessation of the engines turns the ship's movement into a dream.

Trees grew at the edge of the spit of land, mangoes. And the red roots, bared of earth, and reaching to find water, were draped with oysters. They said the flesh was red.

The day we neared Jamaica an inner life began. It must have, for I never remember anything earlier – of ecstasy, or admiration for nature. Beauty never hit me until I was nine. But when we landed, the lack of mist, flowers higher than I was, emerald leaves, or leaves of black leather, the shine of black people, their thrush's eyes, the zigzagging quiver of air hit by heat, the tropic leap into the spangled night – this was the first page of my life as someone who can 'see'. It was like a man idly staring at a field suddenly finding he had Picasso's eyes. In the most startling way I never felt young again. I remember myself then just as I feel myself now.

Arrival at the house in Up Park Camp is blotted out. But next morning is as bright as a button. We were got up at five and had breakfast on a veranda with light pouring through banana leaves. In fact the conservatory again. It was as beautiful as a pantomime, and I had seen one. No heat at that hour – and oh, the giddy air! As white as bird-song. My head sprouted receiving-horns like a radio station. Put back to bed at eleven in the morning (very strange), the beds stood in saucers of water because of ants.

Captain Tarver called in the afternoon, riding: with a coloured groom to hold the horse.

'Can I see the pony? Can I see the pony?'

'Don't bother now, Enid. Go away.'

I slipped out to see the pony. It was all of fifteen hands.

'You like to get up, Missie?'

I was in the hard shiny saddle and the groom put the reins in my hands. Then he turned to talk to a friend. The horse moved off.

First it was a walk and a shout from behind. At the shout it was a trot. I couldn't have lasted long at that but then it was a gallop. Shouts came from everywhere and dogs barked. We were headed for the stables. No stirrups, nothing but the terrible polish beneath me and the rising and falling of the hogged mane.

The horse turned sharp at a corner and I flew on through the air to be impaled on gold-tipped railings. I fell two inches short. In my father's mind for days they were sticking through me. I heard him tell it. I hadn't a scratch. It was my first ride.

My father decided that the children, Ralph and I, could not live down in the heat in Kingston. He rode up to Newcastle (in the Blue Mountains behind Kingston) to look for a house. Newcastle was then a small military camp, and a mile or so short of it stood a disused coffee estate on which was a large and battered house – Coldspring House. He set his heart on it.

William Hickey had once stayed a night in it. In Volume 2 of his memoirs this is what he says:

On the 1st January, 1776, after a light meal at one o'clock, we set off, myself and most of the party on horseback. We ascended the Grand Leganee Mountain full four miles, and when at the perpendicular height of a mile and a half (as they told me) above the level of the sea, suddenly came upon one of the most romantic and beautiful spots I ever beheld, where stood an admirable mansion consisting of fifteen spacious apartments, from every one of which the magnificent city of Kingston, with the shipping, Port Royal, and intervening rich and fertile country met the eye; a spectacle so sublime and magnificent I certainly never did see. The temperature of the air was delicious, forming a wonderful contrast to the extreme and burning heat we had been in only one hour before. At the back of the house rose the majestic and awfully grand mountain towering above the clouds in which its summit was completely enveloped.

While partaking of a sumptuous supper Mr Richards laughingly said to me, 'I hope you have provided yourself with blankets, for I assure you they will be requisite at night.' This I could scarcely credit, but found it very true, sleeping most comfortably under two, upon a nice soft bed exactly as in England. Indeed the moment the sun disappeared the air became so sharp and keen we were glad to have all the doors and windows shut. Then entering my bedchamber I was agreeably surprised at seeing a fine, cheerful coal fire.

The next morning I arose at Daylight, going to the window in the hope of seeing the effect of a clear sun rising, instead of which there was so thick a fog I could not see a yard before me. Much disappointed I dressed myself and went down to the breakfast room, where most of the gentlemen were already assembled sitting by an excellent fire. On my lamenting the thickness of the weather, Mr Richards said, 'Oh, never mind the weather! Come and warm yourself', pointing to a chair next to his. I obeyed and was placed with my back to the windows. After chatting about half an hour Mr Richards desired me to look whether it was clearer or not. Upon going to the window for that purpose I found as bright a morning as ever shone, when Mr Watling told me what I had imagined to be fog was an actual cloud passing over us, both above and below, as was generally the case a short time before sunrise.

This truly charming place was called 'Cold Spring', taking that name from a remarkably cold and beautifully clear spring of water that issued from a fissure in the rock, supplying the family with the best water I ever tasted. To the touch it was like ice itself.

All this, knocked about by time, my father rented from the War Office for £24 a year. There was startled jealousy in the Camp, as no one had thought it habitable. But no Royal Engineer is defeated by a thing like that. Starting in the dark, we drove from Up Park Camp in our two-horse buggy, with Zinc the coachman, to Half Way Tree. It seemed a long way and was a dusty plateau (with a tree) where one changed from carriages to riding animals (chiefly mules and donkeys).

A donkey led the procession. My mother rode it like the Mother of Christ with her child on her lap. Her golden hair was done in a bun and she had leg-of-mutton shoulders.

I had a mule, with a mule-trunk strapped on either side and a cushion on top. Other mules followed with our thirteen mule-trunks. My father, I suppose, had a horse. The Negroes, walking, hung on to the animals' tails.

Up the mountain track we went, and as I was stuck alone on my mule I couldn't grumble *'This* isn't riding!' There was only the mule to hear.

As dawn broke we rode over a night-filled hollow of grass. The sun was rising, blazing, but this secret meadow, shielded by a mound, was blue with dew. The hoofs made a sucking noise, and the hoofs of the mule ahead tore black patches in the dew. These things, remembered for ever, broken from nature, are not so much magic in themselves as they have struck what is magic in the heart. *I gave that meadow life by the power of my sensibility.* But how? But why?

'This admirable mansion with fifteen apartments' had had several lives since William Hickey, but its last life had to do with coffee. And even that was over.

It was built uphill on the mountain's flank, and divided from top to bottom by a huge wheel, once worked by Hickey's 'spring of water' (now diverted round the house in a rough cement gulley). The wheel stood motionless from the top of the roof down to a deep pit below in which frogs barked all night. The drying-barbecues (for the coffee beans) lay downhill in steps like concrete tennis lawns, and a derelict coffee plantation spread around and up the mountain, the bushes bearing flowers, berries and leaves all at the same time.

Jamaica in 1899 was as poor as a church mouse. Nothing got mended. Negroes were Negroes then and not barristers. The roof of the house from inside is described in my mother's diary as 'moving several inches in a gale'.

On the other hand, you could buy eighteenth-century furniture from bankrupt planters for a song. Thus was our house furnished and my father sold the lot for £25 when we left.

The kitchen was a hut upstream, and when the cook killed a turkey she shut it in the kitchen door with the head inside and pulled hard. I saw the body-convulsions and was told the old tale that it was 'nerves after death'. She threw the innards in the drinking stream.

It was the loveliest spot – as Hickey said. Daturas grew round the house. The white trumpets could be filled with fireflies and shaken out after dark. The water from the high fissure jumped down its first ten feet in a cascade. Mossy tracks where the water spilled grew silver fern and gold fern. These, if you laid them on your father's black dinner jacket and banged, left a lace pattern in gold or silver powder.

The house was full of bats. I was told to take a towel and

knock them down, put tumblers over them and throw them out of the window. I did it once. The bat that lay squeaking on the floor was like a thwarted baby out of a nightmare. I rushed shrieking from the room. After that the bats and I settled down together.

Butterflies were as big as bats. Grasshoppers were delirious about white. They jumped at you – ping – ten foot at a jump.

I read nothing and the house had no books. . . . This is what I was going to say. And then in my mother's diary there is a letter to her mother.

'The book Enid is reading now (1901) is Tolstoi's "War and Peace", 4 vols. I daresay you know it, all about Napoleon's march into Russia and retreat. It's so difficult to get suitable books for her' (as though it was *Little Women*).

Could I possibly have sat still inside that house and read '4 vols.'? Was darling Mummie boasting to Grannie? I can only say that *War and Peace* – read in full admiration twenty years later, and in boredom forty years later, left on me no mark at all. What doesn't feed you doesn't exist. And nothing between covers lived for a moment beside the soaking beauty of Jamaica.

So (to me) I read nothing and the house had no books. But cavemen painted before pictures and wild men sang before books. I broke into verse. Just as I broke into a canter. It was up and down between the coffee bushes, the ginger and the daturas, that I plunged with my little paper horses, the horses that had a second life in one of my books. I cut them carefully from the pages of old magazines, sporting ones with luck. It was quite hard to get the collection for they had to be much the same size, and they had to be right-facing ones. Paper was thicker in those days. By gentle rubbing I got a kind of coat on them. Holding a horse in my right hand and a twig in my left I galloped and plunged, flicking at my legs with the twig. I sang, tuneless (no ear), pouring out jingles. I laid my hands on rhymes like someone handy with *The Times* crossword. I knew where they were. In my room full of whirling bats I knelt up in bed and wrote by the yellow moon.

My father, riding up for the week-end, sent for me.

'Your mother tells me you write poems in bed.'

'Yes, Daddy.'

'That leads to insomnia. I want your word of honour you'll keep it to three nights a week.'

'Yes, Daddy.'

The 'word of honour' impressed me. But on the nights when I didn't write poetry I drove instead. With long tapes on my toes I took out the chestnut in the buggy or the pair of greys, or lunged the roan. This, too, was lived again thirty-five years later. Except for my little brother and Mary Adams, the daughter of the army doctor, I had no companions. The children at the Camp at Newcastle were too far away. Only Mary was allowed to ride a horse at ten. She was my 'friend' but quite unintimate. She shared my Miss Evans-lessons with me but not play.

The first quarrel I ever heard (and pretty well the last) between my father and my mother was about poor Miss Evans's feet.

'I can't – I can't tell her, Arthur!'

'You've got to. *I* won't!'

'I won't I won't I WON'T tell her!'

Their voices terrified me. How could I have heard about divorce? At once I thought: 'They're going to leave each other!' This quarrel struck a temporary death into me. I was on the look-out for results for days.

My mother worshipped my father. This was the only and unique time I heard her rebel.

Miss Evans had her fare given her (could it really have been her feet?) and was replaced by Mademoiselle Gattey. This poor French lady was afraid of me so now there was perfect freedom, and Mary's and my lessons were a farce.

Mary's father liked her to go home for lunch. My galloping and the paper horses annoyed Dr Adams. He thought I was hysterical. Even my father thought I went too far. But he was away all the week in Kingston.

I didn't care to let Mary share the paper horses. If she galloped beside me there was no room on the tracks and the twigs hit her face. The horses were unsharable. They needed uninterrupted belief and invention. I know they gave me a besotted look. The doctor didn't want Mary besotted too. But she must sometimes have stayed for lunch because once her plate was broken in front of her by lightning as she ate stewed apricots.

And that was the day – after lunch – when I got my third whipping.

We chewed oranges on a bank above the bridle road (the only road). We chewed for juice and spat the pulp. A platoon of soldiers marched below us towards Newcastle, a sergeant at their head. I spat pulp on to a cap.

I was pleased with the aim, but frightened. The sergeant looked up, told the men to mark time, halt, stand-at-ease, and walked round the path to the house.

I was sent for. It was a week-end and my father was there. 'I'm sure it was an accident, and I'm sure she is sorry,' he said. I said I was sorry. My father paid for the cap and the sergeant went.

'It wasn't an accident,' he said quietly.

'No.'

'I'm going to beat you.'

So he did. It never crossed my mind that it would do me any spiritual harm. Nor it did.

There was no particular pleasure in Mary staying beyond lessons. Much better alone. Besides, two couldn't ride the donkey. I had got my desire at last: I was allowed to ride.

Queenie was a big Egyptian donkey, bought from Lady Hemming, the Governor's wife. Their time was up and they were going back to England.

I knew nothing about riding and nobody taught me. Everyone moved on horses then. Children rode to school. It didn't mean you could ride, as we mean it now. I had never heard of 'legs' or how to use them: nothing about the bit except you pulled left or right.

I sat far back on Queenie's rump as the Negroes did.

We had a mare too, for my mother. If I rode her my father said to the boy (a grizzled coal black man of sixty), 'Give her mash, not corn. The child's riding her.'

Mummie had never heard of the rape of little girls, and never thought of murder. I was allowed to ride Queenie alone from tea till bedtime, all over the mountainsides, far beyond the limits of the coffee-bushes. Often I came on small camps of natives, who laughed and asked if I wasn't afraid of duppies. Alpine strawberries grew wild over sunny slopes: very red because the leaves got burnt off.

There was a bank, my height, near the house behind the stream. Its earth had a tacky quality, like plasticine. My mother built a long village for me, on the crest and up and down the natural crevices; twig-houses, roads, bridges, stockades, and a pool lined with rubber. On every walk we hunted for scraps that would suit: cones, bamboo, bright stones.

I spent hours murmuring up and down it in a sleep-walking voice. In May and October the rains washed it away, but she built it again.

One day I was murmuring and Ralph, wanting to be near me, played by the gully that carried our stream. I heard him tapping quietly, murmuring too, as good as gold. He was prising out the concrete that had splintered away round a stone. The conduit at that point was headed towards the house, as the old mill stream had been. Then, at a vital point it was turned away. What Ralph was tapping at was the corner stone. He got it out.

Out came the rushing stream, delighted to be free, and tore through the house to find the wheel. Missing the wheel it searched through drawing-room, dining-room and two bedrooms.

Ralph's kitten was drowned in that stream. I was wheeling it, dressed in doll's night-clothes, in the doll's pram. A native dog appeared from nowhere and tore the kitten out of the pram. I screamed. My father came running. The night-dress was scarlet. My father took one look, then held the kitten under the water till it drowned. I hammered on his arm howling 'Brute! Devil!' When the kitten was dead he vomited. The dog was gone and the kitten had been disembowelled.

I was in love when I was four, with a woman called Esther. At least I was in love with that name. I used to sing the shining sound in the back of the trap. I always droned about what I was in love with.

Now in Jamaica I fell in love with a man. His name was Lieutenant Usher. He came often and perhaps he was in love with my mother.

One day when he was there she picked up my hand, saying 'Darling – your nails are *filthy*!'

I went out of the house and cried and cried against a dry rock. After that I couldn't live without loves. I have written of this once in *The Loved and Envied*.

She could see the little creature clearly now (herself) as she ran and played – intoxicating worships swinging in her heart like hope in the wind, like lanterns of ecstasy – for after the golden lieutenant she had invented other loves. She told nobody, but had chosen among her parents' friends heroes on whom to hang her adoration – stimulating her heartbeats – a little drug-taker; so that, playing alone among the coffee-bushes, that spangled olive bush-sea that surrounded the house, and called in at last at sunset, she would come tipsy with secrecy, as though she had taken alcohol. She remembered these premature emotions. . . . 'Once one has written oneself into one's name one can't look back,' she said to herself, 'except as an amusement. Youth's not a serious memory. The past is consumed. I'm here. I'm unconsumed. I'm what has happened.'

* * *

Sir Sydney Olivier was the next Governor. There was head-shaking.

'Socialist-chap. Says he won't have any servants. How's that for running Government House!'

Sir Sydney and Lady Olivier had three daughters. How or why I got asked to stay with them I don't know. They had a country house half-way up to Newcastle. I was to ride Queenie down with Major Townsend. He was a little man, worn-looking, in middle years. We picked our way over bilbery and rock country like Dartmoor, and after a while he said, 'Let's get down and stretch our legs.' We both dismounted. I looked round: he had disappeared. Walking round a rock there he was, his horse's rein through one arm, holding something terrible and strange in his hand; a piece of his body. I jumped back, shocked, and filled with hatred. I was too old to be so innocent. I thought he was at some nameless practice, some devil's work. It never occurred to me the poor man wanted to pass water.

I climbed back on to Queenie wondering how I could bear to ride another step with him. As we rode I forgot in five minutes. But I have remembered all these years.

The Olivier girls.

What an excitement!

My mother (who was Ethel Alger before her marriage)

Enid, nine; Ralph, three

My father, Colonel Arthur Henry Bagnold, C.B., C.M.G. (aged eighty)

They were older than I was. Fourteen or fifteen against my eleven. I was a big, boastful, unwarned child. And that first lie (and its whipping) wasn't caught in time.

Rapid interrogations. Like two dogs in the street. 'Can you ride? Can you swim?'

'Yes,' to both. 'I can dive too.'

(A lesson never forgotten. Why don't children know they are going to be found out?)

I was thrown, sobbing, into the pool.

They had a sort of racecourse. Ride? I was off in the first seconds, getting up howling, stamping, ready to kill. I remember no more about my Olivier-visit except my humiliation, and my envy of those gallant and terrible girls.

It was nearly over – Jamaica. I stuck flags in a map for the Boer War. Mummie said, 'Poor old Queen.' And in her diary: 'She must be glad that her time is nearly up. Will our dinner party have to be postponed?' (Like Chips Channon.)

Next day: 'So the poor old Queen is dead. Long live the King. What about our dinner party?'

My father's command was up. We sailed for England on the 28th of March, 1902, and into Plymouth Sound on the 12th of April. In the ship love came into my life. Little girls of twelve are fascinated by love. They may mock it but they long to watch it. Faces of lovers, notes, trembling hands – the beautiful and secret disease they have just heard of. In that ship there was a rich young lady – Miss Daisy Epps of Epps Cocoa. I carried her love-letters to the ship's doctor. She had swimming-blue eyes and wrote on a pad on her lap. I hung around. She would look up and hand me the stuck-down envelope and I sped off. Once or twice I scribbled ardent messages of my own on the back. 'Don't despair', and 'She loves you'.

On landing, we went to the dreariest of places. Lodgings in Ryde, in the Isle of Wight. No love, no excitement. It was like being dragged out of a theatre. I had to carry on. So *I* wrote love-letters. There was a mahogany sideboard in the horrible sitting-room, with a coarse lace cover. Under this, hearing my father's step on the stairs, I poked a half-finished letter.

'What's that?' said my father, too close behind me. 'Give it to me.' It was so unlike him that I think he must have found something before. He carried the letter to the window to read.

(What dreadful twelve-year-old heat and passion simmered across that page?) He called my mother.

'Come here and look at this.' They read it together. I began to scream. There was no way out except screaming. I couldn't bear to wait for the first question.

Shaking me, my father said:
'*Who is this man?*'
'*Nobody-nobody-NOBODY!*'
'Enid – I don't believe you.'
'Nobody-nobody-nobody.'
'*I want his name.*'
'There isn't anybody ... ANYBODY ...' – yelling and running up to my bedroom.

Unaware of being followed I fell on my knees in the room.
'Oh GOD ...' I howled at Him. 'God God God they don't believe me!' I bawled at Him. I was tropically over-developed and there might have been a man. But I suppose there really are accents of truth in a voice. I suppose mine had them. I was believed.

I was then to go to boarding school (and needed it). But suddenly I was said to have a patch on my lung. I spent that winter with an unremembered governess (in sleeping bags with hot water bottles) doing lessons in the garden. Even in 1902 my father was up to date with Davos.

It was because of this, and after this, that Daddy said:
'Find her a school on sandy soil.'

And by this remark, this divine frail accident, my life was altered. Theirs too perhaps. But everything alters one's life.

The school on sandy soil was near Godalming, and it was Mrs Huxley's. And Mrs Huxley was the mother of Julian, Trev and Aldous.

How difficult it must be to send your darling to boarding school. I was agog. It never occurred to me what Mummie felt. But Daddy was determined I should have a good education. It was as though he was living now among the 'A's' and 'O's'. What did he think I was going to do or be? Surely he assumed I was bound for marriage? Or did Mummie's trouble with adding-up affect him? ('She *must* learn mathematics.') But as Prior's Field was above all a literary school they didn't lay stress on mathematics. Or I was unable to consume them.

✳ 24 ✳

I went with Mummie for the 'interview with the Headmistress'. A chintzy room, modern with William Morris – a slender lady with a beautifully-shaped small head. Kind, yes, but away and above my understanding. Each time before she spoke she seemed to reflect. I had never thought of thinking before I spoke.

She asked me my bent. What would I like to do, and what to be? I never confessed, though that was the opportunity, that I continually wrote poems, and had since I was nine. I looked through the window at the games field and saw the girls practising over low hurdles for the Sports Day, their numbers swelled by day girls. I thought that of all things I should like that best. To be good at games, to be better than anyone, to be popular, to be Captain of . . . To be a famous athlete. The triumphs poured through my mind.

'I like games,' I said. I had never played them. I had always been alone.

I was still darling Enid, the great nestling, and went home. But soon I stood on the floor of the school – alone. I wasn't frightened but burning with curiosity, trembling with stillness like a new horse put into a field with other horses. I watched, sniffed, waited. Was it to be attack, defence, or the wild joy of play? With me it was play, and a resolve to be regarded, to cut ice. This was to be my world for five years.

I was rough and difficult to snub, and gay. I was clever enough but of that I took no notice. Clever enough not to show up as a 'show-off-er' but I managed very well as a card. Being fat (the result of Jamaica) I was cut out for clowning. To make them laugh one had to spend oneself without counting the esteem-cost. That was not a bad lesson. Often I got it wrong and looked a fool. But that I had to bear, and soon I got the timing. All jokes depend on timing: something unheralded and said at its only moment. Odd that at such a school as this the gym, the games field, and possible popularity should be my heaven. I kept grass snakes in my desk. I cut ENID on my wrist and tattoed the cuts with the dust from the gym floor (after a science lesson on antiseptics). It doesn't sound funny, but they thought it funny.

Margie Wetzlar-Coit broke both her legs because I had dared her to jump from a height I had just jumped from. I was shocked and sorry. But the legs mended. I remember no shadows. I was blissfully, violently happy. I have never seen any of the girls again.

I went home for the first holidays.

My father had been made Chief Superintendent of Building Works at Woolwich Arsenal, and he had bought the house – Warren Wood – on the top of Shooter's Hill, in which I lived, on and off, till I was thirty.

At that date, 1902 or 3, we ran down the drive to the main Dover Road if we heard a car coming. Their single cylinders popped from far off like a motor cycle. Daddy bought a Cadillac with a little door at the back like a horse-trap, and no windscreen. My mother and I drove about with him with screams of warning and swathed in veils.

On Sundays we polished the brass, and there was plenty. Radiator, lamps, horn, all were brass. It had black leather 'sleeves' for articulated parts, with brass oil inlet-holes, and screw-caps with endless threads. The leaves of the springs were encased in black leather as well. My father put in a winch so that when I had pushed the car out (which was slightly down-hill) I could winch her back. He built a pit beneath her, electrically lit, into which you could have put a bullock. Cars have always been women but they were more particularly women then. There was a touch of keeping a mistress. Their waywardness was loved. If something went wrong it was the nature of a pretty woman to have faults.

The Sunday brass-cleaning was after lunch. In the morning was church. If I could write that with a mourning line round it I would.

Up till then Sundays had been gay and military. Now they were civilian. I loathed the people who huddled in that Protestant church.

It had nothing to do with religion – my hate. It was class. I despised them. I despised their standards, their atmosphere, their lick-spittling hypocrisy. It was Grannie again – and her indecent attitude to 'Him'.

* * *

('And what about God?'
'Are you interviewing me?'

'Yes. What do you believe?'
'I believe there is something.'
'That's not very clear.'
'It's not clear. Nor is God.'
'What do you do about age?'
'I get tired. But not tired of living. Of course I have to talk about Wills and so forth. But I find myself "arranging" without believing.'
'What do you do about death?'
'I don't believe I shall die.')

*   *   *

Church made me more and more queasy. I began to hate it as one hates seasickness. My stomach turned over on Sunday morning. On Saturday nights, too.

In church I thought of death. I thought of numbers. All the people who were dead since the beginning of the world ran through my head. The toiling Egyptians in the sand, dissolved, gone.

I looked round, hating the congregation. I hated their sad squalor and their self-satisfaction. I hated the private souls they had brought with them. ('Let me stand out! Make on me a mark so that I shall be different!') From that moment I was eaten up with ambition. I rested my teeth on the wood of the pew in front as I knelt and prayed: 'God, make me famous.' I wanted to beat them. (But they were dead when I'd beaten them.) I hated the vicar because he was allowed such a fling in the pulpit – and said so at lunch.

'Oh, Enid – *Enid*!' (My mother.)

'*You* don't go!' I said, indignant, to Daddy (who was carving the saddle of mutton with two kidneys dressed up high at one end).

'What I do makes no difference.'

'Don't you believe in God?'

'I don't *know*,' he said (suddenly resting his knife and fork on the knife-rest), looking at me sternly. 'Not another word, please.'

He was blunt enough. But so true. He never pretended anything. And when he said, near ninety, that he had felt his mother near him I believed it.

I tried to explain my hatred of church to Roderick when we lived in this village.

'It makes me ill.'

'That's nonsense!'

'Well it makes me howl like a dog then. It makes me think of death.'

'Hadn't you better think of death and get it over?'

(But there's nothing to *think* about death. Except that it's the worst thing in life.)

I used to think, for instance, in church (there with him sitting beside me): 'I shall have to follow his coffin.' I never thought *I* should die. But when I followed it what had gone before was so terrible that the coffin-and-church-business was just junk.

'Why do you want me to come to church with you?' I asked him.

'It's up to us to give a good example in the village.'

'"Us"! – The *Jones's*!'

'The gentry.'

'One doesn't use that word.'

'It's been good English for centuries.' (It was I who was the hypocrite.)

'Oughtn't you to go because you're . . . well . . . holy and so forth?'

'That's too private.'

We were all nimble with our tongues, our mockery, our cleverness, the children and I. But no good. He wouldn't be jeered out of what he had said.

But he let me off all the same.

'It's no good your letting me off if you're going to be a living reproach.'

'I shan't think of it again.' And he didn't.

The children had to go. They had to stand ready in the hall for the last late rush of their father.

'Quarter-to-eleven-Service,' Maurice Baring called it.

*   *   *

There were only twelve girls at Prior's Field when I first went. (But in a flash there were a hundred.) Professor Gilbert Murray's daughter, Rosalind; Maurice Hewlett's daughter, Pia; Conan Doyle's daughter, Mary. Two girls I admired very much were the Vernon-Harcourts. And there was a girl with a square mane of yellow hair which one day I tore almost off her head in a passion about Shelley. She was called Frances Siemens.

Mrs Huxley was the granddaughter of Arnold of Rugby, and the niece of Matthew Arnold. Her husband was Leonard, son of Thomas Huxley. Mrs Humphry Ward was her sister.

Aldous was at a prep school near by and came to lunch on Sundays. Other small brothers of girls at Prior's Field came to lunch from time to time. When they did, and if one sat near them, one was supposed to make an effort and talk. One Sunday I sat next Aldous, at the headmistress's table, which was small enough for everything one said to be heard. I meditated on Aldous. I should have to speak to him. He sat silent, rather green, inscrutable, antagonistic. I suppose he was nine. Heavily bumping it out: 'What did you do today, Aldous?' No answer. I reddened. Then, angry, because I had reddened, and louder: 'I *said*, "*What did you do today, Aldous?*"'

'I heard you the first time.'

I didn't meet him again for forty years. Then it was at a tea party at Ethel Sands in Chelsea.

'You were very frightening, Aldous.'

He gave me a very sweet smile. 'I'm frightening still.'

Julian and I wrote poems and sent them to each other for a time – towards the end of my school time and while he was still at Eton.

Out of the rough and tumble of my first twelve years of life during which, to the two people who mattered, I was the centre of everything (and – to that centre – so attached!), there had been one thing missing – competition. I had had nothing to live up to. Nobody mattered but Mummie and Daddy and me. And chiefly me. There was little Ralph growing up. I loved him cosily in a taken-for-granted way, but he was six when I was twelve. He was born too late for me.

If I thought about women at all I thought of them as 'dependants'. They 'followed' (the drum). Pretty or ugly, disagreeable or pleasant, they were wives, stuffed into Married Quarters. Only my mother had no label. She was mine and apart. So when I met Mrs Huxley I was open-mouthed: I was shaken. To a rough little army girl this was a different kind of 'woman'. I knew there had been great men. I had never heard of great women. This was one.

From the ranks of the school I saw her every day. Either she spoke in the morning after breakfast or she read aloud to us in the evening. I who had hardly read a book voluntarily (and yet dealt already in an intimate way with words) was again dumbfounded. I didn't know people wrote like that. When she read Meredith's *Love in a Valley* she read without stressing the sense: she let the complicated rhyming wave by itself like music.

> When her mother tends her
> Before the laughing mirror
> Tying up her ribbons and letting down her hair,
> Often she thinks 'Were this wild thing Wedded' . . .
> More love would I have and much less care.

In her silvery even voice the words had their head. I became as dotty as I had been with the paper horses. I danced the words in my bedroom. I walked in the field, toes pointing. As a military band lightens the march for soldiers so I moved, haunted, musically light. I never said so. I never told her. Just as well.

I had opportunities for telling her for I often saw her privately. I was sent to her for punishment.

The school was built by Voysey in tent-fashion, and added to again and again until it was like an armed camp of tents, in its many roofs and their many angles. I crawled out on my slope from my bed late at night and looked in at the sleepers as one might look at the dead. I felt a tickling sense of power as though my skin was being run by a battery. The cold clear moon sailed dizzily over my splendid isolation. Hands and bare feet held to the rough tiles, white night-views at angles blazed under the moon as I reached each coping in turn, the occasional slight slip was an electric shock on the spine. It was animal and divine. I was seen and caught by the cook.

Another time I was brought to Mrs Huxley by her sister, Mrs Humphry Ward.

I had climbed down the lavatory pipes to sleep in the wood beyond the playing field among the juicy bluebells in May, but had lain awake and at last had fallen so deeply asleep that I never heard the calling bell. I had savaged the bluebells at first, not knowing how to express myself. There were so many of them. But when they lay about and the blue was gone I stopped. If they had been human it would have been too late.

I wasn't scolded. Hardly rebuked. Mrs Huxley seemed to blush a little before explaining. She asked for my co-operation – without asking. It all seemed unimportant. We seemed to mourn about myself, in a light-hearted way. I was a child and she was soon to die, but the gap was bridged. I didn't argue, though she would have let me. I listened to that voice talking to me with such a new distinction. The words were simple. I couldn't doubt them.

When I was fifteen Mrs Huxley went to a Congress of Headmistresses, where it was suggested that, once in the school-life of every girl, an essay might be set in verse. This she did. She set the Verse-Essay, and the school went mad with worry. Sixth-Formers walked about with knitted brows: girls kept their thumbs in Tennyson. They were in despair. But I – I was an addict. I wrote the long poem, five pages of it, with choruses and constant changes of metre. That had been my great pleasure at night for years.

The great day came, the End-of-Term. Stars sat with Mrs Huxley on the platform. Sir Gilbert and Lady Mary Murray, Lady Jekyll (of the cookery book), a splendid local character, whose two daughters, Pamela and Barbara, were day-girls at Prior's Field; Mrs Huxley's brilliant Staff, two of them outstanding – Ethel Sidgwick and the half-Greek, Emma Neurotsos.

We wore games 'djibbahs', with scarlet sashes. The large box pleats, which should have hung straight from the yoke, were pulled apart by my breasts. I looked like the top drawer (of a chest of drawers) pulled out. My face was as scarlet as my sash with hope, and my miserable hair (called 'fine') stuck out at the back in a small plait. We sat on wooden chairs. I was at the back.

I knew I had written the best poem. But I wondered if *they* knew.

Mrs Huxley came at last to the poetry experiment. She spoke of the 'standard achieved . . .' Then broke off. ' . . . but there is one poem so outstanding . . .'

'(Mine!)'

'Will you stand up, Enid Bagnold?'

There was a grind of wood moving as I stood. Each girl turned, screwing in her chair. The farce and the unsuitability and the wonder of it! Disbelief, amazement. But there I stood, no getting round it, fat, square, scarlet. And *crowned*.

Heady fame. The gods had come down to announce that the clown was the poet. Unanswerable. It was I.

If that was the end of term then it was during the holidays that Mrs Huxley took me to see Yeats in London. She must have known him: she must have sent him the poem. All I can remember is that it was an evening party, that the walls had brown paper, that a man I was told was Ezra Pound (I am told now that it couldn't have been) sat on a stool. Yeats asked me nothing but said that if I wanted to be a poet . . .

'if you want to do creative, imaginative work – *never* interest yourself in politics, welfare, or the conditions in which people live. Only in their aspect, their hearts and minds, and *what they are*'.

He meant exactly the opposite to what happened to poets in the Spanish War. He didn't live up to his own advice but he meant it at the time. I wore a dress of strawberry-coloured alpaca, a boned upright lace collar (called guipure), and boots.

At the beginning of the next term Mrs Huxley was ill when we returned, and almost in no time she died. Leonard Huxley, her husband, wrote a poem about her and read it aloud to the school. We were shocked. That wasn't how we had felt.

The new headmistress, an excavator in Rome who had lectured to us, took on my tiny 'fame'. I was removed from the curriculum and taught Greek in the Rose Garden, personally, by her, on a rug. It didn't work. I lost myself. I never learnt Greek and I never rose any higher in the school. I remained 'Remove'. Not even Fifth. And never a prefect. I grew up, heard talk, read newspapers, worshipped Mrs Pankhurst, and became a muddled, badly-arguing socialist. But the wonder went out of the school with Mrs Huxley.

Chapter Three

✳

WHAT they spent on me....
I don't know how Marburg was arranged or who knew someone who knew a German family. I went to it for three months. I couldn't stand it longer.

There was something called a '*Bummel*'. I have stored the word and perhaps it doesn't exist. It seemed to mean men walking up and down the street in the evening, wearing mackintoshes and looking for girls.

Though always accompanied I glanced back at their glances. I was flattered. Fat didn't seem to matter in Germany.

I came home with very little German. Then I was to learn French. Somebody's governess had been discovered socially. That was a mistake. She set up a small school in Lausanne and I travelled out with a guinea pig in a box.

From the moment I got there I sniffed meanness. The food was mean, the suspicions were mean, the woman was mean. There were eight girls.

At the end of the week (quivering with dislike of everything) I learnt there was to be a dance. Six Swiss boys were invited. I understood it was a dance to learn manners.

On the day of the dance, about tea-time, we stood for some reason with a governess at a tram stop. All the trams went by full, and if anyone got off at our Stop a leather strap was hooked up so that no one should get on.

As the third tram stopped I called out, 'Come on!', leapt on to the platform, threw my leg over the strap, tried to go inside, but was ejected. The girls laughed but the governess walked us home in silence.

I was 'sent for'. I was accused of 'exposing' myself. For a minute I hardly knew what was meant. True I was seventeen, but never in my life had it crossed my mind sexually to attract anyone. My disgust at the accusation went all lengths. I had never lived with mean people. I said so. I was sent to my room, supperless and danceless (about that I didn't care) and locked in. In the morning I was dangerous.

Again 'sent for'. To the woman's bedroom. She lay in bed with a bed-tray on four legs across her. The tray with the food was covered with black oilcloth. As she re-accused me (and owing to a missing tooth) she spat on the oilcloth.

'You lifted your leg' (she said again – incredibly – the expression reminded me of a male dog) 'to attract men.'

I opened my mouth to deny it. Then saw the spittle. I took her by the shoulders and shook her head backwards and forwards with a murderous strength. I might have broken her neck. My whole life's journey depended on one bit of gristle. It held.

I looked at her. I saw she was alive, and left the room. I packed a small case, went to the station, and took a ticket along the line to Perroy. I think it was called Perroy. It was where Paderewski lived.

My father knew some friends there and they helped me send a telegram home. I stayed the night. Then went back to the school.

No one spoke to me. I find, looking back, their whole attitude extraordinary. I think they really thought I was mad. In my room I went on packing. A note was then pushed under the door to say that my luggage would be retained to pay the fees. I came down to meals, passing twenty-four hours in silence (though the girls glanced at me with longing awe), and then a Cook's courier, a Miss Deakin, came for me.

Everything melted before her. We left with the luggage and the guinea pig. What about quarantine? Didn't it exist? Or did I smuggle it through?

At home I walked into the drawing-room. Mummie (lying on a sofa) held out her arms. – 'Oh my poor darling!'

'Are you ILL?' (in horror).

'I've lost another baby,' she sighed. 'Never mind.'
Daddy came in. 'That woman was a bitch, it seems.'
That was all. On his daughter's side without a question.
And all through my youth the same.

           *   *   *

Paris was a dream of happiness. I stayed a year.

It was a large and expensive school at Neuilly called the Villa Léona, owned by a Madame Yeatman, who was quite famous in her day. She had retired (I never saw her) and was succeeded by Miss Eastman.

There was the opera (which I couldn't bear) but there was Sarah Bernhardt. This is what I remember. It was *L'Aiglon*.

Opening Act One. People on the stage talked of the young Duc de Reichstadt. He had not appeared. They went. Then in the garden in deep thought he was there – tapping his riding boot with his whip. Actress and duke conveyed together that he was alone, unaware of the audience.

Suddenly – (the tail end of his bitter thought) – unintelligible words ran like an arc through the theatre, like a hand striking a harp.

It was a line of Rostand's of course. I am not going to look it up: it's how I heard it. It was how it was done that night. That lovely voice – in that line – had not been used as a voice. It had instead this startling effect – of thought escaping. It was so private we were stunned.

Then, looking us over, the young man knew that he was not alone. The play began.

I can't have invented that effect. I couldn't have invented such mastery.

On Thursdays we went out in small groups to museums and when possible I slipped across a particular road to chalk 'Vive Sarah!' on the wall of the Boulevard Péreire.

This must have been about 1906–7.

There was also Mounet Sully. And there was Coquelin. I suppose no one falls in love with Napoleon now. Hitler has seen to that. But I did. Recollecting that golden fire I can hardly separate Napoleon, Rostand, Madame Sarah's white-uniformed youth (at sixty), Coquelin's back against a tree ('*Ce sont les cadets de Gascoigne!*') – and Napoleon. On Napoleon's death-day I borrowed a black dress from a girl called Edith Jordan, who was in mourning, and with the stretched back fastened together with chains of safety pins came ponderously down to Morning Prayers.

Miss Eastman fixed the shimmer of her pince-nez on me from where she stood.

'Turn round, Enid Bagnold.'

The broad white vertical band of petticoat from neck to hem was displayed to the rostrum.

'And why is this?'

'It is the day Napoleon died,' I said in the ringing tones of Hyde Park Corner.

'There is no need to make Napoleon absurd,' she said. 'Go to your room and change.'

It was a radiant year, fighting to conquer the French language – poems, plays – entering French literature. I should never have learnt as much French as I did but for my devotion to Mademoiselle Ruth Charpiot, the literature teacher.

An American girl, Carola Stuyvesant Fish, tried to do my hair. She was concerned about my looks. But Ruth Charpiot read Verlaine aloud to me. (Verlaine against Miss Fish? I couldn't waste time on my hair.)

* * *

The Paris year was over. I was 'finished, burnished, ready'.

* * *

1907. And now we have the parents with the great gosling come home. Awkward, clever, bubbling, in touch with life but not with graces, mad about herself, furious with her face, not well dressed, unable to dance, suddenly shocked, struggling, imprisoned by strange standards.

Dear and beloved Warren Wood. It was from there I rose like a dragon-fly to my adventures. Always returning.

It was from there I went to my Chelsea life, and from there, later, to my high society. But always to come back and tell and tell. Not the whole truth. And how my mother listened. She always remained as she was: she never grew older: adoring, amused, delighted. Whatever wrong I was doing I couldn't do wrong.

I see perfectly well where I got what Cynthia Asquith* called my 'luck' from. It was this confidence that my mother gave me that I have had all my life (and which only the theatre has broken). Now that I know that I am gifted, which then I only hoped, it's strange that I should have ended up with the one form of art that obscures it.

There was so much love in the house, such gaiety at my return, such pride in presenting me, such beauty in the garden. It wasn't that my mother was so good with flowers – not as good as I am. It was the garden itself, its extraordinary position, as it hung, hidden (query existing? Was it real?) at the edge of the Old Dover Road, on the crown of Shooter's Hill, traffic pouring from London, not a sound reaching in. Eight miles from London Bridge and in May the bluebells were solid; in June the bracken. The ancient trees grew there since Henry the Eighth (whose Shoot it had been). Our garden had two and a half acres. The rest of the forty acres of the old Shoot went with Falconwood next door, a Palladian house come down in the world that belonged to nobody in particular.

Dear and beloved Warren Wood (in winter ice cold), each room marvellously important. Each room different, very personal, the whole enclosed in a 'Gothic' villa with a turret, built (Daddy said) in a bad period, and sinking a little at one side.

His study, on the right of the front door as you went in, could have been no man's but his own. He lived in it like an engineer-fish in its shell. There was no convenience-contraption that he did not turn on his lathe in brass or mahogany (he collected Victorian mahogany W.C. seats because the wood was so seasoned) to make his surroundings serve him. Things were to hand, or arrived to hand electrically, or on hinges, or on wires. Two inches of brass tubing, stuck upright on a crossbar, held his personal dusting brush. A pilot jet burnt day and night for his pipe. A metal rod had a swivel-head attached to the gas tap (no need to stoop). And beside the gas fire was a gas ring for melting glue. Glue bought in tubes was frivolous. One bought

* Lady Cynthia Asquith.

it in slabs and melted it in a jacketed copper pot. His typewriter swung away from him on a hinge at a touch. He could ring a bell from wherever he sat in whatever part of the room. A slender metal rod (pulled by a string) made contact (within a ring) from whatever angle it was pulled. His desk was a battleground which he commanded. Water, sponges, compass, coloured inks, contrivances simplified from the experiences of a lifetime, all had settled positions. It was he who taught me to suspend a large piece of hardboard on the wall for basic tools, outlining each tool in coloured ink, so that you could exclaim in fury on entering the room, *'Who's taken my hammer!'*

When called into this room, or temporarily allowed in it, I couldn't keep my fingers to myself.

'Ethel!' he would shout to my mother (long before *Pygmalion*), 'can't you take this bloody child away!' I was brought up to bad language and, hardly noticing, have always used it.

The drawing-room was miscellaneous. Nobody had set out to make it a woman's room. There was a band of pale blue above the picture-rail. And this – for a man who hated art and decoration – greatly pleased my father, because it was he who had thought of it.

An upright cottage piano was draped with an Indian cloth on which the peacocks had looking-glass eyes, worked round with turquoise and silver. The sofa and two armchairs sat round the chillyish anthracite stove. Daddy couldn't bear the front opened. To open it contradicted the theory on which the stove was designed. My mother would put out a slender toe and tweak it open.

Here again, as in every room, there was a gas ring. This one was for the legendary making of Turkish coffee. When serving in Egypt he had watched the women grind coffee beans in stone mortars and he would have liked me to do the same. Only thus could one get (and it's true) the almost-greasy, face-powder-quality which coffee should have for its finest taste. Failing the mortar (I had rebelled) he found a grinding machine, a shiny copper tube so dreadfully designed that it turned round and round in your hand as you tried to hold it. The rules were (and this was for every day) that I grind the coffee fresh immediately after lunch, that it came to the boil (but never boiled) in sugared water – sugared because the immersion-period was longer than in water without sugar. I affirm this: Daddy said it: it *must* be right.

Coming near the boil three times (twice stirred and the last time not) it was stood on a brass Egyptian tray so that the chill of the metal decoyed the grounds down through the coffee-water. It was poured with care so that the guest got the froth. It was a long business. Roderick said that he married me for my coffee.

Tea also was dictated from knowledge and care and was a nuisance. Daddy designed a plated teapot with a pendulous sieve inside. Into this the tea leaves were put, the boiling water poured on, and a metronome set ticking. At the moment between theine and tannin the metronome gave a yell, the sieve was taken out like lightning and I was sent running to the bottom lavatory to wash it, since tannin stained silver plate if it was left on.

THE DINING-ROOM. It deserves caps. Everything that really happened happened in the dining-room. Meals grouped us firmly together. It was then that things were said. Rows and plans and decisions about my life broke out in words at breakfast. There is something in me pulsing and impetuous (and not wise) in the early morning. But my father, faced with his office day, needing quiet for his newspaper, faced too with a lavatory-anxiety about which I didn't know then, was in the lowest and last mood to encounter me.

The long oak dining-table filled the centre of the room. Over it whispered and sibilated the incandescent gas mantles of the hanging chandelier; brass, and shaped like a crown. All through meals in the dark of the winter the mantles listened to my chatter, and chattered in my silence. There was an open fire, two armchairs, two cabinets. One held Crown Derby, never used. The other had sugar, jam, and particularly tins of sweetened Nestlé's milk. This I often stole, winding half a tin on to a spoon, and dashing the shine off my lips as the door-handle moved. The instinct for stolen food is deep. It lives in some wild animal-pocket, quite suddenly accessible. People who are poor eaters will eat if they can steal the food. I throw out this psychology-suggestion.

French windows opened on to the garden. Trees filled the panes. Outside was the dog kennel.

My forebears hung on the walls. Busts of my father's father and my father's uncle (brothers) stood on columns in two corners of the room. They had been done by Susan Durant, a woman who did most of the sculpture round the base of the Albert Memorial.

The two old gentlemen looked out at me eyeless, from their Parian substance. I, too, had long become blind to them. My grandfather had been a general in the Honorable East India Company. My great-uncle Tom a sea captain. He had been cashiered for twenty years; and reinstated.

In those long reaches of adventure (to come – I am speaking backwards) between twenty and thirty (when I married) my father retired. Creatures of that age (mine) tend to think that what their parents are keen on is tedious. Tedious, because it comes out of a special layer of life, the 'retired layer', and often holds the fort in talk at mealtimes.

In what's called old age (but he had thirty more years to go) my father took up his genealogical tree. He and my mother went to Staffordshire and roamed about among tombs. She spent hours at the British Museum and the India Office copying things. My grandfather's career wandered in and out of that period in India. I paid no attention to this. I was swimming too hard. Waves of life rose in foam for me to dive under or over. I thought it all just a hobby and hoped not to have to listen. When Daddy died he was ninety (and Mummie had died fifteen years before), my brother and I brought boxes and boxes and trunks to this house in Rottingdean. It was all carried to my eternal 'Tower Room', a type of high room which I had in each house and which dates from the one in Warren Wood. There were military tin boxes with 'Major A. H. Bagnold' painted in white on them, and earlier boxes, lined with Regency wall-paper, belonging to my grandfather. I took a brief glance, and felt that my father had taken immense trouble; but felt too that he didn't know where to stop. Out of respect I meant to read it all – all the histories of cousins who had married cousins, their 'pedigree-tables', the ship-owners, the sea captains who had sailed under them and married their daughters, but I quailed at the pedigree-tables in my father's beautiful 'drawing-hand', taught long ago at the 'Shop' (the Royal Military Academy). The Indian ink shone, spotless, the children 'descended' in table-legs – crossbars for marriages – through Larkins's, Tickells, Pascoes, child by child, through the Indian Mutiny and the eighteenth century, middle-class, robust, seafaring, soldiering, through graves and births, coming nearer and nearer to me. The boxes were stacked and dustsheets thrown over them. I meant to look at them 'one day'. But the sea of life was still in a rage.

Then disaster.

Alone here in this house in Rottingdean, in my seventies, the cold tank on the roof froze, thawed, broke. Water came down through five floors, beginning high up with the boxes. It was terrible. I felt my father's wrath. I had never looked at them.

I carried them down to the kitchen in endless journeys, and knelt, drying the books and folios and handwritten diaries inside the plate-warming compartment of the Aga stove. Feverishly I separated pages with the point of a knife as the ink tried to stick. I was guilty, guilty as I saw the dates, the private letters, words of life – lived. In the end nothing is undecipherable, though the ink ran and some words are blotched. It all went back to India. Cawnpore, dying letters, a mother writing at her last gasp, my grandfather's jovial diaries of dinner parties, of rajahs and their English or French mistresses; my great uncle's diaries, his inventions, his court-martial, his dryness, and the way he handled death. Without this water-accident I might never have looked at them. Old stuff. But suddenly not old stuff any longer. Not old-fashioned. Diaries of two men from whom I came, who never knew me. These were the loins. Sperm has been ejected through two hundred years to arrive at me. I am navel-y attached to a man who wrote in his own clear sepia hand how he fought the French and buried the dead and what he was and what was his life. Those chalkwhite busts in the dining-room at Warren Wood coloured up and moved their lips. No young person would be lit up by it. Only at my age does the marvel work.

The 'Family' is curiously detested now. I have not that feeling. I grew out of the dead and I can't forget it.

The material here, that my father tied up in boxes and labelled, grows more important and strange as time goes by and the dead recede. All over England there is menace to the private past, as the people grow thicker on the ground and the houses smaller. These valiant, tough, middle-class soldiers and sailors of mine have only me to look after them. And I am too interested in ME.

My great-grandmother (I read) Thomasin Bagnold, born in 1756, seventh daughter of a bell-founder, was said to have a hot temper. One judges the dead by the accident of a letter here and there. My father had a hot temper. I had a hot temper. But why pin it on Thomasin? It may have trickled down since Adam. At any rate her husband left her. She had three sons. She managed somehow. I can't believe she loved them much for they all sailed away from her.

My great-uncle Tom, the eldest, was born in 1780. My grandfather, Michael Edward, in 1787, and John (I think) in 1792.

John died at twenty-nine in India, and in his last letter home to his eldest brother he said: 'Mother always preserved a silence regarding them (his father's people) which I have remembered with painful sensations. I have often longed ardently to know them – something of our Father's Birthplace and Burial. The only person I ever saw was a good-natured, honest, farmer-like looking man who called at Knightsbridge. I went with him to Town and recollect his taking me to a stable in Piccadilly to see the large cart horse, Monarch, 22 hands high.'

So Thomasin was implacable. And, later, she married again 'a gentleman from Winchester and a man of considerable means' (*Gentleman's Magazine*, Vol. LXXIII, page 986) 'the Revd James Pile Ashe'.

Before she married, my grandfather Michael Edward sailed from Gravesend in April 1802, not yet fifteen, in the *Sir Edward Hughes* as volunteer Bombay Marine. He arrived in India in that August and 'was employed against the piratical States of Malwan'. Still fifteen, he was at the capture of the forts of Muckey and Soosoo on the coast of Sumatra.

An episode on the voyage out changed his ideas about the Bombay Marine. They were a rough lot. Landing on an island they found the Innkeeper in his coffin on a table, dead from typhus, the rum at their command. As the fumes rose they tipped out the corpse and put in my grandfather, carrying him to the edge of the sea. He woke (rum too?) to find himself rocked on the incoming tide. Sailing on to India he got out of the Bombay Marine and into the army. In 1804 he became an ensign. In 1805 a lieutenant. And so on . . . till in 1854 he became a major-general.

I would not answer for it but I think he never saw his mother again. She sounds an old bitch, but how do I know? I can make a mistake and she is vulnerable against me.

The last I hear of her is a letter in which she asks Michael Edward (then a full general) to come home and look after her and her old second husband. He wrote back – 'If I give up my career for you what are you leaving me?' She replied: 'Nothing', so he didn't go.

My great-uncle Tom, the eldest, sailed in the *Mars* (Royal Marine) in 1797.

'I witnessed' (his diary begins), 'the general mutiny of the Channel Fleet.'

On the next page: 'This evening made Barbadoes.

'In consequence of a drunken quarrell at Nancy Clarke's Tavern a duel was fought next morning between T. Tappen, Surgeon of the *Arab* and Lieut. Dundas of the Army, the latter had his thigh shattered. In the evening the Capt. came on board drunk and confined all the Officers in a most extraordinary manner leaving me in charge of the ship. Next morning he released all but the Master . . .'

He 'observed' a Flying Saucer and described and drew it too. No explanation. This happened twice.

April 13. 1804. 'Saw a curious phenomenon as follows: There were two large luminous rings in the sky which was thick, damp, and hazy: the larger one parralell to the Horizon and a small one at right angles to that. The orbit of the larger one passed through the center of the small one. In the center of the small one was the sun and on either side of him where the circles intersected each other, was a luminous reflection looking in all like three suns, and on an opposite side of the circle appeared two more thus:

```
        April   04
 3  Sailed from Lerwick
12  made the Ferroe Islands
13  Saw a curious phenomenon
    as follows — there were 2
    large luminous rings in
    the sky which was thick
    damp & Hazy the larger
    one parallel to the Horizon
    and a small one at right
    angles to that the orbit of
    the larger one passed thro'
    the Center of the small one —
    in the Center of the small
    one was the Sun and
    on either side of him where
    the Circles intersected each
    other was a luminous
    reflection looking on all
    like 3 Suns   on the
```

```
    opposite side of the Circle
    appeared 2 more thus

    This Memorandum not being
    made till the 24th I am not
    certain whether it was the 6
    or 13? but it was on a friday
    I rather think on the 13. —
              May
12  Off Peterhead & heard of the
    Bills return to power
13  arrived in Cromarty sent
    the Gool Gawl round to
    Inverness for Wine —
21  made the Coast of Norway
22  near North Bergen
23  Anchored
24  Weighed & made Sail in
    chace of a Cutter
```

'*A curious phenomenon*' (*from my great-uncle's diary, 1804*)

In May 1807 his ship was ravaged by yellow fever. His diary: At eleven this night died Thomas Nealands and at 8 at night died James Halford. Our situation now dreadful. Every officer laid up with the fever but Capt. Edward Dix, Acting Captain, and myself, who kept watch with 11 men in one watch and 10 in the other.

(next day) The surgeon ill. The decks strewn with sick and dying, ranged alongside between the guns, having no strength to get into their hammocks and not being near enough well men to look after them. In this situation I cleared the booms which in this ship were very high and levelled them, spreading spare and old sails upon them to make a large bed. Put a gangway ladder and two handrails up to it, the ship being flush fore and aft, and made them lay there with an awning over them. This system in a great measure seemed to do good and having from former experience found Ginger tea efficacious in allaying the violent retching in this disease, I carried a quantity from Barbadoes

with me and hardly found it fail whenever it was used. I am now Surgeon-Officer of the Watch, Marine Officer, Chaplain. In fact was obliged to try all things and fortunately a good constitution and spirits carried me through.
Died Norman and Maria Burrell, a brown woman. Mr Pilkington sickened at four.
Died Thomas Green – marine. Died Edward Glass, John Benson and Elizabeth Norman. Died Mr King William, John Lowe, Pilkington, buried them in the evening.
Observing a smoke ashore landed in the yawl and found we were abreast of the Suramaca River. The shore here low, muddy and swampy and covered with forest timber to the water's edge. Shore covered with Flamingoes and thousands of other birds and the water full of sharks, sunfish etc. On my return on board found two men dead, names forgot, but was called to bury them while dining with Captain Dix who had waited till my return.

He was court-martialled in 1808 – apparently unjustly. He petitioned during twenty-three years, and was reinstated in 1831 and his name restored to the Navy lists. On August 3, 1835 he puts down the word 'Married'. And under it:

> Inveni Portum Spes et fortuna valete
> Sat me ludistis ludite nunc alios.

On October 30, 1836: 'She took to her bedroom.' Otherwise the lady isn't mentioned.
'August 4, 1833 . . . my brother [my grandfather] landed at the Customs House Stair where I met him after a separation of 41 years (and the 31st of his absence from England).'

My father had printed one small page of all his father's achievements to the point where he retires, buys a house (14 Upper Hamilton Terrace) and dies in 1857. My father's special touch at the end:

> (Kensal Green. Grave 14. 194, Sq. 62.)

He had a kind of ogre-ish delight in the stuff you throw away.
 'Be tidy, label it first, number the parts.' – (i.e., the bicycle I later took to pieces.)

As a child it made me wince. It does still. 'The filing cabinet,' he seemed to insist, 'outwears the body.'

But was it because he himself resented death? And by kicking the horror faced up to it?

It was the same when he brought back to Warren Wood his brother Lexy's gold plate from his dead mouth.

'Oh .... Arthur!' (horrified, my mother).

'Why not? He won't want it.'

Tom would have done the same, of course, for Michael Edward.

UNCLE LEXY. Like the dining-room I give him caps. He was a special man, a 'Desmond'* sort of man, the only one in our family. Gay, subtle, indulgent, never cross, patient – but patient from philosophy as well as nature. Odd things made him laugh. I was too young to understand why, but I loved the sudden bubble in him. He wrote poems, and even a play in verse, but this I only knew after his death. He wouldn't, of course, have told a child, and no doubt he pretended to think his own specialities unrespectable in his army family. My father pretended to think so too, but he treasured them later with a wary pride, as though the writing of poetry had a kind of dynamite mxed with shame.

Alexis (Lexy) was the old general's eldest son: my father was his youngest, born in 1854. Older than Lexy came Alice, and in between came Clara. There were other children, but either they died of cholera in India or were buried at sea.

Lexy was a stout man with beautiful manners, a barrister, well off, chairman of some big insurance company, and unmarried. Unmarried for a sad reason, and it marred his life. His sister, Clara, was ugly. Women are not often ugly to that extreme, but she was. Her lower lip drooped out like the old Queen's. When my grandmother died she left that Victorian Command – so terrible and strong – a deathbed wish. 'Look after Clara.' And this Lexy did, for he knew what was meant. Clara was cursed by her looks. She would never marry.

So he never married either and he took a mistress. He was as loyal to her as to a wife, and by her he had two charming

* Sir Desmond MacCarthy. F.R.S.I., Hon.D.Litt., Hon. LL.D. (1877–1952). Theatre critic, Essayist.

daughters. My father and mother helped him with their upbringing in every way they could.

The other, older sister, Alice, knew nothing of this. My uncle shrank from letting her know – perhaps because she married a canon. I remember her (from one visit to them when I was thirteen) sitting at the head of her Sunday table while my uncle carved. She had thirteen children and twelve of them were there. She had a square, strong, sweet face, and red hair. If I had been Uncle Lexy I would have told her.

At my mother's funeral, half a lifetime later, the only thing that was near to fun on that dreadful day was my introduction of one cousin to another.

'A *cousin* . . . .' the legitimate cousin probed. (They were hot on relationships.)

'Take it or leave it,' I said – 'Have some tongue.'

Uncle Lexy stayed with us. Not often. Our house was cold and his was warm. And we didn't have wine. Of if we did it was Graves: you can't sink lower. He generally came because he wanted advice about his daughters. He worried about them; deeply feeling his guilt. But they married happily and well; the husbands prospective being told, of course, of the illegitimacy.

At meals, like all people who live by themselves, he had lonely tricks. He started to hum; and stopped. He played the piano on the tablecloth. But the trick he loved and that my father hated was to thread his knife inside his silver napkin ring. Then watching it carefully he moved the knife up (chink) and down (chink). My father frowned, we held our breath, but Uncle Lexy attended thoughtfully to the napkin ring.

Racked by apprehension that my father would remark on it, I sometimes drew the ring farther away. But while talking to his brother his Unconscious sought it again, and suddenly, if he couldn't find it, he bent his Conscious on the search. This fascinated me. At what point did he make the change?

As a matter of fact my father would never have burst out. The brothers loved each other. Or if love isn't the word they would have liked me to use they were 'fond'. My father valued Lexy's opinion but he qualified – 'These lawyers. . . . They're undermined from the start – taught to see both sides. It's weakening.' And it's true Lexy saw two sides to everything, and weighed things so long they didn't get done.

After Aunt Clara died the five-storeyed house in Warrington Crescent was much too big for him. He sighed that it was so: useless to try to help him. Though he secretly thought my father must be right because he was a man of action he couldn't take that step. 'If I could be wafted in my dreams into a flat'... he said. A Zeppelin bombed him. He was found in the night on his area steps, and taken by ambulance to an open ward in a hospital. The wound wasn't bad but he was there some weeks. He wouldn't be moved to a private ward.

'It's the first time,' he said, 'that I've met poor people.' A whole new life spread before those inquisitive eyes. He made friends whom he stuck to until he died.

At six that bombing morning we were rung up by a voice that grated and shook with fear and courage. Maria, a tough old tree of a parlourmaid, in black and white, who had upheld him for thirty years in her branches, told us of her night. Daddy and I got a lift on a lorry outside Warren Wood and arrived at the picketed area of the seven broken houses about eight. Daddy seemed more enchanted that the telephone could still ring in the house than he was upset by Lexy's predicament.

When he moved him from the hospital to a flat in Kensington Lexy never gave a blink backwards at the Edgware ruins. He shopped SW instead of W. It was a fascinating geographical change.

But before all this happened, and for many years, we had all stayed once or twice a year at Warrington Crescent for a night for a play. Each time it was going to be a straight play, something you could 'live'. It was each time promised. Each time he lost his nerve and made it a Musical.

To a Musical you can safely take everybody – such various people as Mummie and Daddy, Aunt Clara and me. He couldn't face sitting with the four of us through drama and emotion. So I, who hadn't any ear, was each time disappointed and deceived.

We went in a horse-cab, rubber-tyred, and the horse's hoofs seemed rubber-tyred too. The Musical of course held some pleasure for me, but the principal lady seemed to sing the same song so often, and the 'story' got mislaid among the songs. We trotted home, had cocoa, and went to bed carrying lighted candles in candlesticks of Sheffield plate, with snuffers. The house was gaslit but at night it was turned off at the main.

In the morning I woke at six because of the milkman's song and the hoofs of the horses. They were hollow and watery down the empty road.

* * *

But once it was a play.

I was fourteen. I don't know what it was about but as the evening (and the 'story') went on something got transposed, and *I* had written it. The Calls at the end were for *me*. It was I who felt the triumph. I wore a blue sash on the stage and bowed – a genius. That glory drifted through my life – asking to come again.

I had no idea then what a strange art it was – nor what a strange art I would make of it. I thought then it *was* a story. Better for me if I had gone on thinking so. I didn't know then that the transmuting of life in my hands would need the cunning . . . 'the cunning of a crime'.

('A picture is an artificial work, outside nature. It calls for as much cunning as the commission of a crime.' – Degas.)

When I read that it seemed to explain to me my obstinate labour, my edifice of hints and distillations. The theatre is a gross art, built in sweeps and over-emphasis. Compromise is its second name. What I do cannot easily be remade in the bodies, movements, voices of human beings. Ah, if I had known the delicate and bitter labour far far ahead – at a time when the little rough girl became a secret orchid, working in a hot-house of everlasting words – if I had known the agony, the lost and spilt meanings – well, I would have done it all the same. Almost now, at my age, I would write for no public. I would sit like a woman lost in the pleasure of her game of patience until she falls dead-face down upon the cards.

* * *

We are back in the dining-room. I am eighteen. The two old men had not spoken then; they still looked at me with closed eyes, their white lips moveless. No portrait does anything; it has to be the living word. But they drove me out all the same, to risk and taste life.

But what was there to risk – as yet? Where were those men I had grown up for? Where was the boiling world – drunks, lovers, wits, poets, beautiful women, I amongst them? Where was my beauty? What about my composure? Why hadn't Marburg and Lausanne and a year in Paris done more for me? I don't believe, till I thought of men all in a rush that summer, that I had thought of them at all.

I was eaten up, at each foreign school, by the curiosity of my immediate surroundings, and my surroundings had been girls. I hadn't troubled about the future.

What an odd education it was, at that late age, eighteen. Violence and energy and fun and stimulation right up to the edge of going home. And never a thought about men!

And now they were on me and I was undolled-up and unprepared. I was to 'come out'. Men had to be conquered. But what did one say to them? How to talk as I read in books? How to make them tremble with my womanhood? I didn't seem any different from a boy.

My mother couldn't help me. She didn't think there was a problem. She had been beautiful at the right age. At eighteen with golden hair and large violet eyes she must have looked like Juliet. She had had no troubles with men except that she was frightened of them. She had been besieged, but being so shy it hadn't flattered her. And soon she only had to put her hand eagerly and for life into my father's. Then she abandoned, with his blessing, all the puzzling business of 'appearance'. Daddy was still 'Victorian' – though he went on growing all the way to ninety – and he had at that time, and I think always kept, an odd, illogical (or perhaps not?) attitude to women 'decking themselves'. It was right that a girl should dress prettily to catch the male eye, but that eye once caught, she might leave off the adornments. When I asked him 'How do you like my new dress?' . . . 'Very nice,' he would say, but there was a warning in his voice. 'Don't push me too far about clothes.'

Nothing I had asked my mother would have shocked her. She only would have said – 'Wait till Mr Right comes along.' (And I wanted Mr Wrong.) Then I would scream with impatience at her. That she never minded. She laughed. She had baskets of clichés. She knew when she dealt them out I would scream at her. She knew I was as raw as a broken egg but she had her own way of talking and wasn't going to change it. She accepted herself as she was and loved me. But that was no help to this jam I was in. No *man* – and I would be old in a second. It wasn't a physical longing. I had no yearning stamens like a flower. I simply knew that the road up was by adventure, and adventure with men. Road up to where? I wouldn't have minded a throne. I was bursting at the seams, but now we have to get down to thinking of a dress.

So there was Miss Somebody at Blackheath. And what material, and what shape? It must be like nobody else's. It was of cream satin, with a black satin apron in front. I wanted one behind too.

'Like a sandwich man?' she said sharply.

'Yes,' I said, equally sharp. She couldn't see along my lines and I couldn't draw along hers. So – with my 'originality' and conceit and bluster I got my way. I sailed out in it. To my first dance. Oh, Miss Bagnold.

The dress, taken out of its box, had been hung in the steam of the bathroom while my hair was curled with irons. Nobody had asked me to dine first, and so in a horse-cab with my mother we drove together down the Hill. Mercifully it wasn't the Gunner Ball, the coldest, the most hurting of all. It was at the 'Shop' (the Royal Military Academy, then at Woolwich, now at Sandhurst). Partners were found for me but they didn't stay with me. I was returned at the end of each dance. They were my age, cadets. But I could really only hop.

Yet the cadets also had their failures – hot hands, burst gloves, spots. I only got the young ones, but I saw, as we bumped and charged, that there were older cadets who were Stars. I saw the General's daughter dancing with a Star. She had that mysterious poise that attracted him. I saw in his eyes she was offering him something he was liking. It must be sex.

But how did you get sex into your conversation? There was never a gap where a fly could get in. I talked fast to cover my shyness. 'Have you seen a theatre, have you been to the races, what about the Drag, do you know Devonshire?'

'Yes, I know Devonshire, where shall I take you?'

'Take me to my mother. Thank you. Thank you.'

I saw my mother's blue eyes on me – not anxious. She was proud of every inch of me, and I was fat.

And in the cab, going home, 'Did you enjoy yourself, darling?' Enjoy, enjoy! I made her laugh with my set-backs while we had our soup in the kitchen. But my father called down the stairs, 'It's late enough good heavens!' Men don't really like to hear women's conversations.

Alone in my bedroom I moved the furniture. This was something I had done before and that night did again. I don't know what it means when you want to move the furniture, but in V. S. Pritchett's enchanting Memoir, *A Cab at the Door* which I have just read, he says his mother did the same. Was it an excess of strength and jubilance and joy? The dance hadn't been so joyful. But, like coffee, it had woken me up. The familiar and ugly furniture in my room needed to be . . . what? I needed to be drunk to 'see' it. But I wasn't drunk. It needed to be moved to be seen. But the word isn't 'seen', it's 'perceived'. It's the mescalin that is within.

Till dawn I shoved, inexorably pressing, noiseless inch-by-inch angling. The chest of drawers changed places with the marble-topped washstand (its jug of icy water lop-lopping. I disdained to lift it off). The shoe-cupboard had a new corner. And last of all the Elephant of the room (bare toes clinging to the floor) the vast wardrobe grunted over the linoleum to a new position. It was a strange, battling ecstasy. What was wood? – What was power? The brass bed on its castors crossed the room like a dancer. I heard the first bird. It was summer. Soul and body shook together, as on the roof at school. I fell into a heavy sleep and woke to the cosy astonishment of my mother (who had had the 'removal' before, but knew when to be surprised).

'I let you sleep on.'

'*What!*' – I wailed. She had lost me an hour of my life.

'Girls always sleep on after dances.'

'Why, that whole dance wasn't worth losing one hour!'

Must I go to another dance? Why, of course. Things would brighten up. But what (I knew) needed brightening up was the way I did my hair. I didn't spend hours in front of the glass. I looked at it with fury, and left it.

There was no make-up then, or very little. White powder like flour. Rouge was unthinkable. I hardly knew there were hairdressers. I frizzed my hair myself.

I had small successes with older men. But then, as now, they were married. It wasn't that I wanted to marry them, heavens no. And I mistrusted, too, what they might say to their wives in bed. Might they not mock me. . . . I had no knowledge of the intimacy of married people. I understood things in compartments, and never got them put together. To know what's called the facts of life, the breeding arrangements, is nothing. What I was desperate about were the tiny moves, the spots the dice put one in, what to do in them, why one slipped back like snakes and ladders. I didn't know how to be gone-further-with. I couldn't keep it up.

In theory I wouldn't have minded being seduced, but in practice I couldn't be touched. If a man's hand came near me I didn't know the rules. To encourage? My skin winced. To reject? Then I was dull.

All this was called, officially, to 'come out'. To be introduced to the stage of manners and customs that I was expected to occupy for life. To meet, to fall in love, to marry. Then Married Quarters, India, Egypt, the world full then of our army stations. All the 'abroads' enclosed in Married Quarters! *I wasn't going to!*

The Huxley school had given me a sharp taste, and I wanted it again. I knew I must break through this social layer to grander lands. To mountains.

If titles and money provided wider platforms to meet brilliant people, then it was those platforms I wanted. I must climb. But there was nowhere to climb to.

(What do you do when your daughter so curiously wants a better social life than your own?)

But at any rate I was the daughter of a Royal Engineer (I thought) and that's a free thing. A Royal Engineer, anyway in those days, was a man prone to be eccentric. They were the Top Twenty, the cleverest of the batch as they passed through the Royal Military Academy. They were the (mechanical) intellectuals of the army. They were never in groups, but sent alone to special jobs, often in antagonistic relationship to 'army types'. They were often brilliant, tended to know best, to grow inwards, to become mathematicians, explorers, astrologers. My brother Ralph too, began as a Royal Engineer.

'Queer fish' the army called them. My father had made few friends, but strange ones. One was Sir Wallis Budge, Keeper of the Egyptian Department of the British Museum.* Another was Colonel du Paty de Clam of the Dreyfus Case. There was a civilian Higher Mathematician. He would also grow very attached to his non-commissioned working man, his sergeant, his corporal or his quarter master, if he worked with him for a long time.

Suppose then I had no one to marry but a gunner! Or an officer in a line regiment, or in the Cavalry (but there were none at Woolwich). I should spend my life going about with the wives, toeing the line. I determined never never (in spite of the Royal Engineers) to marry a soldier.

But thoughts of marriage didn't fill my days. Yet men did. Men so enigmatic. And, good God, somehow so dull. All this love and sex, hidden behind black and white, or khaki and scarlet, and no way to get at it. There had been no boy in my life, and Ralph had always been too young. What a difference it would have made if I had been three and not six when he was born. The gap was due to the miscarriages. I was twelve and at school when he was six. I was fourteen, fifteen, sixteen, when he was at prep school. At twenty I could have talked to him but he was fourteen. We came together in later life (and now), but we don't remember, in childhood the same things. How much there would have been to say and confide and laugh about if when I was twenty he had been seventeen. He is as brilliant as my father was. Perhaps more brilliant. But brilliance apart I should have loved to have shared my man-troubles with a brother man.

'Oh damn the subject of men!' – I thought. It's like A Levels and O Levels and I wouldn't sit for the examination. Yet I knew I had to.

The truth is I had nothing to do. When you 'come out' – what do you do (in between failures with men and failures with clothes)? It was just beyond the period when you 'helped in the home', and before the period of the secretarial course. Mummie ran the house with two maids, and that was half a maid too

* Sir Ernest Alfred Wallis Budge, (1857–1934), Keeper of Egyptian and Assyrian Antiquities, British Museum, 1893–1924.

much. I thought I was emancipated, just as girls think now. I wouldn't learn to cook, or garden, or sew. These arts came on me twenty years later in a blaze of pleasure.

The maids got £20 to £28 a year. They had no bathroom but carried cans for a hip bath. The hip bath my grandmother had – and would never do without – was a royal thing. A blazing fire, warmed towels. But the maids' hip bath must have taken determination. Our house was as cold as a medieval castle. Mummie said that at the Registry Office in Woolwich they had begun to ask her if the maids could use our bath.

'Over my dead body!' said my father. That closed that.

Our one bathroom was square like a bedroom, with a tree in the window and a row of shining cans. The cans hypnotized me as I lay in the water. I thought long thoughts about life while the water cooled, or broke into tears, looking down at my body, thinking 'It will never be used!' When moments like this came I went for long walks. It never failed. I was gay in a mile. My particular cure-walk took me to Well Hall, past the beautiful old house where E. Nesbit lived. Her husband, Hubert Bland, had a 'reputation with women', or so I'd heard. Passing the house very slowly I murmured the opening words of his (invented) attack on me. Violently attracted, he called me his Enigma. The 'New Age' had had a drawing of him and I would have known him by his broad eyeglass ribbon. I never met him. He never came out. But his coffin came out as I was going by one day, and like a fool I hurried on. Next day I read in the papers that Bernard Shaw had been at his funeral.

In between going for walks and plans to be seduced I took my bicycle to pieces. I made a mess of putting it together again. Next it was my Empire typewriter (a very old one). But this time Daddy showed me how to number the pieces on a board, and after three weeks I got it back together. I watched Mummie add up her weekly accounts, sucking her pencil and desperate. It was nonsense that every penny had to be accounted for, but Daddy was meticulous. 'I'll *never* do that!' I exclaimed. 'No man shall make me do that!' And almost in tears she laughed, not contradicting me. She knew I would have to. Or if not accounts then similar chores of marriage. But at that time I didn't see myself married. I wanted bigger relationships. 'Love', – and no duties.

It was then I had my first proposal. In a conservatory.

'Miss Bagnold . . . May I call you Enid?'

This was the uncertain voice of a lieutenant called Hill. Not a hint of preparation. It was as frightening as rape. I was at once hysterical. To marry into the army when I was just thinking of getting out of it! For a moment, as though looking down the muzzle of a revolver, I stood still.

Then – 'But you don't *know* what you're getting! You don't know what I *am*! . . .'

How he had fallen in love with me, why he had come to the brink of binding himself for life to a young girl who was more like a cavalry charge, who can imagine! I hoped he wouldn't touch me. He didn't. But he told me he had already asked my father.

'What . . . what. . . .' (outraged) '*Asked* for me . . . I'd sooner. . . . I'd rather . . .' (wildly) 'I'd rather be your *mistress*!' But as this was unthinkable too, I ran.

I got home shaking. I never thought of it as a triumph; only as a cutting-short. How could my father imagine. . . . How could he have let him loose on me! He was sitting with Mummie in the little study by the front door.

'How could you let me in for that!' I burst in. 'You *knew* it!'

'Did he propose?' said my mother.

'Yes he did. How dared he!'

'Don't you want to be married?' she said, comfortable and quite unmoved.

'Not to that, *that*!'

'What then?'

'Someone *tremendous*.'

They laughed. 'You may never get another chance.'

But I knew they didn't believe that. They were so proud of me. My father didn't always laugh. My mother always did. She thought it was a joke, having me. And she was never afraid. Yet I think she must have been later, when I went through, for 1909, unheard-of-risks. But if she stayed awake at night then she never let on.

I had another proposal at a Hydro, another from a doctor, and a fourth from an Indian Civil Servant. Each was written in a letter. I say this because it had a bearing later on. They astonished me. Those proposals seemed to have nothing to do with love: they were more like a Take-Over. I had no sense of being attractive. What – then? I pondered. Those four men who might have changed my life (like the near-murder of my headmistress) obviously found in me something to attract them. I was unconscious of being anything but a noisy failure (noisy – to cover the failure). I think now it must have been my vitality That's a thing one doesn't number among one's charms, or even recognize, because one is never aware how much other people lack it. Then, if a male eye looked with love, maybe it saw my intelligence, in spite of the state of blockage I was in. Under my fat I had good looks but I wasn't yet tailored into them. The face-battle, the hair-battle, the figure-battle never abates. It doesn't grow less with age, but it takes on a new relationship (with oneself, not any longer with men). The difference is that now if I can't look as I want I forget it. Then I never could. At sixty-six I had a face-lift done by Sir Archibald McIndoe. This, if it is ever read, will amuse my grandchildren. Either by then they will belong to a harsh Welfare State that frowns on such things, or face-lifts will be the necessary toilet after thirty. For me it was an adventure.

I simply, in 1907, couldn't get to grips with a man. I was lucky if I was asked twice to dance or taken out on the stairs. There was no tremble. The situation was without a current. There was a battery there but it was wired up wrong. Men wore white gloves and there were programmes with white tassels. I never kept one. I felt so 'offered up'. I wouldn't have minded being offered up, but it was the wrong market. And yet, before each dance, there was the quiver of dressing for it and the quiver of what might be. And, in the lighted glass – 'Tonight – this very night?'

'In a month I may be in China or sweeping a crossing.'

It was a little Eastern. In those days, on the whole, men altered your life for you. But looking round I wasn't sure I was going to let that happen.

The dance above dances was the Donaldsons' dance. Not for happiness, but because I could go alone. They were next door, and there was no question of a chaperon. My mother could stay with my father, which was what she so much liked best.

Decked, kissed, and wished luck to, I was let out of one

world (the house), and not yet in the grip of the other (the dance). I hung about in our garden, sniffing at its timelessness, like a house-dog turned wolf. Or, in my absurd satin dress, pretending that I had 'beauty' and was 'fatal to man'. I did see, I did admit, that after the workaday day women had to be something else in the evening. Some sort of trinket. But how to be a trinket? Five foot seven and seven-eighths – eleven stone. I had to get some of that off. Fever of life does it, not fever of fret. (These are the thoughts of later.) As soon as men began to fancy me (not yet) I got thinner. Being in love oneself doesn't do it.

Reluctantly crossing the lane between our gardens I heard the Donaldsons' music, walked up to the lighted windows, watched a moment and went in.

The dining-room where they danced was lined with mirrors. One saw oneself from every angle being wheeled around. 'If I were thinner there . . . or pulled in here . . .' I thought as I turned. And what to say when the music stopped?

The Donaldsons were gunner-women. I despised them and they despised me. They were 'up' to gunners, and I wasn't. Gunners were older men. They knew what they wanted (not me). One compliment would have changed me but it never came. I suffered with the gunners as I never had in all the years at school.

When I went home no one waited up for me. Crossing the garden again I shook off my dance-pangs and disappointments like a duck coming up out of a pond. Two wags of my tail and they were gone. In those days I slept all night. In those days I got up every morning made perfect by sleep. To hell with men. I threw off the beastly necessity of a love-life. I was beginning to write.

Remembering the title of a weekly paper which used to lie in the Mistresses Room at Prior's Field, I bought the *New Age* at Woolwich Arsenal Station. They published things called 'Pastiches', short prose-poems which didn't get one very far, and had to be very good indeed to be accepted because they were so short. They seemed to me easy. They weren't. Mine were rejected. But the *New Age* all of a sudden published a poem. Daddy, who thought the politics of the paper near treason, was pleased about the poem. He felt then, suddenly, that a sitting-room of my own would solve my restlessness. He gave me one. It was my first 'Tower Room'.

Up from his own dressing-room wound a narrow stair. It came out in a Gothic turret which sat for some reason on the roof. It was a pinnacle with a door on to the leads between two slopes of tiles. It was cold, but he put in a gas fire, running up the piping himself. And of course a gas ring. 'You'll want that for glue.' I never questioned the remark. Of course I should want glue. And I did.

He ordered (from the workshops in the Arsenal) a solid carpenter's bench, with two vices. I could never use two, but he must have had some need (from the past) in his head. If you really get used to a vice in your life it's a handy thing.

My life simply thundered in that room. It took on a momentum that has never stopped. I became (beneath the sprouts of youth while eyeing the man-world and uncertain of my suitability, bursting with health, *rowdy* with health) – bit by bit I became, the disciplined writer.

Who wants to become a writer? And why? Because it's the answer to everything. To 'Why am I here?' To uselessness. It's the streaming reason for living. To note, to pin down, to build up, to create, to be astonished at nothing, to cherish the oddities, to let nothing go down the drain, to make something, to make a great flower out of life, even if it's a cactus.

I wrote poems in that room, and my first book (later on). I had a friend called Kitty-K*, who spent her life moving between adorations. Me she adored, to the extent of thinking every word I wrote better than the last one. I didn't believe her but that made no difference. It was the Food of the Gods, the Vitamin B.12 for the Ego. And it's the ego that drives.

Ah Kitty-K's Pill of Praise. . . . What would I give to have it now, to read aloud egotistically each evening about six with a glass in my hand the words I had written in the morning.

So, Cuthbert,† when you came I thought it would be you! But, poor Cuthbert, you are writing for your own life, for dear life.

* Kitty Foord–Kelsey.

† T. C. Worsley: theatre critic, who lived – adding greatly to my life – for four years in my cottage in the garden: and whose woes and triumphs I have shared as he has mine.

Chapter Four

*

S HOOTER'S HILL had large houses on the north side of its descent. It was a dramatically upright hill. When it froze the coal horses fell, generally opposite the drinking fountain. Fallen horses are terrible. One doesn't see them now.

Broom Hall, Blomefield House (where in 1880 the skulls of twelve horses were found under a floor), Ramsey House, Campbell House (where the clergyman lived who had too long an upper lip).

And on the other side of the road Castle House (where the Phillips's lived), Severndroog Castle (not a castle but a memory of a battle), Castlewood, Hazelwood, Forest Lodge, Summercourt, and us.

They were houses of size, with gardens. So there were garden parties.

At Blomefield House lived the General commanding the Garrison, General Tylden. He had a daughter called Dolly. It wasn't a name that suited her and she changed it. But not then. Chic, composed, smart, with a cheeky nose and a dog's melting eyes, she looked to me as though she had the key to life. They gave a garden party.

While the Gunner Band was playing behind the trees she spoke to me.

'D'you like reading?'

'I don't know.' (Taken aback.)

'What do you read?'

To show off I said, 'Browning.'

'What about Bernard Shaw?' (I'd missed him at the funeral but I had also missed him in books.)

'Galsworthy?'

'I've never heard of him.'*

A pause.

'I hate it here!' (With sudden intimacy.)

'Where?'

She indicated the surrounding country, making it mental as well.

'You'll . . .' (I tried to be intimate too) . . . 'marry.'

'Never! My family's too old, it's played out. I'd give birth to an idiot.'

I shivered at this freshness, as one shivers with delight when one first hears French.

'I've never been kissed,' I volunteered, again to imitate her intimacy.

She looked round at the men. 'I'm not much of a kisser,' she said gloomily. 'I'm too finicky.' Then suddenly – 'Let's go and live in London.'

It started like that. There was the fuse but the cotton wouldn't burn. Not then. Three days later a kiss was given and received. But badly received. I had been with the Donaldsons to the Garrison Theatre. (Sir Frederick Donaldson had yet to be drowned with Lord Kitchener.)

There was a major in their party, a sophisticated man, I thought. Bit by bit I was getting prettier (so slow I didn't notice it). No mirror gives one any idea of oneself, and in age it's just the same. I couldn't, when I looked in the glass, see my own eagerness.

This major was attracted to me. Since I couldn't find my attraction in a looking glass then perhaps I might find it in him? He asked me to tea in his flat in London and by a miracle I was going with my mother to the dentist. By a miracle I managed an hour free.

When I got there he had a used sort of face and kept the gramophone on; there was a fire and tea, and a sordid mirror

---

* I knew him later when I had written *A Diary without Dates*. He asked me to go and see him. The light came from behind him as he stood on his porch. He had shellpink, transparent ears. Holding out his hands he said: 'Come in – Heart of Pity!' He was quite out of my generation.

in front of a sofa. When he kissed me, which was as soon as he had poured out the tea, I caught sight of my face in the glass as my hat went sideways. How far would he have gone, how ridiculous his watchchain, and in fact how like a father. That in itself was unpleasant. I fled, crashing on my knees at the door of his flat, one knee broken and afterwards needing band-aid. My mother saw my knee.

'I had a fall,' I said.

'You should look where you're going.' I was amused at that.

Thinking over the man, I wondered if I ought to have stomached him. It was a great loss to have lost him. But how shocking the kiss had been. Should I tell Dolly? Yes, always tell. It's the only thing that's fascinating. What's the good of anything? It's words that count.

'Dolly . . .'

'I hate my name. It doesn't suit an Intellectual.'

I by-passed that and pushed in my story. 'What made him like you?' she said.

'Could I be pretty?'

'Not yet. You're too fat.'

'Then what did he see in me that I don't know I've got?'

'Your eager eye and your vitality.'

'I can't do much with that!'

'Why did you go?'

'I went exploring.'

'That's no good unless you feel something.'

'How do I know if I feel unless I try?'

'Don't worry. He was just a bloody bastard.' She, like my father, was long before *Pygmalion*. She swore when she chose, but she was thought no more than fast. Her mother was dead and her father didn't dream of correcting her. He was a frightening man but he didn't frighten her.

'Dolly. . . .'

'Call me Violet.'

'So soon? Are you certain?'

Was she to be Violet for life?* And should I remain Enid? But it doesn't weigh on one that one doesn't know anything that lies ahead. She changed my life. I was nineteen and she was twenty. 'Loose talk – loose talk! How marvellous!' By which I

* Now Mrs Violet Henson of Hammamet.

mean that at last I could talk about men. I had nothing to say. But she had. She was a real contemporary. My first. She said it again at last, and made it concrete. 'I'm taking a flat. Come and share with me and the Brockmans.' 'Share' was a fourth share of a rent of 12s 6d a week.

Now I had to put it to my father.

I never could put a case, not all my life, not now. I choke with indignation at being refused before I have the first word sticking out. I turn my listener at once into an opponent. It was of course at breakfast. What a meal to choose!

Yet such a locked-in meal, so cosy, fresh, euphoric (perhaps only to me?). Why was the food so good, with those changing servants? Mummie said she enjoyed changing. 'Such a change to have a change.'

Whole kidneys that never shrank, on toast that had caught the blood: things called kromeskis, rolled in vermicelli that when fried ate like tiny twigs: things fried (Daddy loved twice-cooked meat – we all did): a plated breakfast dish on legs, with a double belly for hot water.

There was Devonshire cream that morning, sent by an uncle. 'Cow Grease', Daddy called it. It always made him angry, and even sick, to see Mummie and me eat it just as it was from a spoon. He longed to read the morning paper in silence as he ate. If he was crossed and made to lose his temper he left the dining-room and took the *Morning Post* to the lavatory. I knew all this but I couldn't let the whole glorious day go by without asking my question. Or making my statement.

'I want to go and live with Dolly Tylden in London.'

Why couldn't the silly fool (me) put it better? How could he know all at once in that one line that this was a point I'd got to that was far beyond reason?

'Dolly TYLDEN ... ?' He didn't seem even to know her name.

'General Tylden's dau —'

'Yes I know I know. What do you want to go and live with *her* for?'

Skipping every reasonable answer ... 'I want to live ...' (making a great gesture the shape of the world) ... 'I want to LIVE. ...'

'Isn't this living that you do with us?'

A father is always making his baby into a little woman. And when she is a woman he turns her back again.

This little feminine thing which I had never been, this doll, this darling, had said an idiot thing. Point blank, like an enemy.

He couldn't eat any more. He was on his feet, passing my chair, going.

'But EVERYBODY, everybody... wants...' I said up into his face as he passed.

'Who's *EVERYBODY*?' he said furiously. And was gone.

'Darling,' said my mother as the door slammed, 'you *do* upset him.'

'And now now NOW' (desperate), 'I'll have to do it all again!'

He had me into his study that evening. He had thought of it a lot, probably, that day – and while walking slowly back up the Hill with his hands behind him.

Perhaps I had been right after all to say it in the morning. It needed two sessions – with a gap for thought between.

'Sit down and tell me why.'

'You see, I'm like a man, Daddy – I want experience! I *must* have it!'

'But you're supposed to be a girl...' (looking down at his hand, finding a bit of loose nail, even picking up his scissors to chip it off – but I knew his mind was sailing over his actions).

'I want to meet artists and people.'

'Artists!' I shouldn't have said it. From being reasonable he was off balance again. If I say he hated art I mustn't be got wrong. He hated what he thought was exaggeration and misrepresentation. All this 'presenting' and re-seeing and transposing that we do when we paint or write, that was anathema to him. The word 'art' could drive him beyond reason. When Lovat* came to stay with us later (and they quite got on) he said, 'I've never known anyone so blunt about art as your father. It's almost heroic.'

Having got on to the wrong foot about artists I was silent as he calmed down. He said at length. 'Let's get this all over this evening. I don't want to have it again. What are you going to do all day if you live up there?'

'Go to Walter Sickert.'

* Lovat Fraser.

'Who's that?'

'It's a drawing school like the one at Blackheath.'

(I had been to Blackheath Art School for a time, taking sandwiches and drawing in the Life Class.)

'If you want to live under a separate roof I can't afford more. You'll have to live on your allowance.'

'I will. I will.' It was seventy-five pounds a year.

His side of the talk was carried on without a word of love. He was deeply hurt but he was determined not to get angry.

'Have you thought about your mother?' (I had, I had.)

'It won't be for ever, Daddy. It won't be for ever. It won't be for long.'

'No. Don't kiss me. Go to your mother.'

The first time your child finds the house you have built around her stultifying, the first time she takes somebody else's side against you, the first time she wants something from a contemporary more than from her mother and father – then you know you are left behind. It happens with each generation. But it's astonishing how astonishing it is. And what astonishing pain.

So I went to London – with many a pang and backward thought for them. But I knew I must do it, or else be odious at home.

The flat Dolly found was in Rectory Chambers in Lower Church Street in Chelsea. It stands there still, its door open, the discoloured tiles still line the walls by the stairs. Dreary to look at, but not to me. Three bedrooms, a sitting-room, a kitchen and a bathroom. Twelve and six a week.

By what native genius did Dolly (who didn't succeed with 'Violet' for another twenty years) hug the group so soon – so close – around us? She had a circle-making gift. Lovat Fraser, Gaudier-Brzeska, Sophie his 'sister', Kenneth Hare, Haldane Macfall. These are the names that stick. But there were others.

With her long cigarette holder, stuck in that face of a little Pekinese, Dolly sauntered through her day with an easy friendly intelligence, with a nose for the best. She was cynical, without bitterness, amused without shyness, debunking, chuckling, commending, with no ambition for herself.

People who want to create are restless, upsetting companions; but not to Dolly. I was never a circle-maker. Without her (and

I have no 'Dolly' now) I strip my life of companions. And then complain I am lonely.

But in those three or four rooms in Rectory Chambers it was all done for me. At night we filled a zinc bath with hot water, sat with bare legs in it to talk till near morning, and thought we were saving on the gas meter. Lovat was a real friend. Perhaps too period a manner for cosiness. Gaudier not a friend. More like a dagger in the midst of us. He had a hungry face (we didn't know how hungry) and a mind made of metal. He talked like a chisel and argued like a hammer. Too many things tore at him. He was so deadly poor – (how to buy paper, clay, food) – and Sophie so treacherous, suspicious, easily affronted, violently hurt. I remember their poor bed, never made, on which they slept together. We didn't know she wasn't his sister. She seemed mad even then. He had to cope with her, soothe her. After we had all been together, talking, or wandering about London, arguing in tubes after the last train had gone, then she took him home, pestering him with her suspicions. 'Did you notice how . . . ?' 'Did you hear what she said?' 'That Bagnold despises us. . . . Did you notice?'

And Katherine Mansfield, momentarily touching our group, was clawed and held by the sleeve because Sophie's burning eyes and foreign accent couldn't get over to her what was meant. 'Did you see that writer-woman pull away from me?'

Gaudier asked if he could model my head. Not as a compliment but lacking a sitter. I wrote the account of it in Jim Ede's book – *Savage Messiah*. Sophie said nasty things about me. She couldn't help it. She was jealous of any woman near her Pik. She said I had the failings of a social woman. (There may have been something in that!)

Looking at *Savage Messiah* I see that in a letter to his sister he says:

> Yesterday evening I met Enid Bagnold in the King's Road. She asked me to do a plaster cast of her head. [I didn't! *He* asked me.] I told her it would cost three pounds, so I shall make 35/- on her, which will do for casting a statue, which I will begin to-morrow. I have sent Parlanti to get the model from Fraser. [Lovat.] She asked after you and wishes you etc. etc. anything you like. She asked me if I wasn't lonely.

I replied rather evasively that I was working. That made her laugh in a rather cynical way and say 'O well, I don't think you mind much' . . . – *sale garce abominable*! I'm not quick at repartee, and while I was chewing over what to say she started talking of something else.

I don't recognize myself. Nobody does, when they hear the inner effect that their words have had long ago on other people. The innuendo that he drew from my asking if he wasn't lonely must have been a transmutation from his own acid.

On Wednesday evening I went to see the Bagnold because of the plaster cast. She is staying with Dollie and another girl whom I don't know. There was a boy there called Lunn. [Hugh Kingsmill.] We spoke of Murry but I don't want to see him again: I don't dislike a person easily but when at last I do, it's for good. We arranged with the Bagnold that she should take the plaster for £3 – with what is left over I will bake one or two little statues and buy a decent book for Christmas. The Bagnold still has the same peculiarity. In the middle of the conversation she rushed away to the Embankment without saying a word. Affected, of course – but in spite of that she is the most interesting of girls – she at least tries to understand and to get into touch with things. [Sophie didn't like that.]

A letter dated 7th December, 1912 (to Zosik):

Sappho, I understand that the important thing for you is intellectual intransigence, but for me the important thing is sculptural intransigence. Till you can understand this there will be no possibility of our discussing things with any accuracy and consequent possibility of agreeing. As usual, your pride detaches itself in its omnipotence, and you don't take the trouble to think what you are writing. Your wailings on what I wrote to you are ill-placed – those on the Bagnold erroneous, those on the studio etc., unreasonable.

I quote this because his Zosik (Sophie) was so jealous that one word from Pik of admiration for anyone, or even of justice, sent her mad with rage.

Here is an account (from Jim Ede's book) of a meeting at Haldane Macfall's, in fact a party.

Sophie's visit to the Macfalls was not a success. The fatigue of getting there, the heat of the rooms, and the unwonted meeting with a number of people, went to her head, and she became over-hilarious. In the course of the evening she dirtied her hands on some charcoal, and Mrs Macfall took her upstairs to wash. She was there persuaded to have a glass of whisky to steady her, but instead of doing so it made her ten times more excitable. When they returned, Mr Macfall was telling one of the guests, Miss Bagnold, that a drawing she had made was full of genius [this was the sort of nonsense one says to a guest] (he had set his guests to do caricatures of each other) and Sophie, unable to control her irritation any longer, said in a loud voice: 'Not at all, her drawings are stiff and photographic, their only merit is that they strike a likeness. Miss Bagnold is a writer, not an artist.' Her manner was strident in this drawing-room, and soon everyone was on their feet to leave; and Mrs Macfall was telling her that she would miss her last bus, and Macfall was holding her coat for her.

Miss Bagnold describes one of these dispersals:

'One night we came from Macfalls', Dolly, Gaudier, and Lovat and I, and we were again on a Tube railway station. Though we still expected it, the last train had gone. It was winter, and a wind like a wolf galloped down the Tube tunnel. We stood in its passage, Gaudier talking. He did not drop a subject when he had added a little to it. He did not throw a word in here and there, and make a crisp sentence sum up a bale of thought. What had been talked of a quarter of an hour before at Macfalls' was still being followed up. Gaudier, his long front hair hanging in a string down the side of his white brow, was throwing his future and his past and his passion into the discussion. We lazier English stood and shivered, and tried to back out of the wind. Gaudier felt our bodies moving, grouped, away from him, and I remember as he talked, and his eyes and pale face shone, he put out his thin arms and surrounded us and held us fast in the wind so that our edging movements should not distract him.'

Lovat was the first to be excited by Gaudier's extraordinary talent. But soon he drew away from him. Lovat, most indulgent of men, would never express dislike, but he would not waste time on Gaudier's burning, voluble, cascading talk, though he deeply respected his art.

I didn't like him either; and Gaudier on his side found us both middleclass. We had no idea then of his crippling poverty. He had no time for talk because he was out of work. Too proud to say so he talked instead of eating. He didn't want to know what people were like. He rushed at them, held them, poured his thoughts over them, and when in response, they said ten words his impatience overflowed; he jabbed and wounded and the blood flowed.

* * *

It was at the Macfalls, as we have seen, that Pik met Miss Enid Bagnold, and he thought her extremely beautiful. [Ede's text continues. (Author's note: It's ravishing to read this after so many years, but my recollection was quite other, and a sculptor has special standards which don't cut ice in daily life. Still – at seventy-nine I bow and thank him.)] She came to sit to him, and he expected that she would come every day; but her own activities diverted her attention, and week after week went by, filled with excuses and postponements. She herself tells the story of her finally sitting to him:

'I went to his room in Chelsea – a large, bare room at the top of a house – it was winter, and the daylight would not last long. While I sat still, idle and uncomfortable on a wooden chair, Gaudier's thin body faced me, standing in his overall behind the lump of clay, at which he worked with feverish haste. We talked a little, and then fell silent; from time to time, but not very often, his black eyes shot over my face and neck, while his hands flew round the clay. After a time his nose began to bleed, but he made no attempt to stop it; he appeared insensible to it, and the blood fell on to his overall. At last, unable to stand it any longer, I said: "Your nose is bleeding". He replied: "I know, you'll find something to stop it in that bag on the wall"; and all the time he went on working, while the light got less and less. The bag was full of clothes belonging to Gaudier and Miss Brzeska, most of them dirty, most of them torn. I chose something, long-legged drawers, I think, and tied them round his nose and mouth and behind his neck. "Lower!" he said impatiently, wrenching at it, unable to see properly. I went to my seat, but after a time the cloth became soaked through with blood. The light had gone, and in the street outside there was a terrific noise. It was a dog-fight, one large dog pinning another by the throat, and Gaudier left his work to come and watch it. He watched it to the finish with dark, interested eyes, his head against the window, and the street-lamp shining on his bloody bandages.'

Gaudier had found the previous uncertainty of Miss Bagnold's sittings a great trial to him, since he could not start a new work while he was expecting her from day to day; he therefore decided to give it up, and asked Zosik to sit for him instead.

So the book says. I don't remember being so 'uncertain', but I may have been.

At any rate he did the head, I paid the three pounds for it. The head I have still. Epstein had a bronze made for me from it for fear the original would break, but there is no other copy. The three pounds, I should think, could be multiplied by a thousand.

Meditating what to do with it about ten years ago, I thought of giving it to the Tate. I stood next Sir John Rutherston at one of the Hultons' marvellous parties, in Cleeve Lodge, Hyde Park Gate. Sir John was talking eagerly in an attendant manner to an elderly man. Waiting till he seemed to me to have stopped – 'Sir John' . . . I began.

'Excuse me,' he said with the waspish irritation of an interrupted man, 'but I am talking to my director.' So I didn't give it to the Tate.

*   *   *

Lovat's family were comfortably off and lived in Kensington. He loved and protected his mother's old-fashioned paintings in gold frames on the drawing-room walls. Why not? He had no ferocity and needed no rebellion. He was loved and adored by his family, and his own character was sweet to the core. He had a studio then in Roland Gardens, with a gallery round the top. Here he was busy all day long, sharpening quills, hunting for end-papers, making wooden toys, decorating everything, every bit of paper, every letter; even the menus as we ate. Later I think he had another studio in The Boltons, and there I think he did *The Beggar's Opera* drawings for Nigel Playfair, for the Lyric, Hammersmith.

Everything that came from his white indefinite hands (not the hands of a painter in oils) had a fascination, and perhaps too limiting a perfection. He made his talent like a round O that you couldn't break.

He was sunny, gay, and a wonderful companion (one year younger than I was). I wandered about London with him. I

Two self-portraits by Lovat Fraser, 1911 and in the trenches

had never had its freedom; it was like a city abroad. He loved evening expeditions after his day's painting.

'Let's go and see the tarts in Leicester Square,' I said. I had never been sure I had seen one, and wanted a man's corroboration. We ended up hanging over a blow-hole on Ebury Bridge while Lovat drew the girders, the engines, the bonfire-ish station from the top.

He gave me some of his wooden toys. Forty years ago I reached up above my front door here and put the figures on a shelf. There they are still. I haven't noticed them for so long; but now I 'see' them sharply.

The dining-room here at Rottingdean is full of his framed drawings. Many with exquisite decoration round the mount, which he did himself – and taught me to do. Others are illustrated letters he wrote me, or drawings on the backs of menus. I have somewhere some of the 'Flying Fame' chapbooks, particularly one of Hodgson's *Eve*. Also 'The Rhyme Sheet' No 1; the 'Twopence Plain and Fourpence Coloured' sheets and booklets with Lovat's illustrations to poems by Hodgson, and De la Mare.

* * *

Soon – (mindful of my promise to my father – the 'chaperonage' of an art school) – I said to Lovat —

'What about Sickert?'

'What?'

'Let's go and see his school.'

'Why should we?'

'Don't you want to learn more?'

'I don't think I do.'

Lovat's god then was James Pryde, but he said he would come with me. He was so good natured. I carried my Blackheath portfolio of huge, badly-adjusted, charcoal nudes. As I seemed always to start at the navel, very often the heads or the feet wouldn't fit in.

Sickert was Walter then. His hair was dark gold. The play of the muscles round his lips had a strange ironical – a fascinating movement. What an ass he was, when he became Richard, to wear a beard and obscure that attraction. Perhaps he got tired of women.

When we got there – to one of those odd broken houses that seemed to have had another house torn from its side, overhanging a railway (was it built on a bridge?) I was 'seen' first (though Lovat sat and listened) in a large room full of sun and students.

Sickert took my portfolio. Slowly he undid the tapes, delicately opened it. The art students watched and listened, half hidden behind their easels. He turned every large Michelin sheet in silence till he came to the last one. As he retied the tapes – with a swift wicked smile —

'But perhaps you *paint*?'

The room crackled with laughter.

All the same me he took, Lovat he spurned.

'No, no,' he said to him. 'I couldn't help you. Your talent is formed already. It may be it's full grown too early. I couldn't teach you anything.'

I read in Lovat's *Life*, in a chapter by Albert Rutherston, that Lovat did work with Sickert, twice a week at the Westminster school. I don't know whether Albert got it wrong, but when Lovat visited Sickert with me he certainly walked away sorrowful. And besides – the school I am talking about was in Camden Town. There he certainly never went.

Silvia Gosse was a pupil. Harold Gilman worked there too, coming in and out, not exactly a pupil. McEvoy the same. The rest were women, devoted and dull. Sickert liked his pupils as the Old Masters liked them, protective, disrespectful, chiding, kind and half contemptuous. 'My flock – poor creatures.' He hammered their heads with his wit. I understood from him, and never forgot, that one must work a lifetime – humbly, hard, never comparing, never looking round. 'Lift your head after ten years,' he said. 'You'll see you are one among thousands. Another ten years – among hundreds. On, on ... And *one* day, on a Monday or a Tuesday – with a peacock's feather of luck, you may do better than you know!' He wasn't speaking of me.

He loved dust. Especially dust on mirrors. He loved the abated light that got muffled in the glass. 'Blonde,' he would mutter. It was a love-word. The folds of a dirty sheet in shadow, the model's naked body on the bed, her flesh, green-shadowed, melting into the surrounding wood, rep, leather, reverberating softly in a splendour of unpolished light.

He knew his way among the half-shades. The pencil lightened its hold on the paper, the shortest moment of acid bit a fawn shade of fog. But in fog nothing fogged him. His practical half-German brain held to its plan; his brilliant tongue pinned it down. He was such a teacher as would make a kitchen-maid exhibit once.

('Kitchen-maid?' What can *she* be? Such words have gone in thirty years. 'Stillroom' went before I was born. And now 'scullery', 'pantry', 'servants' hall' have followed it. I'm not sorry. The domestic structure took a hell of a holding up. I don't regret the structure, but I hate the loss of words.)

Later (I don't know how it fitted in – past time is so uncharted) – I went to etch with him in Red Lion Square. I pre-

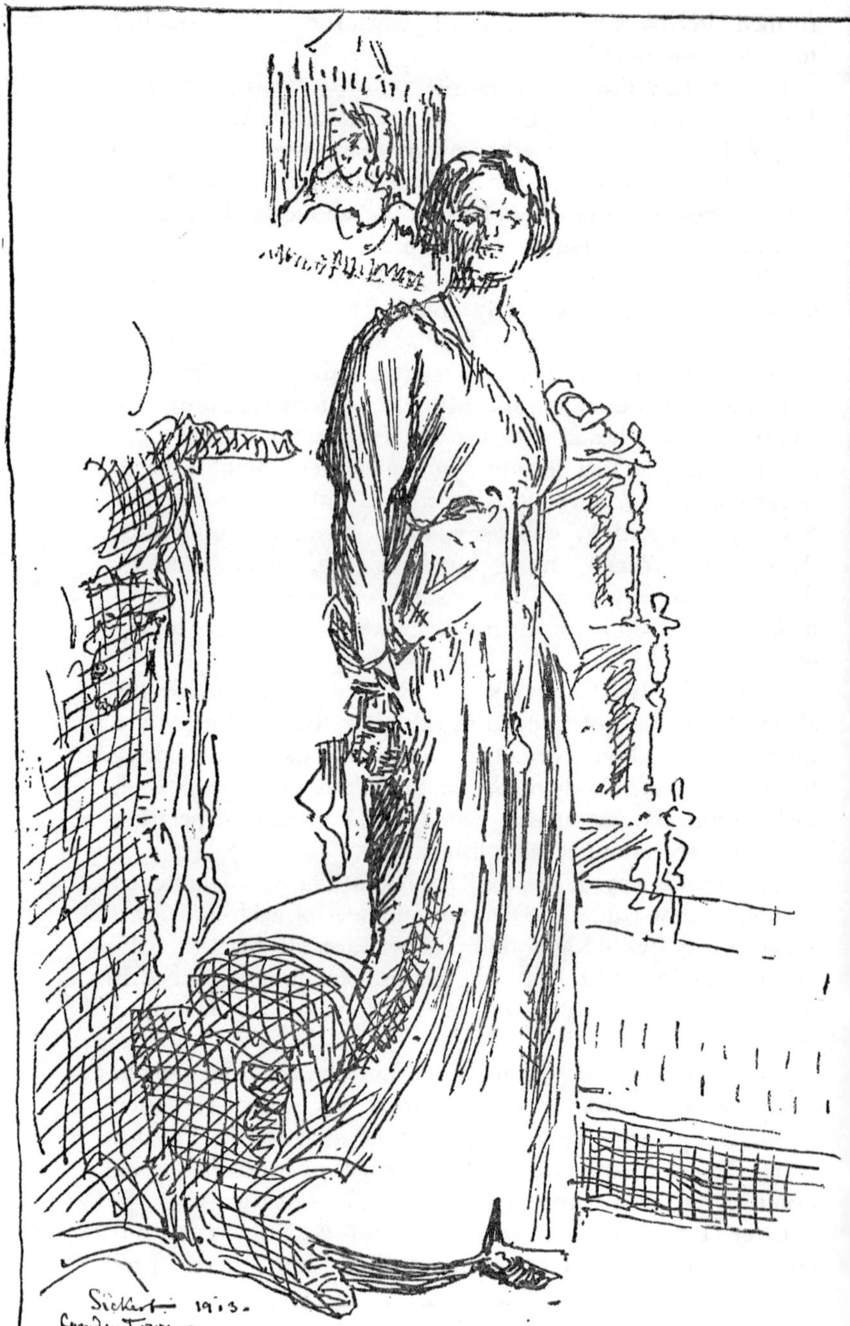
Sickert 1913.
Camden Town

pared, waxed, smoked (with a candle) his copper plates. I have first pulls of so many of his etchings. 'Ennui', particularly. Thérèse Lessore, who afterwards married him, poured out mugs of coffee in the earlyish mornings as he talked and worked and sat, in an old dressing-gown, having come from swimming in the Public Baths in Chelsea. I arrived one day in a new dress and he drew me in it. He gave it to me – the drawing – and it hangs here. *The New Age* published it and fifty years later Claude Rogers gave the reproduction to me, framed, as a Christmas present.

I didn't fall in love with him. Or hardly. We were all enslaved, enchanted. The day glittered because of him. But he had a doctor's morality about his students. Women on the whole were kittle-cattle to him. Like Tonks (then Head of the Slade) he would sigh and say —

'So brilliant girls are! And then the damn fools marry.'

'If you write,' he said to me, 'you can carry all that along with love: you can pour love into it. But drawing, painting – it's for nuns!'

His lightning-teaching tore across clouds of muddle and broke them up. For a time. His danger was he gave short cuts to success. He struck a match to me and held it to my intelligence. I flamed like gas and two of my drawings were exhibited at the New English, and one was mentioned in *The Times*. That didn't make me an artist. I never trod that long, long road.

Often we lunched together at Shoolbreds. 'Eat!' he would say. 'Look at those women of mine back there!' (the studio) – 'Grey with buns!'

'Perhaps that's all they can afford.'

'No, no! They're simply sheltering! Perpetual students! They won't face up to competitive art. Let them get out and try to draw commercially! That'll teach them!'

I got a long way but I was only a Sickert-product. When Lovat saw my drawings exhibited at the New English he did a charming mockery-drawing which hangs downstairs.

When I brought my 'Sickert-produced' drawings home, Daddy preferred the Blackheath nudes.

'Where's the *outline*?'

Stumbling and flashing with enthusiasm I tried to say—

'The truer, sterner, kinder friend', Lovat Fraser

'You map the lights and shadows. You bounce the light off it. And if you manage it right there sits the creature, living, in the middle! You don't *need* an outline!'

'Easier to draw a line!' Daddy snorted. 'What is – *is*. Why make it different? Better still – use a camera!'

(When Sickert *did* use the camera, first arguing with a little guilt, and then, reassured, determining – it was to catch the extraordinary transparency, new to everyone, of Lenglen's flying skirts. But at that time I answered Daddy —

'What are art schools *for* – if we go there photographing!'

'I don't know what art schools *are* for!' But he paid the fees all the same.

He allowed one exception to his art-antipathy – his old drawing master at the Royal Military Academy when he was a cadet. The teaching was high-lighted in jingles of which alas I remember only one.

> Turn your pencil round and round –
> And trees will spring up from the ground.

There is a strange skill, never lost, the military drawing-legend. I saw it in the beautiful eighteenth-century pencil-landscapes done by young officers, in the museum at Gibraltar. Leaves, bushes, small trees, not done *en bloc*, nor single, but, in that mysterious manner of the Douanier's forests – a conquest of repetition.

Here is one of Sickert's short notes to me. It sounds too loving for innocence. But it was airy love.

> Frith's Studio,
> 15 Fitzroy Street.

Dear delightful & amazing,

Do you ever *sleep* in London? If so would you *breakfast* here at 9 sharp? Any day including Sunday.

I should then get you *alone* for which I thirst – and have always thirsted – and shall continue to thirst.

Yours in persistent gratitude for your radiant existence and your dear warm friendship.

W. S.

The lunches with Sickert gradually gave way to lunching at Eustace Miles Vegetarian Restaurant, somewhere near Leicester

Walter Sickert

Amy Lan McCartie's letter

Hjelt's Studio
15 Fitzroy Street

Dear delightful Ermajinis

Do you ever sleep in London? If so would you breakfast here at 9 sharp? I should then get you alone for which I thirst and have always thirsted — & shall continue to thirst.

Yours in persistent gratitude for your radiant existence & our dear warm friendship

W. S.

Square. Here Ralph Hodgson was permanent king of a special table. When I first knew him he was Editor of C. B. Fry's Magazine. How he squared that with the hours – from lunch into a vague tea-time – that he brooded tipping back his chair at that table I don't know. He wasn't in the zinc bath circle. He was older, had a wife and went home at night. She was a Canadian and they got divorced later.

And much much later, long after I married, he went as lecturer to a Japanese University and brought home as wife the daughter of an American missionary (and a cage full of canaries). He brought her to our London drawing-room and said to her face that she was amiable.

'Amiable,' he said, 'is the sweetest word about a woman.'

She was called Amelia and she was a darling.

In the long long 'end' – he didn't die till he was over ninety – they lived in a cottage outside Cartor, Ohio, a place wild enough for him to 'wait on his gift'. He never wrote until he wanted to write; but the gaps grew very long between. I don't know what fruit that last long waiting bore. He seems still so strangely unknown. Amelia wrote to me when he died. I have a feeling that the last years were terrible.

But Eustace Miles. We were none of us vegetarians. The restaurant was chosen by Hodgson because the management allowed his Staffordshire (straight-nosed) red bull terrier to sit on a chair beside him. Such a dog was called in the north 'a business dog'. It was a companion to man but death to dogs. He kept it on a thick chain and close to his hand. 'I don't like other dogs to find out I am going about with a lethal weapon.'

R.H. dictated that no one should join our table except the Pure. He had a very special meaning to this. I knew what he meant but I disregarded it. I wasn't so mad about the Pure. He knew what he meant but he didn't trouble to explain. If one possessed a gift one was only pure if one lived like a hermit hungry for God. All petty pleasures must be foregone: especially if the gifted creature was a girl.

'Pure' was compounded too of a little jealousy.

He did a six-months' expulsion of Lovat once because he charged him with repeating himself in his art – that tyrannical puritan! Those who came to that table had to be pure by his own choosing. Edward Thomas came. Bill Davies came, the tramp poet. I am taken aback at finding letters from him dated a few years later. Quite intimate and forgotten. How can I forget a warm friendship with a poet? But I have. Is it part of a frivolity in me, a lack of respect for the best? No good analysing. Here are the letters written a year or two later. If I could be ashamed I would be.

14 Great Russell Street,
W.C.
Oct. 12th 1916.

Dear Miss Bagnold,
 I think you and I ought to get married, and then we could help each other in many ways.
 I like this poem very much and, if you can agree to the three little alterations, and say you forgive me for taking such a liberty with your work, and then return it to me – I'll try to get it published for you. Editors are afraid of new names, and they like to have the opinion of a writer they know. There's a fine imagination in the fourth verse – fine enough to satisfy any judge of poetry.
 No. I have not been to see Sickert yet.

Yours sincerely,
W.H.D.

14 Great Russell Street,
W.C.
June 18th 1917

Dear Miss Bagnold,
 Your first poem was accepted at once, but was mislaid. The second would have been accepted long ago, but I have been waiting until the other was printed. They have both appeared now as you probably know, in last Saturday's 'New Statesman' and the 'Nation'. I like this other too, and cannot find the least fault with it. If you write such fine things when you are angry, what a sweet life you would have as a married woman!

Yours ever,
W.H.D.

P.S. The 'Nation' does not pay until about 6 weeks after publication – the 'New Statesman' varies.

14, GREAT RUSSELL STREET,
W.C.
Oct 12th 1916

Dear Miss Bagnold,

I think you and I ought to get married, and then we could help each other in many ways.

I like this poem very much and, if you can agree to the three little alterations, and say you forgive me for taking such a liberty with your work, and then return it to me — I'll try to get it published for you. Editors are afraid of new names, and like to have the opinion of a writer they know. There's a fine magnificin... in the fourth verse — fine enough to satisfy any judge of poetry.

No, I have not been to see Sickert yet.

Yours sincerely,
W. H. D.

Letter from W. H. Davies, 12 October 1916

I who was the flimsiest, in the sense of being the least attached to intellectuals, nearly got flung out from the Holy Table. I met a man at a dance. His name was Slattery. He wrote me a note signed:

> Yours without flattery
> Sincerely – Slattery.

I asked him to lunch.

'You think that *funny*?' said R.H. savagely when I showed him the note. Then suddenly – 'You haven't *asked* him?'

I had. I turned my head nervously towards the door. He was that moment coming in. Throughout the meal R.H.'s long-lipped lantern face hung like a lit turnip at Christmas in terrible silence. The guest's hour was hideous.

'How *could* you!' I said when he'd gone.

'*Never* do that again,' thundered the turnip. Oh God, he was an unrelenting man! He stood aloof as the picture says. But he was close as a husband to those he loved; in the sense that one has to study a husband and mind his whims.

I have drawings he did of his dog; but I don't know where they are. One doesn't keep track of things when one is young in the hope that one's friends will be famous. . . .

I have found them! Done at Rottingdean (when the telephone number was 56. *That* will date them).

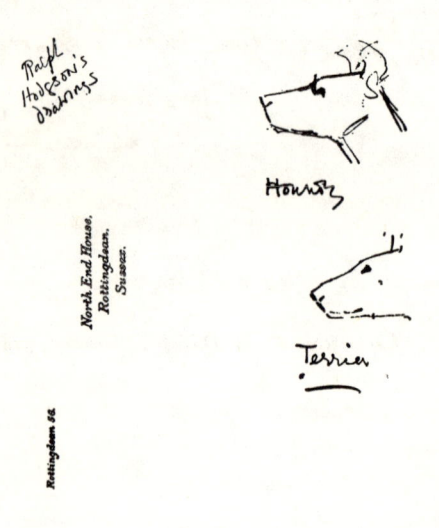

Long after we had gone from lunch R.H. would sit on, hour after hour talking to friends who dropped in to see him, or silent, smoking his pipe, the back legs of his chair creaking under him – waiting on his gift. When the poetry didn't come he stayed at the door in attendance. He suffered greatly from piles. They made him miserable and often short-tempered. When he asked us to his home he lay on a sofa while we discussed over his body whether it was safe to abandon life on the chance of inspiration. Once he sat up suddenly and said: 'You can only write poetry on a breath. At first it's a short breath. And if it stops you mustn't pad. If you keep waiting and waiting the breath gets longer.' He said that after he had been up on a hill all night and had written *The Song of Honour* in a single burst.

One of his first letters to me, addressed then to 'Miss Bag-, nold', was written from Fry's Magazine, Effingham House, Arundel St (undated).

> The thing that is most like your poetry is Durer's 'Melancolia' – 'The Melancolia that treasures all wit', or James Thomson's 'City of Dreadful Night' – though don't read that poem for ten years. I've not seen the picture for a long time but your writing brings it back vividly to me. You are wonderful, passing up and down among the crowds with a head reeling with glooms and spaces and smoking stars, and few people guessing at you. The things in the verse you've shown me that I value most – come and cannot go again – are 'The scum of moths flat-floating', the 'height piled up on holy height' bit, and the remarkable and beautiful 'Night' I spoke about. The last's your high-water mark in my mind. But always I like your original full strong way; and your freedom from cant adjectives, the things that beset nearly all writers in their early work. That was my main reason for liking 'Eblis'. But I think you are finer today than when you wrote that in spite of your halts and fears. Bellingham Smith came into lunch yesterday, and went to the New English with Vere. I like him. You must forgive Fraser,* he wouldn't hurt a fly if he knew it. I hope you are with your muse and that She is not using her hooks in you too savagely. Do you know

---

* I don't know what the reference to Lovat was about. Some small irritation I had felt and, alas, as always, given voice to.

that line in Adonais where Shelley refers to himself and his thoughts 'pursuing like raging hounds their father and their prey'. I hope you don't mind my writing.

                                         Yours R.H.

Vere Charteris was a strange and beautiful artist: a young woman on whom a talent had alighted when, apparently, it wasn't wanted. She drew like an angel without caring to draw.* Whether she had left home, whether she was without means, I

* I have one of her line-drawings.

don't know. Never knew. I wasn't a close friend. But I do remember that there was an arrangement by which Hodgson, and, I think Lovat, together contributed a small sum so that she could live in one room in London. But this was to the end that she should draw. When Hodgson found out that she was going to dances he arranged a wardership with her landlady. When her goings-out were reported, he blew up in a series of rows, and denied her the ordinary pleasures of a girl. She also should sit 'waiting on her gift' as he did. She rebelled, and for a time disappeared. Later she married Hugh Bellingham-Smith, my art master at Blackheath, and I met her twice years later, very coat-and-skirted, at a Sussex gymkhana with a daughter. I didn't dare ask about the 'gift'.

* * *

How can I write of my life without writing of writing? It has accompanied the travel of my days like the telegraph wire that rises and falls beside the carriage window of the train. In my red, bloody brain, like a herring's roe, behind my skull, this marvellous brain that I can't manage, this Rolls-Royce given to a child – what tumult, thoughts rapider than thought, what self-appraisal, annotation, a film too fast to watch.

On the whole never discuss it. The net that might have stretched to take shapes stranger than I could have hoped for may shrink in talk. But I liked to talk of writing with R.H. It didn't happen often and it didn't do an injury. He talked in pointers and always stopped before being precise. But except for him I was tired of talking of art and writing. It spilt the secrecy and took the gilt off.

In the evenings round the zinc bath I fretted to be more extrovert. I longed for more practical adventure. I loved roving about at night and bacon and eggs in the morning. I dare say I longed for love.

All this time the fat-battle with my figure was off and on. Food caught me sideways before I could wrap on my armour. There was a wicked secret beauty even to be alone with a bit of toast. But on the whole I was fining down and more bone-structure was showing. The effect began to give me more authority.

It wasn't long before the seventy-five pounds a year began to pinch. I loved to buy things. I had rather buy things and go hungry. (After all, there was the fat to melt.) There was a small restaurant down the road on the Embankment called 'The Good Intent', and when I ate there I stole a roll from the folds of the pleated napkin on the next table. That saved on breakfast. It was mock-hunger and mock-poverty because I could always have gone home, and Daddy would have given me more if I had seriously asked. But one had pride; and a job was the answer. With whom? Under whom? To work for whom?

* * *

There was then – it has been written about in Haldane Macfall's book on Lovat, and in Ede's book on Gaudier – a little bookshop in St Martin's Court, ruled, presided-over and lit by the life-loving, welcoming personality of Dan Rider. Behind a curtain, behind the front bookshop, was an inner room with a small coal fire where young writers and painters sat and talked on stacks of volumes. Lovat took me there. There I met Katherine Mansfield, and later Murry. The first time I met her she rushed in in a rage with a key in her hand. 'Tell him I've *left*!' she cried out to Dan Rider slamming down the key.

'Left who?'

'Left *Murry*!' (She called him that.) She looked like a whitefaced cat with a tiger in its eyes. Whirling out as she had whirled in, she was gone. I knew enough to know who they both were, she and Middleton Murry, and listened breathless. But it was only a row and it mended.

This is how – in an autobiography – one mustn't tell the past. This stale little tale comes out of its corner like a stale mouse.

'I knew her' is just what I didn't. *Never* till I read *Bliss* fifty years later and found the girl! – I missed when I met her – imprisoned for ever in the crystal of her own words.

* * *

A few days later I went again. Before I had lifted the passcurtain I heard organ-tones from the inner room. Then Lovat's voice —

'Here she is.' I think he had been saying I wanted a job.

So it was Lovat who let out the Jack-in-the-Box. The lid of life flew open and out came the Jack on a spring.

Head by Gaudier-Brzeska (*photograph, reproduced by permission, from* Savage Messiah *by H. S. Ede*)

E.B. at about twenty

Walter Sickert, 1912

Ralph Hodgson, 1912

Frank Harris, February 19
(*Radio Times Hulton Pictu*
Library)

I was struck into silence. His chest was deep, his eyes were deep, he spoke in tones of gold and thunder.

Could it be Lord Kitchener cut off at the legs? No. It was Frank Harris.

In our modern world of 1912–13 Katherine Mansfield, Murry, Gaudier, Lovat, Dolly and I behaved as though we had seen a flying saucer.

His picture is opposite. When I met him he was about fifty-four or -five. He dyed his hair and waxed the ends of his truculent moustache.

* * *

'So you want to be a journalist,' said Frank Harris, looking me up and down – practically lifting off my skin.

He had just become editor of *Hearth and Home*. He needed to staff it cheap. There and then he offered me a nebulous job at thirty-five shillings a week (more than doubling my seventy-five pounds a year). I took it. I became a sort of journalist.

Next day he took me to lunch at the Savoy – where I had never been. My portrait round about that birthday of risky life faces page 103. Long skirt, cigarette (I didn't smoke), bogus look of sophistication.

The luncheon was shaming and fascinating. Not yet in love with him, his faults of taste came out on my forehead like a cold sweat. He talked loudly of his three companions, Christ, Shakespeare and Wilde. The name of Jesus went round the tables like a bell of bronze and heads were raised to listen. Dishes were sent back as uneatable (a curious claim to sophistication that I have noticed in other men. Korda, for instance). Waiters were recompensed with half-crowns built in silver castles. I was ashamed. But soon I grew ashamed of being ashamed.

For let me do justice to myself and my thraldom. And justice to him. He *was* an extraordinary man. He had an appetite for great things and could transmit the sense of them. He was more like a great actor than a man of heart. He could simulate everything. While he felt admiration he could act it, and while he acted it he felt it. And 'greatness' being his big part he hunted the centuries for it, spotting it in literature, in passion, in action.

There were yet a few more luncheons at the Savoy, but funds were going down. At one of these he invited Max Beerbohm, who had just married his American actress wife. She wore her bracelets outside her black net gloves. I was thrilled by the way the top of Max's head steamed in a spiral.

Harris's whole environing world was so much older than mine that I only partially understood whom I was meeting when with him. I had no idea why, one day on going with him into the Café Royal, he pushed me behind a pillar as a small man with red fiery eyes (it was Lord Alfred Douglas) sprang up in a fury and tipped a marble table over on to his feet. I would have liked to stay and watch the fuss but someone (the Head Waiter?) pressed me back to the door and into the street.

Our little group, expanding, had made friends with (or slightly included) Katherine Mansfield and Middleton Murry. They joined us in the shock of the spell of Frank Harris. But soon they were dusting their knees and sneaking off. Katherine Mansfield was the first to go. Murry lasted a little longer. Lovat wobbled, made excuses, and disappeared. Dolly, who had no disapproval in her nature, tried not to be chilly but ceased to be interested. I hardly noticed that only I was left.

Imagine – after Woolwich – to be courted by this ugly, famous, and glamorously misunderstood man. How could I escape? I didn't want to escape. I tripped eagerly after him on his detonating trail, hand-grenades exploding. It was life all right.

I introduced him to the friends I had made. They couldn't bear him. Ralph Hodgson wouldn't speak to me while I knew him. I was cut off from Eustace Miles and isolated, but proud to be a martyr for this 'meteoric, fabulous and fantastic man'. (Vincent Brome's *Frank Harris*.)

In his anger and sorrow, R.H. wrote his poem 'Deep in the bells and grass' about it. Lovat read it, told me, but was forbidden to let me see it. When I was finally forgiven R.H. gave it to me, with an inscription.

The 'journalism' began. I was sent first to report on the Mansion House Party for Children. What a thing it was to see one's own words in print for the first time!

I did various dreadful articles. 'The Home Beautiful'; 'In Aid of Gentlepeople'; 'Mrs E. M. Ward: the veteran art-mistress to the Royal Family'. And (a bit better) 'Young Women Writers: Miss Rosalind Murray and Miss Katherine Mansfield'. 'Orange Galettes and Fruit Jellies' followed; and after that I was sent down to Esher to interview Mrs Annie Besant, who had taken a house there with two young Indian boys, one of whom she had brought to England as the Theosophist Messiah.

When I got there she was taking them for a drive, in a wagonette with two horses. I asked for an interview but she shook her head. She was dressed in white, and the boys seemed younger than in fact I now know them to have been.

I waited for her return. It was then late afternoon. She said, 'Since you've waited then come in while I give them their supper.' It was, oddly enough, bread and milk. But I know now that Krishnamurtri had at that time a weak stomach.

'Do you know anything about me?' (when we had sat down).
'No. Nothing.'
'Anything about what I believe? My religion? Or these children?'
'No.'
'I wonder why they sent you.'
'I was told in a hurry, half an hour before I started. It's my first interview with anyone.'
'I see,' she said. 'Well – do you mind if I write it for you?' Which she did. As the boys ate their bread and milk.

'That's how it should be. Like this. Quite short, and clear,' she said finally. 'Now you can take it and fill it out with descriptions. Of this room. Of the children. Of me. There'll be plenty to say, you'll find, when you begin to think what you remember.' It was my first lesson in journalism. Not long afterwards I heard her speak in that hall near the BBC, near the Langham Hotel. She was again all in white.

When she came on to the platform she was different, she was burning. Her authority reached everywhere. If I had heard her speak like this before I went to Esher I couldn't have talked to her in the way I did.

One boy died. But the other I got to know later, when I was married. Before he disbanded the Theosophists we stayed with him in the Castle of Eerde. And later, when he had thrown off all his sources of supply and refused any longer to believe himself a Messiah he came to see me – at the end of a lecture tour he had made in Europe.

'You're very smart,' I remember saying. (He loved good clothes.)

'Yes,' he said, absently glancing down, 'and isn't it curious...'
He stopped.

'What is?'

He fingered his coat, as though some ghost of his 'smartness' still tickled his mind.

'... that all over Europe after I had spoken people only asked questions within a limit of five. It frightened me that that was the range of their curiosity.'

I have no idea now what he has become, but at that time, without thinking him an anointed saint, I thought him a saint in nature.

Soon Frank Harris had slipped out of his editorship of *Hearth and Home* and bought a tainted little property called *Modern Society*. This had a scandal-page with a newly-invented spice, called 'What a Little Bird wants to know'. Now I was really and truly a journalist. I was up to my neck in it.

Harris took on Hugh Lunn (later Hugh Kingsmill). We were the staff. We filled the paper (except for the scandal-page which was the paper's claim to fame).

Here I must break off to say that I have just found Hugh's book on Frank Harris in that home for lost books, a long-unused guest's bedroom; and I discover, as so often, that my bright story, swinging loose in my memory, has landed in the wrong place. Hugh says he was only on the staff of *Hearth and Home*, quarrelled with Frank Harris, and never saw him again for seventeen years. Well – I don't believe it. I can see him with the eye of a camera in those gay, noisy rooms (one up and one down) in King Street, Covent Garden, where violent schemes – as violently disrupted – flew in and out like blackbirds, and one caught a tail-feather or a bit of wing-fluff as the bird escaped.

I can plainly see him down in the yard at the back as he caught the end of the rope by which I was going to let down the First Folio of Shakespeare* (but it was fake) when the bailiffs came. If he says in his book he wasn't there I don't

* I have this 'First Folio' here in the library. I must have stolen it.

believe it. He is dead: I am eighty. There's no arguing with either of us.

There was also a slim girl who worked outside getting advertisements. As Hugh was lazy (and in any case studying Frank Harris and not the paper) I did the bulk of the work. I faked things. Or plagiarized. I stole. I rewrote stories from Maupassant and signed them myself (needless to say, at my chief's suggestion): I drew, or traced, legs and girls from *La Vie Parisienne*: I lifted cookery articles from foreign papers.

I had no conscience. 'I obeyed my Chief.' That was the answer I heard years later from a Basuto in the dock in a tent in Basutoland, accused of ritual murder. 'I cut off his lips and his tongue. I did it for my Chief.' If I had been sent shop-lifting, I would have been off – flags flying.

The thirty-five shillings never grew any larger. I had to ask for it every week. If I hadn't I shouldn't have got it. But I never thought of asking for more. Half the paper was under my control. I was as happy as a lark.

Horatio Bottomley came in and out. There was talk of Wolfie Joel. Lemoine jingled diamonds in his pocket, showing them by handfuls. I asked a seedy man what he wanted one evening and he said he was the man who spent his nights posting letters in different pillar boxes. 'Mr Harris's lottery, miss. It seems the police spot it when too many letters go into one box.'

My mother was anxious and my father angry. But I was headstrong and insisted this was life.

Hugh – in whichever office he says he was – was a glorious friend, but a deep temptation to gossip. It was always a risk like a knife-edge what I should tell him, what I could withhold. If anyone could have got me to laugh at Frank Harris he could. But nobody could. I was sliding into madness. Frank Harris was roaring about London looking for 'loves'. And there was I, prick ears, like a puppy, sniffing for everything. For life, experience, a dead partridge, an ashbin.

Hugh's special decoy-to-gossip was to get one to talk about oneself.

Something in me frowned as I answered his fascinating questions. He had the brilliant technique that Cyril Connolly has also. A gleam of mischief, a question too near the knuckle, put so that one felt one was adding to one's personality, impossible to resist.

Years afterwards I was never sure how much he knew.

For what happened, of course, was totally to be foreseen. The great and terrible step was taken. What else could you expect from a girl so expectant? 'Sex,' said Frank Harris, 'is the gateway to life.' So I went through the gateway in an upper room in the Café Royal.

That afternoon at the end of the session I walked back to Uncle Lexy's at Warrington Crescent, reflecting on my 'rise'. Like a corporal made sergeant.

As I sat at dinner with Aunt Clara and Uncle Lexy I couldn't believe that my skull wasn't chanting aloud: 'I'm not a virgin! I'm not a virgin!'

It was a boy's cry of initiation – not a girl's.

And what about love – what about the heart? It wasn't involved. I went through this adventure like a boy, in a merry sort of way, without troubling much. I didn't know him. If I had really known him I might have been tender.

'In love' doesn't make one tender. It makes one furious or jealous, or miserable when it stops. It's the years that make one tender. Time, affection, *knowledge*. 'In love' is the reverse of knowledge.

I went home every week-end. Once home it seemed it hadn't happened. Lies were told. You can't grow up without lies. A child is so much older than her mother thinks she is. I risked so much. It was their happiness I risked: not mine. Nothing could have foundered me – I thought. But if they had known (that's what I risked) could things ever have been the same?

There was plenty to tell at week-ends, without thinking of sex. The office was so thunderingly alive, F.H. in and out, struggling in despair, or blazingly optimistic ...

*   *   *

What was he like?

I can't tell more than I have told. I have nearly forgotten him. He didn't exist, for one thing.

'Frank Harris was born in two different countries on three different dates and his name was not Frank Harris.' (Vincent Brome.)

But how could I know that? Vincent Brome's book wasn't written.

I myself had to wait for the cruelty of age before I could write as I did in the *Sunday Times* (it was ten years ago – I was sixty-nine):

> The parts he played had one common link – they were all Great Parts. He was the Greatness-Spotter. And perhaps that was the strange elusive fragment that was real. He knew greatness when he saw it. He then sold it, pimped it, pawned it, wore it as his own, and while wearing it (playing the character of the 'Character') he loved best what Simenon calls the 'limit-moment'.
>
> He was *en rapport* with confession-moments, agony-moments. He stood in the prison corridor while Wilde, in a white sweat of nerves, changed his shoes for the prison boots, he arranged for a yacht to lie off Dartford, and the terrible interview he had when Wilde refused to flee before the trial so tore my heart that I could tell my grandchildren I was there myself.
>
> But then, too, I was with him at the Last Supper – broken and astounded by the words of Jesus Christ. I waited with Mary Fitton when Shakespeare was late for a love appointment and she in such a pain of impatience she didn't know she hadn't put on her dress.
>
> What was fascinating to me in him? Everything. Everything one had to 'get over' – to swallow. Even the ugliness. Besides, for ugliness, his theory was that women love ugly men. He made sin seem glorious. He was surrounded by rascals. It was better than meeting good men. The wicked have such glamour for the young.
>
> If a doubt sneaked in he made the doubt glorious. Caught out in a lie he laughed his great laugh, and that had its dash.
>
> But all the time he was a ship nose-down for disaster. He could pull the stars out of the sky but he flushed them down the drain. Yet what a talker! What an alchemist in drama – what a story-teller! It's as impossible to reconstruct the thrall as to call back the voice and powers of Garrick.*

* * *

* From the *Sunday Times*, Feb. 8, 1959.

The end came like this.

Sarah Bernhardt was coming to London. Frank Harris was to give her a great luncheon at the Savoy. (I found later he was only a guest.) He arranged, he promised, that I should go too. I was wild with excitement. But how should I be dressed? I had what I knew was a smart coat and skirt, black, pin-striped, like a businessman's, and so daringly short that it showed my ankles. White silk stockings and patent shoes with a big buckle. But what about a hat?

On the day of the luncheon, in Bond Street near Cartier's, I saw a white hat in a window, with a big gull's feather. I went in. It cost three or four guineas. I had five shillings on me and a pound in the bank.

I poured out the urgency, the immediacy, the total necessity – and the steady seventy-five pounds which, though not there at the moment . . . I pointed out my father's name in the telephone book.

'But how am I to know that you're his daughter?' I still wore my school vest. By wriggling and dragging, the sales lady could see the Cash's name-tape sewn at the back of my neck. I went out with the hat.

I got a wolf whistle in Covent Garden which reassured me (but I didn't need reassurance). What an effect one made in fine clothes when one was young! In those days the bus drivers would whistle when I wore a new hat. Not because I was beautiful, but because I was at last vain. I peacocked and a sort of sun shone out of me of self-delight.

Frank Harris had to appear in court that morning before Mr Justice Horridge. He had commented in his 'Little Bird wants to know' on the Fitzwilliam divorce case. He had told me it wouldn't take long; the case would be finished that morning; he would fetch me for the luncheon at one.

In the office I waited, waited, starvingly waited. Half past two – despair. Then in came the girl who saw to the advertisements.

'Are you waiting for Mr Harris?'
'Yes.'
'He's gone to prison.'
She rather liked saying that.
'Damn!' – suddenly furious. I knew it was his own boasting

fault. The clouds of hero-worship broke for a second. He had cheeked the judge (was the way she put it). ('Contempt of Court!' – that Master of Contempt!) Frank Harris, in court, in the voice of Jove, had thundered at the judge. The Tipstaff then tapped him gently on the shoulder, and he had gone to Brixton in a cab.

Though it was terrible to miss the luncheon, greater things occurred to me. I was now in full control. How, how to save the paper? It would lose its licence at Stationer's Hall if it was one week off the bookstalls. I hunted half-heartedly in the drawers for the 'Little Bird' column. There must be one ready for next week. But I could find no larder where the spicy bits hung on hooks. When I found nothing and no addresses (did Frank Harris write the stuff himself?) – I was filled with inspiration. That 'great man' in prison! I would make other great men save him!

That afternoon I sat down and wrote to Bernard Shaw, to Pryde, to Max Beerbohm, Haldane Macfall, and Joseph Simpson, asking them to fill the paper instead of the usual contributors 'and we will leave the other pages blank'. Shaw replied on a handwritten postcard in which was the sentence, 'You can't put an elephant to hatch hens' eggs', and refused, but said something handsome about Frank Harris. Harris took the postcard from me afterwards. Perhaps he sold it.

This must have been in February, 1914, because there are two letters from Bernard Shaw to Max Beerbohm about my idiotic attempt. The letters are in the Shaw Collection in the British Museum, and these are two short excerpts from them.

(Shaw to Max Beerbohm)

10 Adelphi Terrace, W.C.
12th February 1914.

My dear Max

All this is blazing lunacy. Miss Bagnold's plan, if she could carry it out, would simply kill Modern Society stone dead. It is about as sensible as an attempt to revive the fortunes of the Oxford Music Hall by a performance of Beethoven's Mass in D. If Miss Bagnold cannot write the sort of thing that people buy Modern Society for, she had better get somebody who can, and go home to bed until she is out of danger of rheumatic fever, which will lay her up for months if she trifles with it.

(Shaw to Max Beerbohm)

10 Adelphi Terrace, W.C.
13th February, 1914.

I havnt seen Miss Bagnold. Her conviction that I am won is the outcome of a sanguine disposition stimulated by the favorable medical report.

But the point is that her proposed regeneration of MS. is not a forlorn hope but a torpedo attack certain, if brought off, to send that flimsy craft to the bottom. It is the offer of the elephant to hatch the hen's egg. Turn Modern Society into a penny Saturday Review or New Age, and its sale will drop to 1500 at the outside. The price would have to be raised to sixpence; and thousands of pounds would be needed to tide it over the first two years of competition with the existing high browed weeklies.*

I don't know what Pryde did, but Joseph Simpson sent a drawing. And, best of all, Max Beerbohm did a drawing of himself and Frank Harris sitting at a restaurant table, and underneath wrote, 'The Best Talker in London, with one of his best listeners'. This was drawn and given on a solemn promise from me that it should neither be used as a cover to the paper nor exhibited as a poster. I replied that Frank Harris wouldn't dream of doing such a thing, but I had doubts.

I rang my father, and told him about the prison (which he had read in the newspapers), about the efforts I was making, about the necessity for seeing Frank Harris.

'Would you mind if I went down to Brixton?'

'I don't like,' he said slowly, 'your connection with that man *or* that paper . . .' (Looking back, I think that Ralph Hodgson had already gone far to warn him.) '. . . but you can't sever things at a moment like this. Yes. Go down and see him.' The Victorian, as always, was too generous a man to force an issue at a moment of disaster.

Frank Harris's solicitor, Cecil Hayes, got me a permit, as a 'business associate'. I went down on a bus. The arched prison

* These letters are reproduced by permission of The Society of Authors as agent for the Shaw Estate.

gates opened on to a windy brick tunnel, at the far end of which there was a second pair of gates. Still wearing the gull hat (more wolf whistles – not from prisoners but from passing warders), I was put into a room made chiefly of glass, with a glass partition in the middle. I could see Frank Harris being hurried, almost scrambling across the courtyard, by a warder. In a snap of disillusion I noted that without his usual 'heightening' pace he was very short.

He stood one side of the glass partition – I the other – a warder at the end. Even with the barrier I could see that prison had already taken the stuffing out of him.

Proudly I told him what I had done. When he heard Beerbohm's stipulation he didn't seem pleased with either Max or me, only gratified on his own account. But he promised: he gave his word.

Within twenty-four hours the young girl who did the advertisements received instructions from him to 'go it strong on publicity' with Beerbohm's drawing, and 'damnation take those fancy promises'.

Arriving a day or two later at nine at the office, I found Odham's single-horse cart drawn up and the man delivering a heavy roll of posters with Max Beerbohm's drawing. I think I did not know all at once where Max lived, for I remember ruffling the telephone book with a hand that shook with rage; but soon I was in a cab, had rung his doorbell, and sent up a message as urgent as I could make it by the maid. He was not dressed, but came down in a wonderful dressing-gown, and as he listened his two very blue eyes were serious with anger, though his eyebrows, his mouth, and the rest of his charming face would not go any great lengths. He was angry enough to dress very quickly, and came with me, carrying his cane (which had a loop or bobble at the handle) in the cab that I had kept waiting. What followed was his own plan, and the pleasure he took in it banished his indignation. Driving to the office to examine for himself the iniquity of the printed posters, he dragged the roll into the cab, then we drove on to the printers. There he collected the block, no one gainsaying him, and we went on to the river at the point where the Savoy Steps go down. Keeping one poster for me we threw the whole burden into the river. The plate disappeared, but the posters unrolled

MODERN SOCIETY

February 28th, 1914. Price **1D.**

'The Best Talker in London, with one of his best listeners,' by Max Beerbohm

and floated for a time down the tide. Afterwards Max gave me the original of the drawing as a reward and I have it still with the one saved poster, hanging here in the dining-room.

Frank Harris came out of prison dismal, empty and needing a shave. He didn't make magnificence out of it.

He hardly spoke. I hardly saw him again.

I went home. I had got off scot-free.

* * *

I never knew how much anyone knew (and as time went on didn't care) but by one of those rumours that linger through the years and never quite believe what they are asserting, I was asked when I was sixty-nine to speak about Frank Harris on television.

Roderick, who knew everything, laughed.

'Don't you mind?' I asked him.

'Not at all.'

Having ever since that time (and before it) been a writer, I have no straight and simple recollections, but a memory falsified by cross-lights and often undependable. In the Frank Harris days I lived violently and uniquely for myself and I thought I could only call back the past in a blinkered manner. But not at all! The past jumped back like a goat. For once I spoke well. I even had to choke back the reason for the 'expertise'.

Chapter Five

*

I WENT home again – yes, as I had told Daddy I would. And all the extraordinary things in London, including the seduction, all that might have covered nine years just covered nine months.

I began to write a novel (about Frank Harris). But the prose had a Germanic and smelly texture. The shadow cast by his form of thought wouldn't let me succeed.

I never finished it, because I found I really didn't know my subject.

My father ('You can't write all day!') gave me bookbinding tools and a wooden frame to sew the pages. I was nimble with my large hands, as he was. Bookbinding did quite well instead of Frank Harris.

I had my Tower Room (my gas for glue), coloured inks for drawing on my letters – fun for the hands when the words wouldn't come. There was an ozone in that Gothic pinnacle.

And so began my second life at home, never to leave it wholly until I married.

One summer, and it must have been this one, was so beautiful that it gave its name to a vintage. As each day opened in the garden there was an incandescence more lovely than a fire coming through the trees. Call it the rising sun, but it may have been the light of youth, the light of being agog. I wasn't restless. And what you remember is richer than the thing itself. Time telescoping inside my head brings back the garden, and now it has a cubic depth like looking into a box. The compressed, violet light is on the charcoal branches, and on a sequinned twig a pigeon casts a shadow longer than itself. It must be morning. He makes a noise of hollow and sweet water in between feather-cleaning.

Next door, through the hedge, is that Palladian house, Falconwood, whose terraces go down like decks in the fall of the woods. It was said to have been built by an illegitimate son of the Prince Regent. He buried his wife on the lawn and when they dug her up they found a wolfhound.

The house seems curved on our side because the balustrades of the entrance come out like arms. On the other side it is really curved, each room faintly a bay. A double staircase leads up in grandeur from the hall. Curved also is the drawing-room, and the actual glass of its windows. People had lived in it and gone. It was too grand for the army neighbourhood, difficult to heat, difficult to sell. As I see it, it stands empty. But looking backwards, soon it will be full.

* * *

Life at home was prised open since London. I could come and go. Dolly never came down to stay with me. I can't think why. I think she so hated Woolwich. Lovat came. Often he and I went down together by the romantic way of East Ham and the Free Ferry. You took a ticket for the ferry, paying nothing.

The ferry, which I remember as shapeless and not like a boat, crossed the river by turning round and round, heavily waltzing from side to side of the Thames. There were two ferries. One loaded while the other crossed. The one that arrived let down its ramp and the horses, carts and lorries went on first, bumping up the wooden planks. It was ten minutes each way and ten minutes to wait. One bank you knew: the other was 'foreign'. Then the reverse. And once out on the river, silver, black or scarlet, depending on the hour, both banks had a fringe, at angles, of cranes looking like trees.

On the way over, Lovat drew in ink and in paint, and carried the drawings to Warren Wood at arm's length, flapping and wet. Daddy thought they were the greatest nonsense. He couldn't see how a reasonable man could do such things. Lovat laughed and argued with him.

'You've only given an impression,' said Daddy, using the right word by accident.

'That's what I meant to do!'

'But where's the detail, the *detail*?'

'It's conveyed,' said Lovat. 'You'll see it if you stop looking for it, Colonel Bagnold.'

Then Daddy would be off in deep defence of the 'truth of the camera'. Translation of life into art, dictated by the whim of the individual – that he wouldn't put up with! 'What is – is. Why make it different?'

Lovat laughed. Hodgson laughed too when he came. It was only I who couldn't laugh. Daddy was so extreme he gave no offence. And in between the assaults his manners were beautiful.

Nobody bothered me with dances now. I had 'gone out of the neighbourhood' as far as they knew. I was no longer discontented, no longer fighting. All the same there were gaps in life, *longueurs*. Then the Baroness-rumour began.

She was foreign. She had been seen browsing round Falconwood.

It wasn't long before they said she had bought it. Who was she? And please God would I know her!

Catherine d'Erlanger bought Falconwood as one of her 'jokes'. The expression 'it's so amusing' was fresh then. It was 'amusing' to make guests drive down the Old Kent Road to her parties. Soon there were lines of cars (no horses now) outside her gate, our gate, and topping the Hill. Grandees. Freebreathers. Or so I said to myself. People who breathed freely on the top of the world. Fashion and brains and wit just over the hedge.

Charlotte Brontë at eighteen (*High Life in Verdopolis: 1834*):

> I like high life. I like its manners, its splendours, the beings which move in its enchanted sphere. I like to consider the habits of those beings, their way of thinking, speaking, acting. Let fools talk about the artificial, voluptuous, idle existence spun out by Dukes, Lords, Ladies, Knights and Esquires of high degree. Such cant is not for me. I despise it. . . .

Such cant was not for me either. I turned my ardent, snobbish eyes, mad with interest, on the great world. I came out of the army as astonished as any trumpeter. The sway of the great was then unquestioned. Even Grannie had had her pseudo-great. Perhaps I hadn't escaped her lessons.

My brother Ralph on leave from Ypres. My mother in the background

Just before I married

E.B. in the business man's coat and skirt

A quote from myself years later: 'Privilege and power makes selfish people – but gay ones!' (*The Chalk Garden*.)

*   *   *

The hostesses were there: and they were there right through the war to come, the war of which we didn't dream. Daddy thought it would come. He listened to Lord Roberts. But I didn't believe him, or if I did it would be scarlet-coated and bright with music. Ah – would I meet this baroness? – was all I thought.

For some local reason to do with Falconwood she went to tea at a house on the Hill. I too. And I met her.

She was French by birth, a Rochgude, married to Baron Emile d'Erlanger (German, a banker, a gentle, home-loving man, of a musical family).

She was tall, red-haired, with beautiful nostrils that flared like an Arab horse, and a way of dressing that was not chic, but grand. She had no French art of dressing. She spoke rapidly, a slight accent tingling in her words, and gave out an alarming sense that one's replies must be brief. She had a social cruelty, logical and French. She was haughty and shallow and swift in her judgments. Her health was unassailable. She went to a dentist and he couldn't pull out a tooth. Her delight in each day sprang alive as she woke.

'*Let's* . . . What shall we do? – Let's —'

'Let's have fun, paint, look for briques . . .' (*Objets d'art*, bits of glass-nonsense.) She thought she wouldn't die. She very nearly didn't.

She asked me a question, asked without interest . . . 'And what do you do. . . .'

In a flash before I lost her – 'I write . . . journalism . . .' (not then true) 'I want to write *books*.'

The hook caught a hook, it was enough. I was over: I was *in*.

'Do you play tennis?'

'Yes I play tennis.'

She was building a hard tennis court, and there was a grass one while the hard was being finished. I was asked to play tennis at Falconwood.

I had no idea what sort of society Catherine had around her, but it turned out it was the most uninhibited, cosmopolitan, gay society I could have prayed for. 'Fashion and brains and wit' – yes. And everything that was peculiar, outlandish, of-the-moment. And artists too. Not serious artists – like Sickert (who wouldn't have gone there) nor Augustus John, but *modern* young painters (how that word leaps from generation to generation); and gay and wild young women, brilliantly dressed. Nancy Cunard. And that lovely and kind girl, so long dead, Phyllis Boyd, Diana (but later, in the London house): and older, celebrated women, the Marchesa Casati, who held two leashed lions at her Roman ball, Princess Marie Murat, Maria Carmi, Lady Ottoline Morrell, Julia James, Ruby Peto, the witty Lady Drogheda. And the men – Paul Morand, the young Georges Boris, Prince Antoine Bibesco, Matila Ghyka, Duff Cooper, Hugo Rumbold, Basil Blackwood. They would have gloriously surrounded the Prince Regent.

I know who they are now. But then, knowing no one, I watched, ravished, alight, alert. My seventy-five pounds was exhausted, my clothes were extraordinary. I must have been a curio (but brave). The conquest of this castle lit my eyes and caught my breath. My 'entry into society' was heady. And dangerous and hard and gay. For a long time I had no name. Catherine said: 'My friend from next door.' I was aware of patronage.

How was my equipment? How were the looks going? My mother comforted – 'You never see yourself sideways.'

'What's so good about sideways?'

'You never see yourself as I see you! Moving . . .'

No. I am clamped for ever to that straight look, that front look in the mirror. I asked Paul Morand long afterwards what I had looked like.

'Red cheeks like an apple.'

Perhaps I was more edible than I thought.

*　*　*

It was touch and go. Touch and go with my father too. Emile (the Baron) had innocently arranged that a henyard should be set up against our hedge and just under my father's window. Daddy was a light sleeper; the cocks woke him at four each summer morning. Furious – 'Those damned foreigners!' he exclaimed at every breakfast, worn out with hours of indignation in his bed. Normally he loved the French, the Arabs and the Turks. Henceforward not the Germans. Even the coming war wouldn't have made him as anti-German as the cocks.

He complained, by letter, civilly to the Baron.

'How do you expect, Colonel . . .' Emile wrote back, not strong on natural history, 'to get an egg for your breakfast if you haven't a cock?'

'Nothing is easier,' wrote my father, 'and they are pleasanter unfertilized.'

The row grew. My chance of life was in my mouth. Daddy wouldn't have forbidden me outright, but when I went next door I was under a cloud at home. (And all my life I can never stand a cloud.) It was the worse in his eyes because he despised 'society': he despised a world that wasn't of working integrity. Well, he had had his ideals and lived up to them! I had my ideals and hadn't got near them.

Social life? It can be wondered at now. But the platform then of rich and discriminating women held so much amusement, such exotic inhabitants, things sophisticated – perhaps tawdry – but what I wanted was fun.

Was I a snob? But no more than if I had ached to go to the theatre. I ached in the same way to 'belong' when I first saw that world in the most tempting and tantalizing way, through the hedge, through the trees, like a cage of glittering tigers being wheeled in for a circus.

I trembled about the henyard. I trembled for my pleasures. But I too felt the injustice of the cocks.

'When you see her,' said my mother, 'as you see her every day, can't you ask her to have the henyard moved?' But I knew that my asking Catherine would make her think it 'amusing' to leave it where it was. I asked good Emile instead and it was moved.

Catherine, like a Royalty, liked her bedroom full of people while she dressed in the morning.

With his tired, depraved, olive look Hugo Rumbold would grumble restlessly about the room. Basil Blackwood, Eric Caledon, Duff – anyone who was staying came in. I hardly knew them, but I listened entranced to the friendships of men. Hugo was never very well in the morning, and no wonder.

There was a vast lit night behind him like a cavern. Then, getting better, drinking his coffee, teasing the open bedroom piano with one hand, in between spirals of music he would give out the gossip-column of his night. Born idle, wit like a passport, he was one of those men with a slight genius, who disappear without label when they are gone. He was an amateur who could make a professional envious.

'An amateur at what?'

'Being funny. So that it was literature in its way.'

As Catherine dressed, she put on her jumble-saleish morning clothes. English country clothes she never got the hang of, but in the evening she wore whatever corresponds to Dior today. There would be a palette on her dressing-table, and a paintbrush in her hand as she brushed her red hair – that got scarlet as time went on.

She had no real aptitude for painting but her vigour pushed her beautiful nose into everything. Sometimes she would rattle open her cupboards and give me a dress. That was agony. I had then to wear it, and it was never what was called 'me'. But how did I know? Since 'me' was unreadable to me. Hugo often dressed up as a woman. But much more than that – he almost became one.

Later on, in the war, when he was in the Grenadier Guards, he occasionally saved a week-end for this prank, or vice, or whatever it was. It was highly dangerous then had he been discovered. At one time he posed as a lady's maid at Garsington, and as Ottoline Morrell's guests arrived, walking up the garden path in pouring rain, he helped them change their wet stockings. Another time, in the war, I went with my mother to Bath. A woman spoke to me in the Pump Room, saying that Catherine had asked her to look out for me. We went together to tea at Forte's. Only as she ordered the hot chocolate did there come the ghost of a stammer, and I knew it was Hugo.

Catherine, at her hotel, was furious and sent for me. Nervously furious in advance, lest I should tell. When I got to the hotel before dinner, Hugo, incorrigible, came down the stairs to meet me in a low-necked ball dress.

I never fathomed the sexual life of either of them, whether towards each other or alone. In fact I never thought about it.

How divine that first magic summer, and those that followed

it, as they moved on towards the war. How divine the sense of conquest, the trying-out of oneself as though one were a sword. In that gilt drawing-room with the long windows open on the falling woods, among beautiful objects that I had never seen before, with people who laughed in all languages and knew each other like a family, I was swimming on approval in a new electric sea.

Ivor Wimborne, Freddie Guest. ... Those Guests – there were a number of them – all acted with the same, the identical, lead-up to a girl. It was as though an ancestor of uncommon strength had laid down, 'There is only one way to make love'. If you had attracted one you could attract another: you knew how each would act. I shook with silent laughter. It was as though they were a litter. It was zoological – a multiple birth.

Catherine's was a hard and shining school. Often I had terrors but I hid them. I had wanted this world, more than I had wanted my Chelsea life, and now I must learn to live in it.

And tennis – what an introduction! The euphoria of movement, the sudden intimacy in a tight corner! Catherine's hard tennis court, that later was to be called a gun-emplacement, was a stage. And the stalls applauded from the bank above. While, from the house itself, grey stone and silver windows, came men with trays and drinks.

Dolly came once, I now remember. But she was antagonistic to the atmosphere. She liked clever people. I liked them clever and smart. For the years that I was in this world I liked it better than the intellectual one. And though I loved and valued Lovat I liked better laughing with Hugo. Artists don't feed each other. Each is at one remove from life. I adored my 'high society'. It suited me. I found it such a spectacle. But I made a mistake when I wanted its accolade.

*   *   *

As with everyone, there were two lives running in me – the enjoyment-life, and the notes I made on it. Even at a kiss there was a comment more valuable than the kiss. I was the Recording Angel and that was my protection and my armour. I am not a born writer, but I was born a writer. Something would come of it. Everything would serve. The hallucinated exclamations visited me on buses and in drawing-rooms. But they broke off short, leaving me stranded. Not the way to write a book. Not yet. Ralph Hodgson would have understood.

Cyril Connolly, reviewing Rosamond Lehmann's *The Swan in the Evening*, said that she had 'processed' parts of her life already in her books and that therefore they couldn't come in to her autobiography. Though I don't like the word 'processed' – it's true.

How can one tell again what has once been transmuted? I come back to Degas. The picture and the cunning. One needs nine lives for writing (waiting and waiting: and then not waiting a minute). Though my strength was strong and my patience inexhaustible – I waited ten years to discover the particular 'cunning' I needed. The life I had lived in Falconwood and Piccadilly had to be distilled into a fantasy. There had to be a way of conveying the incredible as though it was credible – or conveying the truth as though it was *in*credible, without winking an eyelash. I can't paint Catherine twice. It's impossible. Does no one quote their own books? I shall.

The Countess Flor di Folio was a Brazilian of forty-five, the cruellest age in women, whether they be enemies or benefactresses. She had the mind of a child, the energy of a wild animal, and the health of an immortal. She was no snob, and though still beautiful and very rich she had a delightful flair for bad society. There had been a time when the most exclusive persons had accepted her invitations, but having everything in the world that she wanted she had tired of them, and her growing fondness for the disreputable, the curious and shady, for all quacks and purveyors of sham goods, sham art, bogus literature, her passion for imitation fur, imitation tortoise-shell, imitated antiquity, had led her at last to the pitch of appreciating an imitation aristocracy, and with the cunning of a child, which thinks it takes in all the world, it had delighted her to palm off bogus dukes upon genuine duchesses. With the result that she now fed at her table a willing menagerie of adventurers, and a few old friends of standing who could afford her reputation, could stand the smell of counterfeit, and came because they delighted in the artful pranks of hungry bandits.

She adored the abnormal and the extravagant, snakes, Arabs and hyenas. Like a child she wanted to teach the worm to swim in water, the fish to sit at table, the dog to mate with the cat. Behind the house she had made a courtyard garden, which now, turned to marble and mustard weed, housed a wild gazelle, thirsty and haggard at the haunches, the indignant parrot, the cries and beauties of the peacock, the monkey petted or deposed. Below in the kitchen lounged the sick Arab, wasting his days, he who had lately been the Countess's Eastern playboy, filled the vacant chair at luncheon, and clamoured in delightful language for the food that went by in golden dishes. (This was the 'cunning'.)

I had thought at the time (such idiots writers are) that it had been transmuted beyond recognition. Poor Catherine – she had half adopted me and she had nourished a viper. But I had no idea that I was a viper. When it was finished I was so pleased with myself that I showed the MS to her. But I didn't take count of what I ought to have known – that she was no reader. Life pushed her at a gallop from morning till night and though she had books by her bed she didn't read them. She fell asleep when her head touched the pillow (and could wake at any hour of the night to listen to anyone). On the book's publication I was instantly banished from Pic (her London house, 139 Piccadilly), and she threatened to sue me. I was married by then and the Pic-life wouldn't have suited Roderick. Sir George Lewis made short work of the suing by asking her if it was true that she really recognized herself.

I am not the heroine of *Serena*. In some curious way I had rebecome a virgin. Frank Harris was forgotten: that step through the Gateway retracted. *Serena*'s heroine is dead now. She was an extraordinary, most beautiful girl.

At that time, rather before the Catherine life, I had made a friend, older than I, above me intellectually, a grave, handsome woman with whom both Desmond MacCarthy and Bertrand Russell were in love. She lived not far away, in the heart of a large family (and it was there that I first met Desmond). I used to walk down to dine with them, and she would walk back with me up my Hill. My chatter was a change, I think, from their own conversation, and they flattered and 'admired' me.

They were apt to talk in low voices of serious things. I used to draw the talk on to my ground. I wasn't at home on theirs.

Among the sisters was a girl, almost a child, very silent. She hardly spoke at table but looked with all her eyes. My friend, when I knew her better, said she was worried about this little sister. 'She's uncommunicative,' she said. 'I feel she's dangerously out of touch with life.'

'How old is she?'

'Seventeen. She looks younger, doesn't she? I'm afraid for her. She's so desperately innocent. And so secretive one can't help her.'

Not long after that talk the young sister rang me – 'Might she come and see me?'

She came. She asked in the same low 'family' voice, but smiling – whether I could lend her a hundred pounds.

'I haven't *got* it! – But why?'

'I want to have an abortion,' she said. 'I've arranged it and it will cost that.'

'Won't the man help?'

'I don't know who he is.'

Somehow the hundred pounds was raised. My brother gave me what he had, which was fifteen pounds. I had a little more than that, and I made her tell her sister (her so-startled sister) and she had savings which she drew out.

The abortion was managed successfully and a strange thing happened. The mother of the girl – herself in a way a child – an innocent birdlike woman, dreamt that very night that just this thing had happened to her daughter. She told it, modest and apologetic, at breakfast, adding – 'It shows how silly dreams are!'

One day when it was all over I asked the young sister how many men she had slept with.

'I've no idea,' she said. She had a way of saying it as though she 'had no idea where she'd left her bag'. 'I don't get pleasure from men,' she added.

'Then what . . . then why . . .'

'Saying "yes" is the pleasure I get.'

'Would you say "yes" to anyone?'

'I suppose I would.'

I took her to Falconwood but she couldn't bear Catherine.

Catherine frightened her. During the time she was there I saw how she attracted men. She never spoke: she looked. She looked across a table at a meal. She looked just anywhere, at anything. And at once she was surrounded by men.

It was her rueful smile that I put in *Serena*. Her acceptance that if you give freely no one pays. Not even in affection. Yet to 'give' was her politeness, her good manners. What became of her? Ah well, I won't say.

It was with the older sister (who was really the innocent and remained so all her life) that I first met Desmond MacCarthy. She had a lofty, gentle arrogance about sex that drove him wild. I don't know how long he had been in love with her. I forgot to ask. I owe her a lifetime of Desmond, and ah what a gift.

I remember almost the first thing he said to me.

'*Never* be afraid to bore. Don't change the subject. Johnson wasn't afraid to bore. In his time they didn't have this cowardly way of hopping off a theme. Johnson went on and on till he had exhausted everyone' – (with a kind of triumph). '*He* wasn't afraid to *bore*.'

Ah the first impact of Desmond. Not visually, but when the first words moved, caressing and inexorable, into position: when armed with the weapons of his mind he trod softly like a hunter after the hare of his thought.

When I met him he was at his best period. (There is a man gone over the edge leaving too little behind!)

Desmond was never at Catherine's. He would have found it too exotic and too light. And his marvellous gift, his table-talk, wouldn't have suited that name-gossip atmosphere. They hopped on and off subjects like crickets. *They* were afraid to bore!

In the first war he was at the Admiralty and wore a charming uniform and took me out to lunch. He was never in love with me, but very fond.

He took me to Garsington and as I was nervous of those total Intellectuals he kept me by his side. I heard Lady Ottoline say (in her extraordinary double voice like the two halves of a wasp) . . . 'that tiresome girl who wouldn't let go of Desmond'. I didn't know that I was holding on to their plum.

But in spite of the Desmond-trouble I was asked to her

house in Bedford Square. It was there I saw Bertrand Russell un-at-ease and also in love with my friend. My only impression of him is that I was glad he wasn't in love with me.

* * *

At the end of a summer when the war came we were at Princetown on Dartmoor at the Duchy Hotel – my father, my mother and my nineteen-year-old brother.

One morning the great gates of Dartmoor prison opened and half the warders marched out to join up. The band played; their women ran beside them to the moorland station.

No war can burst out quite like that again. Semi-historical, almost in costume, it seemed at first. But it wasn't. Before I could turn round my little brother was at Ypres, a sapper nightly between the lines, miraculously never wounded. Hugo was wounded and returned.

Overnight the d'Erlangers became the Er-*lang*ers. The hard tennis court (thin as biscuit) was called a gun emplacement. But by shutting up Falconwood and keeping to the social heights of London they escaped the witchhunt of the middle classes on the Hill.

While I was passing my V.A.D. Certificate I was sent down with a detachment to meet the trains with the wounded at a near-by station called Well Hall. The great trains with the Red Cross gleaming in front of them edged slowly, softly, carefully in against the platform. There was awed silence as the doors opened, nobody alighted, and the stretchers were carried to the train. There could have been no base hospitals in France then: there hadn't been time. The wounded came just as they were, their bandages soaked in blood. Thus they were carried out.

The second trainload was full of desperately wounded Germans. These would not drink. They shook their heads at our cups of tea. They had been told the English would poison them. They had been left between the lines a week. You could smell the gangrene.

Everyone, trained or not, was rushed into the great military hospital, the Royal Herbert Hospital, at the foot of the Hill, to fetch and carry. Operations went on without stopping. I saw legs in buckets outside the theatre doors. No such trainloads came in the second war. The men at the beginning of that first war were simply picked off the battlefields. That was the difference: in the first war one was closer to suffering.

Victoria Station, for instance, was like a sad 'stand at ease'. For four years men in khaki lay all over it night and day, bundled in their great-coats, equipment draped round them, sleeping, waiting for connections to go on leave, or waiting for the trains to take them back to the Front.

At last I became a regular V.A.D. On my night off I went up to Catherine's, staying in a little room with gold stars on dark blue paper.

All through that war the entertaining went on, the hostesses had their houses, their servants, and the men came back on leave.

Catherine's house in London is still there, and as I drive round the whirlpool of Hyde Park Corner I can see as I emerge what she called One-Three-Nine-Pic.

That house was an international playground. In *Serena Blandish* I say it had two front doors. And if it hadn't it had.

I can see, with my glance – which is all the traffic allows me – the fawnish stone frontage, the carving round an upper window. It had been Byron's house, Catherine had said.

With my eye returned to the traffic I can yet see inside it.

Behind the front door at the top of the steps sits a Mozart footman in livery, in a hooded chair. Up the stairs there's an open landing. The footman will pass you up to the butler, who calls your name into the drawing-room.

One night, on those stairs, there was a flutter, a commotion, a loud gay voice and a group of men. Diana Manners came down the stairs like a muslin swan. Her blind blue stare swept over me. I was shocked – in the sense of electricity. Born to the city I wanted to storm, the Queen of Jericho swept past me.

I wouldn't have dared then say, 'Hullo, Diana'. I wouldn't have dreamt of it: though in the frailest possible way I knew her. Did I comfort myself by saying she must be vain, spoilt, shallow and, by the occasional odd vacancy of that thinking face, perhaps even stupid? No, I don't think so. I wasn't as stupid as that.

Years later, at Chantilly, when she was Ambassadress in Paris, I tried to convey my young feeling of outer space, telling it in the sense that for the 'it'-ness of society I had fought my way in. Someone, as I was talking, demurred.

'Let her get on with it!' exclaimed Diana. 'You'll spoil the point. She's trying to tell the truth.'

I did without that marvellous friendship for twenty years more. But when it came it didn't come too late.

* * *

How charming was, and is, the chanciness of being a girl. One has a kind of honey. But not for bees. You walk into a drawing-room and a dark man or a light man or a red man may change your life for no reason. The butler ought to whisper, 'Cross my palm with silver' as you go in.

You might think that a woman of seventy-eight, glancing at a house where she was once in love, would be full of regrets. The extraordinary thing about age is that you don't regret love.

Even in the looking glass there's nothing to be done. The golden veil has blown off the face.

It isn't that I was what's called, rather unhandsomely, 'highly sexed'. But it was such a surprise that one could attract. It was like a stream finding out that it could move a rock. The pleasure of one's effect on other people still exists in age – what's called making a hit. But the hit is much rarer and made of different stuff.

I made my young hit on Prince Antoine Bibesco in that house, in that drawing-room. What an adventure that night to be a girl.

I asked him later how long he had remained in love with me. He answered with his burst of loud laughter – 'Three days'.

To be a victim humiliated him. He didn't like being in love with women: I don't think he loved men. What he liked best was a girl in love with him. Then he had a free hand for torture. I didn't know that it would all change into friendship for his life; or that my eldest son would one day say, '*That* was the man I would most have liked to have been like.'

He was when I met him First Secretary at the Roumanian Legation, and handsome as a Roman coin. Rich, in a then rich world, magically generous, gay but dipped in melancholy, scandalizing, but easily shocked, erudite and light, a specialist on his close friends, whom he tortured out of principle – 'If you like me you must like the whip' – scolding, stimulating, interfering, keeping on those he loved a creative eye. But these perceptions came later; what I saw then was the beauty, the gaiety, and the astounding pursuit of myself.

That night (from *Serena*):

'The dining-room was domed. The walls of turquoise and gilt rose like cliffs. In the crushing heat beneath the starry menace of the chandelier, a globe of living goldfish stood in the middle of the table. "Here is opportunity," Serena mused, "dazzling, bewildering. From this table I may rise beloved of a cabinet minister, a millionaire, a duke. What a buccaneer am I! What a Soldier of Fortune is every unmarried girl!"'

That night the Soldier of Fortune didn't find a husband. But she found an Adviser. That night Antoine fell in love with me. Next morning at eleven he and Georges Boris and Paul Morand took me to have coffee in Soho. I was due to go back home: Antoine drove me to the station. I was now embarked (for the first time) on love.

At the window of the empty carriage – 'I'll ring you.'

'Oh . . .'

'Why "oh"?'

I smiled 'secretly' as the train moved. His dark face looked back mockingly. Secrecy was his, not mine.

The *telephone*! That was what had startled me.

Because . . .

* * *

An early triumph is in itself a sort of love. My father had had this love-affair long ago with the telephone. Certain things in youth are one's own. The telephone was his own.

While a subaltern at Aldershot (and at that time – 1874 perhaps – the Royal Engineers had the Civil Post Office Telegraph Department under their wing) he went up to Gloucester Place to a small telegraph workshop run by a father and son. The son showed him a couple of receivers (without microphones) just brought over from America by Sir William Preece. It was the first telephone: invented by Bell.

To Daddy the telephone was for ever after a message-carrier. It was for urgency. It was lèse-majesté to chat. This was a nightmare in my coming love-life.

He had other theories about the telephone. You must first announce who you are. ('Bagnold speaking.')

Once when rung up by the War Office.

'This is the War Office speaking.'

'Name please,' said my father.

'I am the War Office speaking.'

'Are you?' said Daddy. 'Then I'm God Almighty,' and put it down.

On that day in Gloucester Place he saw the two instruments, went back to Aldershot, sat up with his corporal all night, and produced an identical pair. Next day he got his soldier-servant to run them out on cable-carriers into a wood. When deep in the wood he spoke to his servant from his end. The man ran out of the wood, scared. 'I heard your *voice*, sir!'

Preece came down to Aldershot with what he thought was the unique and first pair in England, in order to test the transmission on the long coils of cable wound round telegraph carts. He made great 'conjurer' play (a mannered lecturer) to those about him over the secret hidden in his bag.

'I don't suppose any of you would know what I have got here!'

Daddy, drawing his hand from behind his back – 'Anything like this, Sir William?'

Our telephone suffered the handicap of this triumph. He wouldn't let it grow up. It was uniquely for messages. 'Ring up and shut off. Don't keep the wires busy.' Those who 'conversed' he thought wanted manners.

But I was in love with the telephone-gossiper of all time. Worst of all, the damn thing was in the dining-room.

Oh, to be made love to on the telephone! What an instrument, what a cruelty! – At a word of love they are bringing the breakfast in!

Antoine wasn't as fond of social life as he appeared to be, so he often went to bed at ten. Thus he was ready by eight in the morning for torture.

'But, Antoine – I *suffer*!' – (kicking the door shut at the entry of the kidneys).

'Only death can make one suffer. Don't make such a fuss about love.'

When a man rings you all day long you should *know* that he

oves you. But I never was sure and how right I was. I liked confirmation.

'Do you love me?'

'I am the Potter.' (Severely.) 'Why should the Potter love his Pot?'

With my princely lover, with my indignant father, on the edge of tears, assailed on both sides – *'Who is this man?'* cried my father. The Sudan, Egypt, the Boer War, Chatham, Jamaica, Woolwich, hadn't prepared him for Antoine. It was the cocks over again.

Somehow in the dear house where I had been a rebellious but lately more obedient daughter, a *modus vivendi* came about, and the teasing, interfering foreign man was partially tolerated. One thing, however, was laid down. He was not to ring at mealtime.

'If you'd come down and call on them they'd think it more correct . . .' I wavered. Laughing loudly at my suburbanism he drove down and made friends. My father noted his extreme intelligence – but also his extreme danger to me.

But danger is exquisite. I was nine feet high and slept on levitation. It's no use pointing out danger to a girl like that.

Antoine bought me a hat.

'But you can't accept . . .' (my mother).

'Yes, I *can.*'

I had such a habit of intimacy with my mother that I told her things which, when she told my father (and she did), made love more difficult.

Antoine gave me a diamond and onyx brooch (which I have just given to Laurian).* I had never had a diamond before: it was like a scholarship. Since pride was the point of the brooch I wore it. My father was stern, but, I could see, baffled.

'It's a new world,' I told him. I thought it was too; and they always think it, the latest generation. That's the way I too have been fobbed off as old-fashioned.

It was after the brooch, perhaps after a sleepless night, that my father said:

'In my day a man would be thought to have compromised a girl.'

I went pale with alarm.

* My daughter.

'If this goes on much longer,' he said, 'he should offer himself.'

To forestall disaster I passed this on to Antoine as a joke with cream on it. He laughed insultingly (I wasn't insulted – only relieved). To mock me he told me what Catherine had said to him on the telephone – that I might 'set a trap for him'. My inability to set a trap hadn't struck her. For this I was furious.

'Why say such a thing?'

'To punish you.'

'For what?'

'Those you bring together you lose when they *get* together. She likes conquests kept *inside* her house.'

'Set a trap' – i.e. marriage – being in his mind he said, 'What a compliment, and what a madness, that a man should offer to keep a girl all his life . . . Show me a proposal of marriage, dear Virgilia,* and I'll know what you're worth!' It was then I thought, ungrateful and disloyal, of the three proposals written in three letters, the Unremembered, the doctor, and the Civil Servant. I found them and sent them to him. And after a lifetime I refound them, pinned together with 'Well done!' in Antoine's handwriting.

This talk was at tea at 114 Grosvenor Road. The house, gone now, had a front garden with a gate on to the road. It faced across the Embankment on to the river. The rooms were the colour of water lit by sun – silver and gold (Japanese paper), but the gold rubbed so faint as to have sheen without colour. And the pictures on the walls were Vuillard and his contemporaries, new then, new almost to themselves.

As I had come in at the front door a door on the left opened. A hand came through holding out a bunch of wet, dying flowers. '*Take them!*' said Antoine in low urgency, his face changing. I took them and the door shut.

This was Antoine's older brother Emmanuel.

* * *

Even now I am nervous.

'DON'T SPEAK OF THIS EVER. AND DON'T SPEAK OF YOUR SILENCE.'

Antoine said this after Emmanuel had killed himself. I

* Their name for me: Virgil's *Aeneid*.

disobeyed him. Forty-five years later I made a play from the suicide, which I called 'The Last Joke'. If Antoine went to hell or heaven he kept the key in his pocket and slipped back. I will tell later on what he did.

'Don't speak of this ever. . . .'

And when the reviews rained on my head, clattering like tin cans, *who* was laughing like a hyena in the spheres? Antoine.

While I can't believe that 'they' hear you, listen to you, read you – there is something in a threat. Since no one has ever known, one way or another, I have as much right as anyone to shiver. When I wrote Antoine's Obituary he was more lately dead (if there is anything in that). It was nervous work. If anyone had the frivolous malignity to come back and take a stick to me it might be Antoine.

I shall know perhaps in ten years, perhaps in two, whether there are fantastic exceptions (as Rosamund Lehman says there are). Whether people get caught up as it were on a doornail on the way out.

When *The Last Joke* failed so noisily, so totally (after having been thought 'certain' by both Binkie* and his stage director, Rupert Marsh) I had a feeling that 'they' meant it to fail. They were having a revenge. Marthe† said to me, 'They are laughing up their sleeves in the skies.' But she's a Catholic.

Emmanuel had what was called in those days recurrent suicidal mania. There were fewer subdivisions in madness then. Before I had met either of them he had been fished out of the Seine and taken miscalculated poison. He had the devil in him and threatened and blackmailed Antoine over the smallest act.

'I shall die if you don't do . . . this or that!' And in a temper he *would* have died. And in fact did.

Secretly I didn't like Emmanuel, but I had to choke that down. Antoine worshipped him.

'Emmanuel,' I used to say to myself angrily inside, 'is not in the least mad!' Then, more angrily – 'except that he is *mad*!'

Antoine would have given the world and all its women to make Emmanuel 'live again'. Perhaps I was 'loved' myself just to amuse Emmanuel.

---
* Hugh Beaumont, of H. M. Tennent.
† Their cousin, Princesse Marthe Bibesco.

They were both fascinated by the story of Frank Harris.

'But you are so re-spect-able, Virgilia!' hammering on his accent). Then he would laugh and laugh, those laughs without merriment which so suddenly stopped. For behind, and always, and over everything, lay the despair about Emmanuel. Lighthearted about love between himself and women, he loved his brother with a losing frenzy. Losing, because Emmanuel must win some day. You can't watch all the time.

Emmanuel had had a stroke, but the signs on his face were slight. Nevertheless he always wore a blue wool scarf round his mouth. He refused to see anyone who had known him in what must have been his beauty.

But I was brand new. I couldn't make comparisons. So bit by bit Antoine got Emmanuel to accept me and he had great hopes of me as an enlivener.

I dined for the first time at 114 Grosvenor Road. Violet Asquith was there.

Cynthia (Asquith) was there too, with her chestnut Romney loveliness: two or three men whom Antoine knew – perhaps Matila Ghyka.

Antoine's method as a host was to flick rather than talk. He had the gift, through his special teasing, of making people intimate. Violet dazzled me. I was spellbound and tongue-bound. I didn't know that talk could be made to fold and flutter and touch with such fingertips such shades and shadows of thought. Cynthia had then, as she always had, her particular wit. Its trouble was that it could hardly be heard. She tucked it into her corsage like a handkerchief, and gave a light spurt of instantly-extinguished laughter. When I looked back on the majors and the gunners I marvelled that I was where I was. And at last at last I had got thinner. It suited me so that I almost had beauty (but it went again). If one doesn't become a 'beauty' in some men's eyes one has missed the big moment. To be a miracle, even for a moment, is an education. It's not to be sniffed at. And in those years between twenty-four and thirty I had got the hang of it. If I speak in this rather disreputable way it's because I rub my hands together when I think of what became of the gosling. And how in spite of danger she feathered her nest with happiness.

A love affair has so few remembered incidents. It only

changes from good to bad. First he was in love. Then he wasn't. Then I was. But I don't know when. I remember most often my eyes full of tears at the telephone.

'Virgilia's back is broad,' said Antoine. 'She can stand anything!'

I became 'adopted' by both brothers. (Though I didn't much want 'both'.) Books arrived at Warren Wood by special messenger. They educated me as it were in the basement below Proust. Proust was alive then and I wasn't thought eligible for the ground floor.

But I 'overheard' his voice (Proust's) indirectly, at a tangent, by allusion. Many of the phrases, catchwords, French slang used between the brothers I now know (through George Painter*) to have been Proust's.

The car journeys began. This had always been a passion of Emmanuel's. He loved to make shrine-journeys to architecture, and the longer they were and the more tired one got the more he liked it. Also they were very difficult to explain at home. But a girl in love will do anything. Antoine only had to say, 'This will amuse Emmanuel.'

At first – there being no chaperon – I had to lie. And there was one morning at Warren Wood (of course in the dining-room) when all was nearly discovered. By a casual remark and an unlucky telephone message I was brought so near discovery it was like a deathwound in the stomach just before it bleeds. I even know where I was standing on the carpet. I know how my mother and father sat, calm and unawakened. I remember turning to the garden as I answered (and I didn't know *which* answer) so that I should never see the first pain on their faces. The peril passed.

Fifty years later I stood on the same spot on the floor. The agony shot up my feet. Call it memory. But I think it was in the floorboards.

It hadn't been that I so dreaded discovery of deceit. It was what would come of discovery – the threat to those I loved.

I managed at last to insist on a living chaperon. To invent one was so mean to my mother.

Marguerite Lahovary, Marthe's eighteen-year-old sister,

* *Marcel Proust. A Biography*: George Painter.

came to England for a visit and delighted in being taken about by her cousins.

She was pretty, gay, and puppy-plump, and often stayed the night at Warren Wood before an early start. We went, for instance, in a hired lumbering Daimler, to see the Seven Churches of Marshland – including all Lincolnshire. Sometimes Emmanuel, hurrying ahead of us shakily to a church porch, one leg slightly dragging, would turn with arms outstretched, pressing us back to the car, crying loudly, 'No, no! It's too beautiful – not a word – I don't want your comments!' If crossed he flew into a rage, which most terribly upset Antoine. As we drove, he would stop the car peremptorily, snatch wild flowers from a bank, and make me clutch them, fading, all day.

We drove to Hertfordshire in order that I might see red sails crossing a field, the boat hidden in the deep canal; to Dartmoor all night in a blinding fog. That was the time when they gave me a gold watch for driving, with 'Virgilia–Dartmoor' inscribed on the back of it. The tyranny of Emmanuel had made the old driver ill and they put him inside the car while I did the driving.

By some impulse of idiocy I made them stop and call on a hunting uncle, my mother's brother, at ten o'clock at night. Suddenly we erupted into the just-going-to-bed house, a niece and three foreign men. The conversation was so maladjusted (like Tibetans talking to dogs) that no one could answer the other. I took them out again and my uncle wrote severely to my mother. This was a time when Georges Boris was 'chaperon'. But I don't think that did any good.

There must be women older than I who had loved Emmanuel. Perhaps Marthe, his cousin? I have never asked her. But when I knew him he had renounced love in favour of making scenes. I couldn't imagine him as attractive.

At this time – of the car journeys – Emmanuel rang me as often as Antoine. And Emmanuel most particularly rang at mealtimes. He had only to discover a thing to be forbidden to do it. The telephone-irritation grew worse than ever. The instrument, too, was fastened high on the wall. One had to stand to speak into it. The devilish princes liked to talk for an hour. Ten minutes the one I loved: fifty the other.

One day, in the middle of Sunday lunch, the bell went. My father, sharpening the knife for the joint, looked up. I answered it, recognized Emmanuel, floundered, divided in mind between two angry men.

From the telephone – '*Pay attention*, Virgilia!'
From my father – 'Ask him to ring *later*.'
'Go at once to Antoine. Don't leave him . . .'
'My God, can't one *eat*!'
Losing my head, stammering, half-hearing, I said:
'Emmanuel, I'll ring back. . . .'
Click. Finish. No sound.
Holding the receiver in one hand I turned round.
'Daddy, there's something wrong.'
'What?'
'I think he's done it. I think he's killed himself.'
Of course this was no divination, no new idea. The threats had gone on for so long.

The cloud on my father's face had gone. 'Try ringing again.'

It was no good. Marlow Exchange (they had a house there by the river) said the lines were disconnected.

'They weren't five minutes ago!'
'They are now.'
'Ring Antoine,' said my father.
'That's what Emmanuel said.'
'To ring Antoine? Then you should.'
I did. And Antoine guessed at once.
'Come here. Come to Grosvenor Road. Wait for me here. I'll go down.'

My father concurred in it all. I went.

It took me an hour and a half to get there – via Woolwich Arsenal Station and Charing Cross and a bus. I didn't hurry. Antoine wouldn't be back. His man let me in and I sat looking at the river, thinking, 'How will he bear it? What shall I do?' I knew Emmanuel was dead. A little later Antoine walked into the room. He was in no hurry either. What hurry would there ever be again? He glanced at me without greeting, went over to the window, looked out also over the river. After a time he said, 'Of course it's happened.'

'You knew it would.'

'But one can't live with a living man as though he was dead.'
Again – later: 'I took every precaution.'
'I know.'
'I had a man on the river.'
(Pause.)
'One can't live taking precautions. Something slips in the end.'
And so we sat. Words came from time to time.
'He's been so gay this summer. I ought to have known.'
'Why?'
'He always said, "Look out for my *gay* days. Look out when I'm at the top of my form." Come down and we'll walk on the Embankment.'
So we did. I thought it would never stop. We walked through tea-time into dinner-time. Once he stopped and leant on the Embankment wall and said, 'I shall go too.' I made no dissent. The pain in one foot – a corn – grew intense. It must have been summer. I don't know the date.
(I could know if I went to Brompton Cemetery where Antoine had made that beautiful grave. Like the cover of a book, flat, with green Cumberland turf and a margin of blue lobelias (then it *was* summer). A book of emerald leather with an indigo margin. It all depended on shape.
But that was at the funeral, when I sat in the car with Antoine (so suddenly, so fantastically woven into their lives).
'You were the last person, Virgilia, to hear a living word.'
'And a cross one.'
He gave a ghost-laugh. 'That doesn't make it less like . . .' (He couldn't say his name.)
At eleven o'clock we went in.
'You'll stay all night.'
'Of course, but I must ring my father.'
He pushed the telephone towards me. When I rang, my father equally said 'of course'.
We sat on through the night. From time to time a murmur. Once he said – 'I've had only two loves – my mother and my brother.' (Thus wiping out all women.)
And again – 'Would you like to be rich, Virgilia?'
I made no answer. Then – 'I might leave you my fortune and my house in Roumania.' Still I made no answer.

It meant his death and he was talking only to himself. I knew all night it was touch and go.

Desmond used to say that Tolstoi dropped his bucket deeper into the well of the soul than any other writer. We were down there that night. It felt like the bottom of the well.

Somewhere in the middle of the night he rang the bell and his man came. 'The prince is gone,' he said.

'It had to be, Highness.'

'Get us some chocolate.'

Hot chocolate was one of Antoine's staple meals.

The man brought it, and in the morning croissants.

All I did all night was sit. And sometimes answer a question. But the questions were seldom questions. Out of what was passing through Antoine's mind some scrap floated loose from the dense, obscure river. He talked at me to himself. I think it was a help. He got up and got me a dressing gown (blue and green like the grave).

Emmanuel had taken poison and hanged himself on the back of his bedroom door. (*He* didn't tell me this.) He had been found and cut down and laid on his bed by the time Antoine got there. His Will lay near, with last-minute scribbles. For instance – to me he had left a hundred and twenty pounds – 'less twenty because I am angry with Virgilia'. (That was the trouble with the telephone.)

In the margin – 'Buy Elizabeth a diamond bracelet. My *marriage gift*.' Emmanuel had wanted Antoine to marry Elizabeth[*]. It had been his special plan, that Antoine should marry the daughter of the Prime Minister of England. The status of Roumania came into it; and England cut ice then. The Bibescos were descended from the kings of Moldavia and every now and then Emmanuel had a nostalgic flash of State-Responsibility.

Another marginal scribble: 'Seven empty petrol tins to go back.'

That night is as bright as yesterday. I can pick the words off the plate like a waiter the silver. But later, what happened later (except the intricate funeral) I don't know. I don't know how much I was with him. The day and night of the death stands so much further out than anything else.

It finished all 'love'. He was a dead man. But he lived. For a

[*] Elizabeth Asquith

long time he wasn't sure he would. Years later I asked him about the pain.

'It's just as bad when it comes. But it comes less often.'

Marguerite, Marthe's little sister, called at the house in Marlow just after Antoine had left. She was taken to the bedroom and lifted the sheet from the rope-swollen face.

'How beautiful,' she wrote to Marthe. 'He defied God and pulled down his own curtain.' She shot herself, for some passing love affair, a few months later in Switzerland.

Should I cram Antoine into one chapter? He went through so much of my life, like a strange and acrid scent. Desmond, looking back long afterwards, surprised me by saying that he had been certain Antoine would marry me. (And indeed I used to pray every night that he would.)

But it was lucky in the long run for me that he didn't. I could never have made myself happy by writing, linked to that impatient gardener – always examining the roots! This he did to Elizabeth: and to his daughter Priscilla. His method was like starting to teach one Latin when the final exam is next day. The husband that I did have was perfect for that. He never asked about the roots till the flower surprised him. Antoine always maintained that he made my marriage. He loved to say to Roderick, 'I got you your wife!' He had laughed, in his taunting way, in a station (Paddington) – 'There are wrinkles round your eyes, Virgilia! You must marry *at once*!' He knew Roderick wanted to marry me and I haven't wrinkles round my eyes even now. Other detriments but not those.

I didn't, at the time of Emmanuel's death, imagine that Antoine would really marry Elizabeth. He spoke of her faults. He had even mocked her. He had told me of Emmanuel's 'absurd wish'. He had told it, laughing lovingly against Emmanuel.

So that when . . .

I will jump to Senlis. I had got to the war at last, though the war was over. I had driven five winter months, uniform stained, a bath occasionally when I found a bath-house on a river, when I got a telegram from Antoine asking me to lunch in Paris. I went, driving in, and put my car (Quai Bourbon) under the lamp by the parapet that looks over the river. Antoine owned the whole house but his flat was on the first floor. That silvery flat was dying even in my time. It was the colour of the river. The walls rose from the black floor in an indescribable shine. On the walls were two big Vuillards. They weren't pictures. They were gardens into which you walked through a frame. Foliage, women, things going on behind the skin of imagination. He left them to an Englishwoman. I wish he had left them to me. But just as I wasn't allowed to know Proust so I wasn't fit for the Vuillards.

('I wrote your Obituary all the same! You never thought of *that!*')

There was a mirror opposite Antoine's bed that mirrored the river. It tilted. You could pull it to dismiss or to show the water. I tried to have it put into *The Last Joke*. But unless you make a thing yourself it never works.

Antoine was waiting for me.

'I have to go out,' he said, 'unexpectedly. I have ordered your lunch here and I shall be back in an hour and a half.'

'You're going *out*. . . .'

'I have to meet my future father-in-law, dear Virgilia.'

('Wait, pain! There'll be time later.')

'*Father-in-law?*'

'Mr Asquith. You don't read the English papers. Your lunch won't be ready for half an hour. What would you like to do?'

('Wait, pain!') – 'I should like to have a bath and wash my hair.'

'Jean . . .' he said to his valet, 'prepare a bath.' And he was gone.

The bath was being run. I looked out of the window. A barge was coming up with its old peculiar hooting. I had known this flat (in love). I went into the bathroom. ('Wait, pain, till I'm in the water.') I did that thing that men do and women don't – sank back, water creeping up the scalp, face afloat.

('*Now*, pain.') But it never came. And this is the truth. I never felt anything about Antoine's marriage. Without exactly knowing it I had passed over already to that long friendship in which so little praise was ever given but such responsibility implied.

Chapter Six

*

THE ROYAL HERBERT HOSPITAL, when I was first there was staffed by old-time Sisters in scarlet capes, who inherited from peace the idea that men in bed were malingerers. At the opening of the war men lived on meat and died on the gravy: there was no light diet.

When a man died his bed was emptied, his mattress taken away to be disinfected. No attempt was made to see that the visiting parents didn't arrive to behold the empty wire of the bed. This attitude and these things shocked me more than the plight of the men themselves. I kept a diary of such shocks. I sent it as a present to Antoine and he returned it with the words 'Why not keep something for yourself?' What he meant was that I should make a book of it; and that is what I did. I sent it to Heinemann's, but Desmond (who was 'reading' for them) lost it on a bus. The only other copy, a carbon without the drawings, was with Ralph Hodgson in an anti-aircraft unit on the East Coast. He found it and sent it back. The illustrations were childish and easy to do again.

William Heinemann was alive then. We met. We liked each other (he in rather a stern way). One of my endpapers shows my state of mind as I bus'd up the Old Kent Road to luncheon. He said he would publish what was called from then on *A Diary Without Dates*, and he asked me to dine.

He put me next to Robbie Ross. (How right I had been about drawing-rooms and platforms.) He had a sweet-tempered, indulgent way of being brilliant. You could mistake him for not being clever; and then find out how clever he was all by yourself and self-gratifyingly.

After dinner he kept me with him, and to talk more easily we sat in an alcove off the drawing-room. I was enraptured – but what was this jarring and sawing? What was this pressure and irritation? I lost half his sentence and he half mine. We turned crossly round.

There sat a strange, leaning-back, immortal woman.

It was Suggia playing her 'cello.

When *A Diary Without Dates* was published, I was sacked from the hospital by the Matron in the first half-hour of my day. The *Daily Mail* had a Leader on it and I sprang into a tiny fame. Desmond called me a Lionetta. ('Not a lion, dear.')

I spent that day of publication of my first book in a dream of pleasure. I had nothing to do but draw my pleasure.

The Leader in the *Daily Mail* wasn't totally an explosion of praise about me. There had been a scandal in a hospital at Rouen (of unfeeling routine) and as they were exposing it my book illustrated it well.

Desmond, with his 'Lionetta', ought to have reviewed it. Especially as he had lost it. But no. 'I give you my friendship,' he said, *'instead.'*

'Suppose I would rather have your review?'

'You can't undo friendship and I don't review my friends.'

'But suppose I was Shelley or Shakespeare?'

'But you aren't.'

After the sacking from the hospital I still had to use the only bus that went to the station, constantly meeting the Matron and the Sisters. I tried out all sorts of expressions of indifference. But in the end, and not long after, the Scarlet Capes retired and a different system set in.

H. G. Wells, unlike Desmond, was prepared to put his opinion on paper. In *The Dream* (page 235) he writes:

> Nowadays of course nobody reads the books of the generals and admirals and politicians of that time, and all the official war histories sleep the eternal sleep in the vaults of the great libraries, but probably you have all read one or two such human books as Enid Bagnold's 'Diary without Dates', or Cogswell's 'Ermytage and the Curate' or Barbusse's 'Le Feu' or Arthur Green's 'Story of a Prisoner of War' or that curious anthology 'The War Stories of Private Thomas Atkins' . . .

I hope the compliment wasn't the greater because he already knew me.

Before the war, when *Ann Veronica* was first published, the Mayor of Woolwich (a literary mayor) asked me to lunch to meet H. G. Wells. Then he got cold feet. He telephoned for me to come a little early. For a little warning.

'I'll put you next to him as I promised. But you must promise me . . .'

'I won't.'

'How do you know what I'm going to say?'

'Because I've just finished *Ann Veronica*.'

'Well, if he asks you to lunch with him I beg you not to go.'

I sat next to Wells and he asked me to lunch.

'Where?'

'The Ritz.' (He was more safely in funds than Frank Harris.)

'No,' I said decidedly. 'In the Cottage Tea Rooms in the Strand.'

(*Why* the Cottage Tea Rooms? I didn't know at first when I wrote that down, but now I find traces, in the books on Lovat and Gaudier, that the Cottage Tea Rooms stood for something in our lives – something I had forgotten: an alternative to Eustace Miles.)

I hope Rebecca* will forgive this story.

We lunched. Shepherd's Pie, paper meringues, cardboard coffee, no licence for beer. He explained to me that I was just his type. I had thought I was.

TELEPHONE.
VICTORIA 3441.

614, ST ERMIN'S,
WESTMINSTER,
S.W.1.

Your servant madam

'But,' he said, 'I'm awfully tied up just now....'

(Pause: we both thought of Rebecca.)

'In fact,' he said, perfectly in earnest, '... if you could wait, you know....'

'Like a tin in the store cupboard.'

'Yes,' he said. And he wouldn't let his extraordinary little blue eyes smile.

(Those eyes of Wells' in that blunted, unmoulded face (the nose so cocky – a touch of Cyrano) were as wildly seablue as Diana's.†)

* Rebecca West.
† Lady Diana Cooper.

I ought not, ought I, to have told that story here and there. But I did. I couldn't help it: it was heaven. I owed him no love-responsibility. But looking back and telling it again on paper makes me a little tender to that greedy little boy.

We were friends for many many years. And I have fifty-two letters from him, mostly with his drawings. Drawings of the attempted seduction and of my escape. We both loved joke-drawings in letters. He was better at it than I. Our two houses, mine on Shooter's Hill, his at Dunmow, threw up shocked chimneys. Their windows stared, goggle-eyed, watching my descent, shaped like a tadpole, to Hell. His tadpole pursued me. But once I had arrived at the bottom I turned as nimbly and re-ascended. In one of the drawings he shoots himself over a hell-fire – both houses horrified. Alas, he used bad sepia ink and the drawings are fading.

He stayed with us here at Rottingdean, and one night, sitting over the burgundy in the dining-room (the burgundy that Roderick so loved), H.G. burst out against beauty. 'Beauty isn't what matters – it's *sense*!' The argument got so hectic that he cried out – 'Show me beauty on a page and I'll show you how meaningless it is!' I rushed for *Orlando*. It opened by itself at the ice scene on the *Thames*. But my absence from the dining-room had cooled him down and he was talking to Roderick about something else.

Another time we lent him the Kipling House here – The Elms – for his 'honeymoon' with Moura Budberg.* When he fell in love with Moura he explained to me (and she was there too) the dignity of love, in age.

'When you're old,' he said, making his discovery a bit late, 'you only look a fool if you fall in love with a *young* woman.' Moura twinkled at me and I forbore to say – 'You might have learnt that before.'

When he asked us to his wedding party in a Soho restaurant there was a long table at which we all sat (perhaps thirty people). I can only remember Low because I sat next to him. I went up to Moura to congratulate her. She smiled up at me with calm. 'I'm not going to marry him. He only *thinks* I am. I'm not such a fool. Marjorie† can go on doing the housekeeping!'

* The Baroness Budberg.
† His daughter-in-law.

H. G. Wells—and the Pursuit

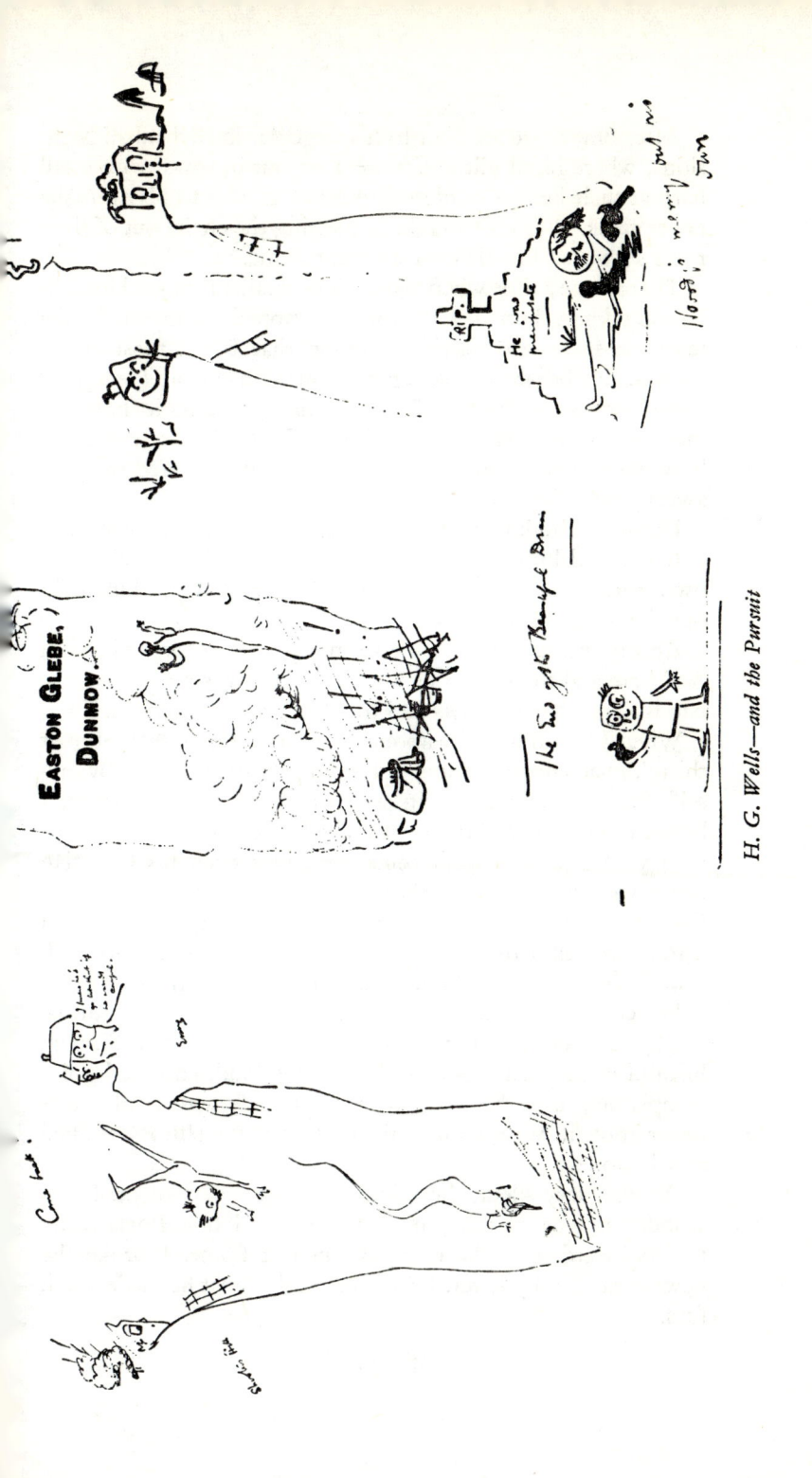

After dinner we all went to his large flat in Bickenhall Mansions, where hired gilt chairs were set out in rows, with a tall harp at their head. Countess Benckendorff was to play but she never came. Nobody thought of pushing the chairs out of their rows so we sat like that till we went home.

There came a time when his glorious vitality forsook him, but I didn't know him then. I got so wrapped up myself in the ten-years-surprise of having children that I lost most of my friends. But before his old age took him I had read *The Crystal Egg* aloud to the children. They couldn't shake off its hold. Its magic of – 'It *might* be so, mightn't it? *Might* it be that that's how we live and don't know it?' It was an invented story so awfully near the discoveries about life.

Dining with him I tried to tell him of the riveted audience. It irritated him. By that time he had something against his own stories – as a waste of his time. He was seeing nothing then but the doom of humanity.

And now is it time for me to marry? I have slipped into a 'we' here and there. Stories won't stay in my 'single woman's' hands. They have sequels and that leads on to marriage.

When I began to write about myself I had thought: 'Stop at thirty'. I had chosen, I thought then, a path to be walked by myself. But at twenty-eight, in spite of my 'mistress' attitude, I began to get engaged to people. The first engagement was to a man whose name I can't remember. Not even his Christian name. He was a friend of a character called Cardie Montagu who lived on Hay Hill. He – the fiancé – was a racing man and I learnt from him that one always wrote out cheques to Ladbroke's on a Monday. Odd things one learns from men.

He came down with me to Warren Wood on a formal 'engaged' visit. In a tram outside Woolwich Arsenal Station, brimful of Arsenal workers, I heard his loud, educated voice complaining that the workers smelt. People with loud voices never know it. We got out at the bottom of the Hill and walked slowly up.

'You're very silent,' he said. Of course I was silent. I was wondering when to tell him what I had to tell him. It was really too awkward with the coming lunch at home. I broke the news next day, by letter. I don't remember that he made much fuss.

It had been odd at lunch. Like talking to a man who wasn't there. 'Did you like him?' I asked casually after he had gone. Daddy laughed. 'It's *your* business to like him!'

Round about twenty-nine I got engaged to a gentleman-farmer-squire. I might have married him but we quarrelled at night on a heath. All his four tyres had punctured because he had that day taken his car out of storage where it had been all through the war. I was going to his home to meet his parents. It was a sweet-smelling summer night. I suggested we stuff the outer covers with hay so that we could roll on gently to a garage. But he hadn't a jack. He had those useless writer's fingers like Desmond's. But he didn't write. Out of this situation the quarrel flared and the bully rose in me. Our characters caught fire and smoked. We were not for each other. I couldn't go through the week-end: but walked three miles and got a train home.

I had, just before this, met Roderick.

These 'successes with men' that I seem to record so often, were spread over ten years, if you start at nineteen. I was a very slow starter but later a little momentum was gained. To attract – I saw – was a kind of trick. I became more expert. I lost this expertise when I married and never quite got it back.

I was just about thirty and Roderick was forty-two. We met at Lady Sackville's house in Ebury Street, before driving up with her to lunch at Eve Fleming's house in Hampstead. It must have been winter because I wore a fur coat, as yet unpaid for. I was still on my seventy-five a year, and I had been to Reveille's in Hanover Square because they had a sale of hats. No one would serve me with a hat. They were clustered round a fur-coat-clientèle buying mink. Or if it wasn't mink in those days it was musquash. Defiant, I picked up a three-quarter-length coat and tried it on. I saw I looked a smasher in it and I wondered what it cost. With more dash than the days of the gull hat in Bond Street I 'sent for' Mr Reveille. He came: he couldn't know I wasn't a millionaire. I explained to him that I couldn't pay for the coat whatever it cost. In time, yes. But not yet.

'It's eighty pounds,' he said. (More than a year's allowance.) 'Wait there while I talk to my accountant.'

I sat in the cubicle looking at myself in the coat. He came

back and said: 'You can have the coat on a down-payment of five pounds if, on your marriage, you promise to get your trousseau from me.'

'I'm not going to be married.'

'Not engaged?'

'No.'

He laughed. 'With that coat you'll be engaged in a month!'

I was due at tea with Violet Keppel at Sixteen Grosvenor Street, later Jacqmar. She was waiting for me in the hall.

'You've got a fur-coat-look,' she exclaimed – just at sight of the way I walked.

On the day I met Roderick, a few days after, we stood by Lady Sackville's famous lapis lazuli table in the hall and he said, 'Let me take your coat.'

'*No one* takes my coat!' I said. 'It's all I have!'

He said afterwards, he always said, he fell in love with me at once. But not I with him.

I never dreamt I should pass my life with him.

I dreamt it so little that when within a week he asked me to marry him I carried out my programme of going to Vienna with the Quakers. I didn't think for a moment seriously of what he said.

Vienna – ice, snow, cobbles. My job was to take milk to children. Often I found in the rooms a hungry general sitting in full uniform to keep warm. I stayed two months: I was what the maids used to call 'unsettled'.

Letters and cables came all the time. Then one day the Vienna Reuter Correspondent arrived, bringing tickets for my return to Paris.

'Sir Roderick,' he said, 'telephoned this morning that he is leaving for Canada for the Imperial Press Conference in the summer. He thinks it advisable that you should return next week as he says there will be a great deal to do before the wedding. He is meeting you in Paris.' (Silence.) 'And may I add my congratulations.'

'The nerve,' I thought. 'The Almighty Nerve.' He handed me the tickets. I thanked him for his congratulations. He gave me a sheaf of minute arrangements. He must have thought I lacked the smiling brilliance of a girl engaged to marry his Chief. I was determined to show no surprise. Any surprise at all would have involved me in explanations. Somehow I got him out of the room.

The tickets, the audacity, got me on to the train. I meant to have it out in Paris.

On the train I told the Sleeping Car Conductor that I was going to be married (just to hear the sound). He got me special hot water in the morning. I still had, though it was years old, the 'businessman's' black striped coat and skirt.

The whole thing was a sleep-walking obedience. I could refuse in Paris. Going to Canada? Nonsense.

Roderick met the train. Antoine (the husband-insister) had lent his flat. Roderick drove me straight to Boucheron and paid four hundred pounds for a ring. Then to lunch at the Ritz. We were engaged. I tried to think. I couldn't. I wasn't in love. But I had been in love pretty often and didn't think it stood the wear and tear. I didn't marry him because he was rich. I have never bothered much about money – always thinking that I could earn it – which I have.

I married him because he made me. I watched myself. It was like a new and wildly-interesting job. And in a way I had no choice. He was an irrevocable man and what he wanted went.

Back to Warren Wood and explanations. But he had well prepared the ground. He had been there several times, and taken Mummie up to London to lunch. But Daddy and she, knowing me, were ready for anything – that I should go ahead, or backslide.

Alone with Mummie – 'Now *don't* say anything to me about children!' I hated babies then and I knew her darling sentimentality. Roderick wasn't really Daddy's sort of man. At least not then. But no son-in-law ever is.

They were both unworldly and took no notice of riches ahead. They watched, and let me go my way. But Mummie's relief when we were actually going into the wedding showed me how deep her anxiety about me must have been.

Lady Gladstone, who had been a close friend of Roderick's in South Africa, asked us for a week-end to Dane End. I had to give Roderick information. It hadn't been possible in that arrival in Paris. I had thought of it when he bought that four-hundred-pound ring. But I simply couldn't, though he could have had the ring taken back. The ring-buying had been sprung on me, the whole thing was like the rush of a First Night at a play – then the journey to England, the losing of my passport (which, once married he would have been furious about, but he didn't dare then).

On this week-end at Dane End we sat in a cornfield. (How could we have? It was in June.)

Roderick didn't sit easily in cornfields but there he was.

So I told him about my lovers. Not with jauntiness, I hope: and not as a confession. He looked away in silence and didn't answer.

At length – 'Well?' That came from me.

He turned round and he was laughing. I stared.

'I'm thinking what a mug I've been!'

'Mug . . . ?'

'All those pretty girls I've known – would they have slept with me?'

And that was all. What an extraordinary way for a conventional man (but he wasn't) to take the past of his future wife.

We were married by special licence in Chelsea Old Church before it was bombed. Lord Northcliffe signed the Register. And Ivor Wimborne, looking like a strange, mad goat, signed too. I got my trousseau from Reveille, plus another fur coat. We went on our honeymoon, two extraordinary strangers. But the man who could take the cornfield so easily couldn't take lesser things.

On the morning of our first night he was missing from my bed. I found him in an ante-room, dressed, ready to go to London, writing a letter to me that our marriage was over.

'Of course I shall arrange,' he had just written, 'that you have an income . . .'

To this day I am not sure what had happened. He said I had kicked him in bed.

'But I was ASLEEP . . . *ASLEEP*!' I said, indignant.

(Silence.)

'Did I *say* anything? Was it anything I *said*!'

He looked at me. He took in the blank innocence of my bewilderment. He undressed and came back to bed. We rang for breakfast.

He has heard me tell this story. He has laughed over it. But he has never explained it. Though it was a kick in a dream it must have confirmed to him his marriage-panic. He had never meant to marry. He was forty-two, ambitious, very hard-worked, and taking on what sort of burden – and for life?

'*Was* it panic?'

'I suppose it must have been. But I can't recall it: I can't call back the frame of mind. But I only know I was *so* afraid of marriage.'

The honeymoon of these two strangers was a journey with a hundred editors to the Imperial Press Conference at Montreal (or perhaps Ottawa). We took ship for Newfoundland and the then Lady Burnham (the Burnhams headed the English contingent) ticked me off for lying in the cabin sick.

'You shouldn't leave him on deck alone. It's your duty to come up.' She was right and I struggled up.

When we landed there were two trains waiting to carry us across Canada – two trains – our home. Restaurant cars, shaded lamps, polished brass, polished waiters (oh lost world of wonderful trains). As we travelled we took on the fruits of the countryside, river-trout, game, eggs, butter, cream. Each night we stopped for some vast dinner at some hotel where speeches on Empire were made by us, and to us from the Canadian Press. We dressed for dinner on the train – a hundred men and women – shuffling and passing each other to the luggage van and dragging from piled trunks and suitcases evening dresses, petticoats, stockings, shoes. The speeches went on till nearly midnight and then back to sleep on the train, which would sometimes be stationary or sometimes moving off to the next halt.

I had never in my life done anything like this. Never had a duty. Never had to behave myself. Never heard anything so mockworthy as all this hot air. The only fun was to laugh at it and I never doubted but that Roderick would laugh too.

He didn't laugh. And the first tremendous row blew up, muted, in the little 'drawing-room' of the train.

He had no notion of what I was, how much of his relationships I might endanger, how much he dared encourage me. These men at whose speeches I laughed belonged to his difficult daily life, some friends, some enemies. Reuter's was not exactly 'press', Reuters was stiff and proud, Reuters ran a course alone. Reuters was de Gaulle, if you like. I had no idea of his passion, his love for this other wife, a woman he had courted since he was seventeen. I had to live with him to get to know it. He was reticent then, and it was his soul. He wondered, as he had wondered on the marriage-morning, whether he had married something that bit. (But he hadn't.)

Such a man of forty-two who could take such a woman of thirty on such a journey – looking back I wonder he got away with it. Did he think he could 'train' me at that age? – Well he thought it and he did.

Canada, fifty years ago, was naïve, touchy, longing to be praised, young. 'What do you think of us?' (said immediately before one had even thought). I was always so nearly saying, 'I think you're a bore.' I wouldn't have thought it if I hadn't been so disgruntled by the haste of the question. The Daughters of Empire were always asking it and always taking me aside. I could see what a marvellous country it was but I never could get into it. I was chained to Empire and the train. Yet really and truly I got to love the train. I heard moose call. And some man of imagination had modelled the train's call on the moose. The same hollow echoing sound, loud but minor. And the way the train took us forward and on, always leaving the horrors behind. But always, as trains are, there was a landscape just outside the windows, a denied paradise. The coolness of pools, the glitter of lakes, alleys in forests, birds in swamps, men's faces upturned and left behind. But all known Canada to me was the press and the press's wives.

It was the dry time, alcoholically. But there were wet spots, much sought after. Montreal was one. In Montreal we met a man, very important to Roderick, who was a hard and successful press man but a poet as well. Some special agreement connected with Reuters had to be come to between them. He was the most attractive man I had met in Canada. Clothes careless and elegant. Face a bit architectural, city-white. Elliptical speech, constantly in brackets as it scooped up double-harnessed ideas. In fact a treasure of a man whom we were to meet again next day.

The lunch he arranged to give us was at the best hotel in Montreal.

At the appointed time there was no one in the vestibule. Deep leather chairs, columns, gilt staircases, lobbies, hidden writing-tables with lamps – no man. Then out of one armchair, overlooked till then, rose a rumpled figure, hair on end, face scarlet, unsteady, advancing a hand. He had ordered a luncheon in a private room. The head waiter led. He followed. We behind. He put one hand on the wall to steady himself as he walked.

It began as a nightmare. He was conscious enough for us not to be able to leave, but not conscious enough for talk. First came the soup. His shirt-bulge, as he slouched forward, elbows planted, drew up the soup in a dark patch. The five ordered courses came and went. He ate nothing. He knew he was drunk and now and then said 'very ashamed'. When he said this we very slightly bowed.

We got used to it and talked to each other while his eyes with curiosity watched our lips. He seemed contented except that now and then he said he was ashamed. The waiter, with no glance of conspiracy (the host was too conscious and too powerful for that) hurried the courses, flashed out the dishes – we were through. We rose. He tipped the waiter accurately, signed his bill with ease, opened the door and took us to the corridor that led back to the hall. Once more, but more clearly, 'I am very ashamed.' It was odd the things he could do and the things he couldn't.

Roderick had his business meeting with him, very agreeably, next day. Nothing was mentioned.

I seemed to be getting used to Roderick, after the amazed storms of the first week. I think he began to be more sure I wouldn't explode in public, to know I was not a fool and not disloyal. We had quite enjoyed together the poor big shot at Montreal. And at Calgary . . .

It was hot. We were panting hot. On the nineteenth floor of the biggest hotel about 11 at night Roderick was in bed: I not. I put my hand on a radiator and said, 'Good God – they've got the heat on!'

'WHAT!' He jumped out of bed and stubbed his toe on the heavy copper spittoon. 'HELL!' – he said, picked it up and shot it clean out of the open window. All his life he punished inanimate objects that hurt him.

I rushed to the switch and put the light out. Then back to the window and looked down. A man was walking nineteen floors below on the pavement *alive*.

We got into our beds. The manager came tapping on the door.

'Has anything been thrown? . . . Out of the window?'

'What's that . . . ? We're asleep.'

'I beg your pardon.'

Nothing more, not a word. But on the bill was written – 'One metal spittoon seven dollars'. It was paid in equal silence.

* * *

Back in London.

Back with the trunks and boxes settling into Roderick's flat in South Street. Back to be waited on (and hated) by his personal cat-valet. He was a green-eyed man with fangs who made faces at me behind my back. He was observed in the mirror. He had to go.

When the excitement and deference to a bride and congratulations and settling-in and temporary adjustments of two strangers – when all this sank shallowly into place – then the real deep maladjustments showed up.

Roderick loved Reuters better than anything on earth – except (now that he had found me) *me*. He had gone into it as a string-correspondent at seventeen, just before the Boer War, and now was Head of the whole world organization.

For it he bore every responsibility. He loved it as Freyberg loved his army. He worked all day and half the night, not as a burden but with passion. He promised me each morning that we should dine at eight. At eight the operator rang from the Reuter switchboard: 'Sir Roderick has just left and is *walking home*.' We dined at 10. No cook would stand it.

Each night a heavy leather bag was sent out to him. After we had dined and he had talked to me an hour he went to his room and his night began. Each morning a Reuter boy came and took away the mountains of paper, pencilled and ticked in blue and red.

This frightfully busy, day-and-night working man had married an untidy, disobedient, conceited, arrogant, and self-engrossed ex-girl. He loved her. The trouble was I didn't know it.

He trained me as he trained his men at Reuters. He praised and blamed and watched and insisted. I fought and forgot and cried and lost my temper. In the morning he left me lists. I put them down as soon as he had gone to the office. We had different ideals and different standards. I considered myself an uppish intellectual. Which indeed I wasn't.

'If there's one phrase I can't stand,' I exploded, 'it's that one about being captain of my ship!'

'You'll hear it again,' he said.

In that South Street flat I felt sick, which was odd. I hadn't felt sick in the Chelsea flat. Later on I knew why I was sick. I was having a baby.

Pass over all that – pass over the night of her birth (temporarily back at Warren Wood) and there I was with a cradle beside me.

Motherhood is a tarnished old word and is used to convey any sentimentality. I didn't feel it for two days. But after that there swept over me the same savage delight in a job which I had had when I married Roderick. 'She'll be astonishing! She'll be the light of the world. Oh – the *next* generation! It's here in my hands.' Is that motherhood? It's what I felt. She had a lousy start. The midwife, chosen because she had been fetched at some time when Emmanuel had failed to commit suicide, stayed in her bedroom and wouldn't appear. The doctor managed alone. The baby had a spot of blood in its eye. It gave me the horrors to try to breastfeed her, but I conquered it.

The responsibilities grew, the possessions grew, and good God I was founding a family.

* * *

I hadn't meant to write about marriage. True in an anecdotal way I have sauntered into it.

And now perhaps I'll go on. And if I go on it's no good sauntering. No good beating a big drum either: I don't want to alarm myself.

When Roderick wanted me to write about it – years, years, a quarter of a century later, I said it was too delicate and much too difficult to do.

'Oh – write about marriage, darling! Our marriage. It's so extraordinary!'

'Extraordinary – how?'

'That we should be shut up together. And fight so hard. And make a success of it.'

'You couldn't have invented, could you, two people who annoyed each other more!' (After forty years of marriage we still stood with broken swords in our hands.)

He kissed me. 'Write about it. Write about it, darling.'

But I didn't think I could.

However . . .

At breakfast in Oxford the other day, Dame Sybil* said . . . (we were together in another of my failures – these plays, these plays – the waste and the pain) 'Lewis,' she said, 'is a very violent man.' (Pause.) 'But I am a violent woman.'

I looked at those serene blue eyes. 'You really are?'

'Yes,' she said. And I believed her. That marriage has lasted sixty years.

Lynn† also said to me: 'I do wish you'd write about marriage – *when it has lasted*. That's the difficulty – and the beauty of the difficulty! Anyone can *part*!'

The Victorian habit used to be *not* to part. But at that time it was a charm for the woman to be meek. In my marriage, in Dame Sybil's marriage, in Lynn Fontanne's marriage the women were not meek.

One mustn't expect to be happy when married. That's not the point. It takes a lifetime to be even acquiescent. It's a huge, huge work. Like Michelangelo and the Sistine chapel.

Roderick, when he asked me to write about marriage, knew that the ingredients were love and war.

One has no idea what goes on between married settled people. Once a pair has weathered twenty years they have closed the front door. That doesn't stop what goes on behind the curtains. The entrancing gossip of bedroom life, the crackles of annoyance, the candlelit battleground, the truces, the fun, the love, the rage. In marriage there are no manners to keep up, and beneath the wildest accusations no real criticism. Each is familiar with that ancient child in the other who may erupt again. For instance – at fifty – at dinner one summer evening the walls couldn't hold my anger and tears. I ran out of the

---

* Dame Sybil Thorndike – married to Sir Lewis Casson.

† Lynn Fontanne (Mrs Alfred Lunt).

house in my evening dress – up the garden, murderously panting, up to the top of the field. Then turning saw Roderick and Richard* in the dusk of the field's gateway and Roderick was laughing. So I was already forgiven! Laughing and sobbing I ran down the field to them as though I was seven.

Such a scene we married people keep to ourselves. We are not ridiculous to ourselves. We are ageless. That is the luxury of the wedding ring.

With my habit of exaggeration, with my 'novelist' mind, if you like, I was always offending the 'journalist'. Roderick minded an inaccuracy more than an infidelity. Which brings me (just briefly) to sex – the great inequality, the great miscalculator, the great Irritator. But it's too large a subject. It's not till sex has died out between a man and a woman that they can really love. And now I mean affection. Now I mean to be *fond of* (as one is fond of oneself) – to hope, to be disappointed, to live inside the other heart. When I look back on the paint of sex, the love like a wild fox so ready to bite, the antagonism that sits like a twin beside love, and contrast it with affection, so deeply unrepeatable, of two people who have lived a life together (and of whom one must die) it's the affection I find richer. It's that I would have again. Not all those doubtful rainbow colours. (But then she's old, one must say.)

* My second son.

Chapter Seven

✷

WHEN I was engaged to Roderick – that brief time – I had told him that I wrote. That was a statement he ought to have heeded, but he was too much in love to bother. It meant that in my married life three hours would be taken out of each day. I was to rule a household with three hours short. By the nature of my first thirty years of living I wasn't a ruler. I wasn't used to having authority and I hated it. When I had to face a human being with rebuke I trembled. When something like courage came it was too violent and too late. After my wobbling socialism and my loving-to-be-liked I had to find out that there was some mystique in being a ruler.

What I think now is quite different. I have more or less discovered what people want. They want, good or bad, their work to be noticed. To blame is better than nothing, and praise is good too. But the main thing is that everything should be noticed, and though that's a lot of trouble it's the only way it works.

All those changing servants all through the years – they may have liked me more than they liked Roderick. But for him they worked. They didn't work for me.

After the green-eyed valet there had been a middle-aged parlourmaid. She had to go too and I stayed awake all night before I gave her notice. Then there was Cutmore. He stayed twenty-nine years.

He was a gloomy handsome man, a family man but with an inborn contempt for women. He disliked me but it blew over. Slowly under his sway the staff enlarged.

It soon became as difficult to write as if I were a shop steward in a factory. I prayed in despair – 'Dostoevsky wrote in prison and wrote poor. Oh God let me write *rich*.'

We *were* rich. Or we lived richly. I knew Roderick wasn't personally rich as people thought he was, because I knew that he had borrowed half a million from the Bank of Scotland to buy out the then Chairman and Board of Reuters when he first took over – and this had to be paid back.

For a woman who is mink-rich or Ritz-rich it's different. But I was the wife of a man who intended, for the sake of his job, to keep up his position. Things had to be run and I had to run them.

In the end we had two houses, four children, Cutmore, nine indoor servants, two nurses and a nurserymaid, a chauffeur, two gardeners, a 'groom' and a strapper. Inverted commas are round the groom, McHardy, because he can't be mentioned in that way in a list. He was God-given, and the answer to:

'If I am good for ever will you give me a horse?'

He had been a jockey and had had some mysterious bad luck (hardly alluded to) racing in Belgium, which had made him for the time a tramp. He arrived in this village with nothing. The village had long been a racing village, which was why we had fourteen loose-boxes round the top of the garden. They were a hundred years old, with ancient bricks, immense iron mangers, and constantly-leaking roofs. The cottage next to the garden had by tradition been a trainer's, and Roderick had bought the cottage, the field above our garden, and all the loose-boxes. They stood empty till McHardy came.

The baby* in the cradle was eight and had one pony, rough, in a field, and certainly not needing a groom. But as tack needed cleaning and bits were a trifle rusty under her slight attentions, I offered McHardy a small sum for one week.

I found he was sleeping in a cupboard off the garage on a cement floor.

'This won't do.'

'I'll sleep in the end loose-box where you keep the straw.'

'You haven't got a room in the village?'

'No.' There was never a Miss or a Ma'am. One didn't need it: it didn't suit him.

* Laurian, my daughter.

The loose-box (he wouldn't give it up) became, with alterations, his bedroom. As everything runs uphill here because this house is at the foot of the Downs, I could see him from my bed through the window as he walked out at six into the air. The stutter of the taps began as he watered the horses and there seemed to be a radiance of life growing up there.

He always got his way: we never discussed it. He stayed ten years till he married. He was more important than a governess: more important in those years than a mother. From one pony he rose us to thirteen. He invented us as a horsebox family and through delirious summers we trailed after success. Laurian had horse-passion. Timothy* less passion but a natural aptitude for winning. Richard† dreaming of trains, forgetful and concentrated, rode, but didn't compete much. Tucker‡, at five, was taken over by the Management (Laurian – McHardy) and forced, like a child-actor, on to our stage. He wore a carnation in his buttonhole, won fivers and First Prizes, and when the war stopped him at eight forgot everything he had learnt.

As the years went by I had taken better to authority and there came a moment when I knew that McHardy had to be pulled up. Our unthinking worship had become too heady for him. Like an old-time Nannie he was beginning to edge me out. He stopped consulting me. I was to have the trouble without the interest. I 'sent for' him. By this time I had learned that much. It had to be on my ground. Also I employed a trick.

He was very frightening himself but I outfrightened him. Having sent word formally I then changed the day. When he arrived to see me I changed the room too.

'Not in here,' I said, and walked, he following me, to a room farther away. When I turned to face him I thought the grim mask was sitting looser. I used the Nannie-symbol on him. 'Keep me interested,' I said. 'It's got to be *my* fun too.'

He didn't say much. His blue eyes listened like ears.

Two days later he whistled me awake under my window at six-thirty.

'I'm going to worm Jenifer,' he said. 'Come and hold her

* my eldest son.
† my second son
‡ my youngest son, Dominick.

head.' It was handsome of him. I went without a murmur and the pink stuff from the bottle dribbled down my dressing-gown.

McHardy was 'Mi Taylor' in the book I wrote, *National Velvet*. He was sent a copy while we were abroad. I trembled to think how he would take his personal portrait. He couldn't fail to recognize it: it was clear as daylight it was he.

I walked up to the stables. He was standing on the cobbles.

'I've read every word right through,' he said. 'Not one fault you haven't made.' Thus with great tact he passed over the question of the 'portrait'.

When Cutmore, as a lad, had chosen, or first been pitched into, 'service' he must, like all men, have wanted to build himself a high place in his profession. Roderick interviewed and engaged him in his office at Reuters. Cutmore arrived with a photograph of himself on a small stool, two footmen one side of him and three on the other. He produced it in silence.

'*Five* footmen?' said Roderick in surprise.

'Yes, Sir Roderick.'

'I'm afraid with us you'll only have a parlourmaid.'

No answer. But he came.

He was a polished handler of fading rituals – things that had come out of the past and had had their uses – but their reasons now unidentifiable. The things he knew aren't suitable now, but all knowledge is fascinating. He understood fine points, situations. With his five footmen I dare say he knew how to manage men. But now he didn't choose to any longer. He had been Emperor of the Servant-Era. It had cracked. It was flowing away. He had learnt a trade that was over. Now he simply watched. If a cook wanted to leave he didn't dissuade her. He didn't help. And me he didn't warn.

The 'nine indoor servants' shifted like a panorama. 'Notices' were mysteriously given, underground quarrels erupted, never explained. I spent my time adjusting, placating, pleading in Registry Offices, my ears full of the rumours of revolution. The nursery, the stables, and the garden 'ran', because in each case the job had to do with life and growth. But 'downstairs' there were legendary boundaries to each fragment of work; nobody helped anybody without infringement. It was much as strikes are now in its small way. The whole edifice of servanthood was rotten at the core. Nobody did a full day's work and nobody was happy.

Cutmore understood this and let it slide. He loved books. Or he loved meeting the men who wrote them. 'Is Mr Mac-Carthy coming? It's time Mr MacCarthy was here.' Ralph Hodgson he equally liked. R.H. often came to stay a night at Rottingdean, carrying an attaché case no bigger than a book.

Cutmore spent the whole afternoon 'unpacking' for him.

At tea (with his C. B. Fry's Magazine manner) – 'What a nice chap Cutmore is.'

'What have you been talking about up there all the afternoon?'

'Oh . . . *you* know what men talk about. He told me about his rheumatism and I told him about my piles.'

Roderick loved to change every night for dinner. Part of the burgundy-ritual. Cutmore came discreetly to see him around seven.

(As anyone who had seen the attaché case would have known) – 'Mr Hodgson,' he observed, 'will not be changing.'

'Oh,' said Roderick, miserable to lose the cherished habit. 'I suppose I'd better not change either.'

'I think, Sir Roderick,' said Cutmore's deepest voice, 'that Mr Hodgson would be very upset if he thought that *any* action of his would alter *any* habit of yours in *any* way.'

He loved babies. His dark face glowed when he leant over cots. He cut his own hair with nail scissors.

With his looks, his height and his gloom, his impassive knowledgeable calm, when they travelled abroad Roderick always complained that Cutmore was taken for the Head of Reuters.

When he finally retired I gave him the signed books of all the authors he had known with us.

'H. B. Cutmore has fed this author.'

I asked him if he liked it that way. He did.

* * *

I found – and Roderick immediately bought – 29 Hyde Park Gate. This was an ex-country house, with a garden, which Sir

Edwin Lutyens rearranged for – parties. (For parties there were going to be. Was I going to be a hostess?)

The charming house had still the curved glass of 1800 in the long windows, the hand-made wooden shutters with their iron bar, and on many of the doors the unchanged locks of that time. The inner front doors (of mahogany, like old Brighton houses) had door handles of black horn and mother-of-pearl (and have still). It had been owned, and perhaps built, by the first Tattersall, and what is now the big drawing-room was then a coach house with stables beyond. Above the stables was the coachman's mews-cottage and above again the hayloft which in our time was the biggest nursery in London. It was marvellous luck to find this untouched house with its big garden, but I took so long over the furnishing it drove Roderick frantic. I would only buy or put on the walls or electrically-light at a snail's pace.

'For God's sake – get *on*.'

'Go to Harrods or Hampton's!'

He knew better than that. He treated me alternately as an office boy and an artist.

'What about the tables?' he said one night.

'Tables?'

'For the dining-room. I should like to be able to seat twenty-eight.'

– So we were in for it. –

It was a marvellous dining-room, of a curious olive shade that Lutyens loved. Long, shady, stretching through the house from street to garden, lit at both ends by windows aflame with green. The street, which is still a cul-de-sac, was quiet then.

Mrs Harry Cust still *just* lived (in the big house opposite, the oldest in the street), and on spring nights when we dined, her garden, through the window, was ghostly with magnolias behind her low wall with its stone urns; and on our side, pressed into the window were the fig leaves of our own garden.

She was ninety. She had lived through a scandal, very intimate, hardly known. Now all was quiet in her house, no blinds moved on our side, no windows opened.

Twice I saw her from her front door come down the steps; tall, thin, her stockings hanging on the bones.

She walked a step or two on the pavement, hesitated and went back.

Then she died. And for a year no housebreakers came.

'Nina' her name was. Lady Horner (herself ten years less than a contemporary) stared through my drawing-room windows at the house.

'So she is still alive.... Do you know about Harry Cust?'

'No.'

(I might have known. But my 'coming-out' in Woolwich had delayed my knowledge of that world.)

'He was the Rupert Brooke of our day,' she said. 'Golden haired, well-born (inextinguishable word), a poet. Irresistible – not to me – but to most women.

'Nina fell wildly in love with him. With all the secret strength and desperation of a shy woman. He never looked at her, not his type, plain, highbrow, awkward. But what a will! She went strange lengths to get him.

'He was on the verge, then, of a dazzling engagement.'

'To whom?'

'Never mind....'

It was then Nina struck. She wrote to Arthur Balfour, and to Haldane. The intended marriage, she said, was impossible. She herself was with child by him.

Few people knew about the letters. But those who knew acted. Harry Cust married Nina. And left her at once. And there was no child.

After many years when he was very ill (perhaps to be so long wanted moved him) he came to her, and in that house she nursed him to his death. Whether she got happiness who knows. For she did that unnatural thing – she laid the rest of the only life she had on an altar for him. She published a book of poems to him. She drew and sculpted his head.

So time went on and all I knew was the bare story.

A year after her death the housebreakers came. Suddenly, overnight, there was a hole in the garden wall as though from a hand-grenade. I had meant when I saw the hole to slip in and steal an urn, but they were gone in a flash. The front door now stood wide open; scaffolding went up and chimneys came down.

Diana was with me one morning when we saw a black

serpent laid across the road. A cable from the electric main went up the steps and inside the house, in the shadows of the hall, and the deafening noise of a road-drill stuttered inside.

It was midday, near the workmen's lunch hour. We followed the cable into the house, the drill still working behind an open door on the left.

Inside the room was a live man astride a stone horse. The drill in his hand had cut the original rider away and only the stone legs clung to the flap of the saddle.

'What is it . . .?' Diana shuddered. (The man stopped his drill.)

'It's Harry Cust. Riding,' I said. I had seen the head on the floor.

'It was the lady's bedroom,' said the man, dismounting.

*   *   *

I move back from this story across the road to our dining-room. To the furnishing. The tables Roderick wanted were a triumph. There they are still. There they will be for a fortnight. For as I write the house is sold. It is now the interval (July '69) between death and burial. The housebreakers can kick the first hole after the eighth of August. Lists are made: vans are ordered: the fabric of which I write is evaporating. I feel no pain. I exorcise it on this page.

There stand the tables. But they didn't make me a hostess.

One was long – for eighteen people. The other round, for eight or ten, with segments that slid in. It's odd that one should write with love of tables. The light strong tops were supported on tripods of brass copied from a Regency book. The tops were painted and 'marbled' by Alan Walton in polished olive and charcoal bound by a fine engine-turned brass rim and inset with a narrow brass filet. When empty they stood, simple and light, in a kind of delight of proportion.

I loved them. I loved the thinness and the strength. They were lovely empty and lovely laid for guests. Twenty-eight chairs with arms could gather round them. They were less lovely when, ten times a year, there were twenty-eight guests.

The furnishing moved slowly on. The big drawing-room that Lutyens had 'seen' through the jumble of bits and pieces which overlaid the coach house emerged as a sort of stage viewed from the dress circle. One looked down upon it over a low wall before descending the wide steps he built. All along the west side four french windows lead on to a terrace and into the garden. One peculiar pillar supports part of the ceiling. It is made of cement but appears panelled, and I remember Lutyens running his thumb down the still damp corners to blunten the sharpness. 'Always do that,' he said. 'It adds a hundred years on.' Alan Walton filled a large recess with a joke picture of Brighton painted directly on glass. The Duke of Wellington told me that a bundle of mahogany pillars and odd sections he had seen roped up on a pavement priced at twelve pounds would turn out to be two staggering and fantastic rout sofas with dolphins, each with an angel and a garland. The garland was lost, but the rest of it might have been built for Mrs Fitzherbert's house in Brighton.

At that time, forty years ago, it wasn't difficult to buy the frailties and oddities of Regency. The stranger the object the less it cost; which is reversed now.

I bought two uncomfortable and radiant chairs, blazing with gold and mother-of-pearl, at Christies for five pounds. And in Brighton a Dresden mirror six foot high with a whole woodland of robins and buds of pale blue and pink for twelve pounds. I got a kind of fixation on twelve pounds and was suspicious if I had to go above it.

On a journey we made to Egypt Roderick was put in touch with a quiet, cultured Arab, part dragoman, part antique dealer in Luxor. Through Arab friends of his, quietly engaged on excavations of their own (before the authorities became aware of the possibilities of certain sites), he fished out for us seven funeral jars of alabaster, two to three thousand years old. These floated in some manipulated and secret way to England. I hesitated long before getting them pierced for a flex to pass in. I knew the sacrilege and felt remorse, but choked it. Lit from within they were beautiful. Unlit just shabby. A Henry Moore, bought when I was twenty-four at the Leicester Galleries and marked on the back eight guineas, hung between two of the ffrench windows. (This, by the way is how Grannie told me to spell french windows, though Georgina* says it will get me in wrong with my day.)

* Georgina Ward.

In the King's Road in a basement, leering dustily upwards through a half-window to the pavement was a row of sculptures, block-shaped, half-human. Scribbled on a card was the word 'Epstein'. One was labelled 'Vice'; but it was simply a toad. Another was the top half of a woman having difficulty pulling a breast out of the ground. The man asked five pounds.

'For an Epstein!'

'Just at present . . .' He gave them a look. 'Well, I can't get rid of them,' he said. Something was wrong, but five pounds wasn't much to risk. What was curious was the weight of the object I bought. The man had to call two sons and the thing fell in among the gears with a crash.

Epstein lived opposite to us, but I didn't then know him. One day in the street I went up to him and asked him to come and look at my Epstein. He was fascinated; took out a pocket knife, scratched the surface, and exclaimed, part happy, part angry: 'Where did you get it. . . .? Have I caught him at last!'

Someone had been casting fake Epsteins in cement. I think it never quite turned out who. But one, he said, was in a museum in New York.

I was the witness in a case he brought against the shop (before Robin Maugham's father, Lord Maugham).

'Did you buy this sculpture, Lady Jones . . .' asked the opposing Counsel slowly . . . 'for pornographic purposes?' There was so much laughter I didn't have to reply; and he didn't risk asking it twice. It didn't save us the case, however. I couldn't prove that 'school of' hadn't been written very small under the word 'Epstein'. Epstein and I came back to Hyde Park Gate very silent in a cab.

'Where shall I write?' I asked Ned Lutyens. But this was earlier on when the house was threaded with ladders and workmen's cups of tea.

He thought. He ended by fastening a room like a ship's cabin into a niche above the drawing-room. It had two doors and one was a silence door, padded with something impenetrable and very thick. We invented a wooden label. 'Stop and think whether your errand is really necessary.' When you had opened the two doors you ran down a short flight of seven steps and the newell knob on the newell-post at the bottom turned on ball bearings so that you could swing round. This was one of

Ned's little joke-inventions. He built me shelves all up one side of the room 'with lipstick on the edges'. My two-vice carpenter's table was the pivot of this room. The writing-conditions had long been an invention of my own. So that my back shouldn't ache I had always had a tilted drawing board for my typewriter, which rested on the arms of a tilted armchair. I could thus lie back and type, and Ned was so delighted he got one made for himself.

Vita, who did not admire, as I did, my dear drawing-room, wrote a poem about these two rooms in 1933.*

* * *

After my marriage I gained cast and lost cast. I exchanged Sickert for Beaverbrook, Lovat for Lord Riddell, Hodgson for Northcliffe. That wasn't Roderick's fault. I had done it before, through the hedge at Warren Wood. But then I was a visitor. Now I had the inviting to do.

Roderick would sound the horn for the Hunt or the Meet.

'There are six Japanese princes coming over...'

'Over?'

'From Japan.'

'The princes' were perhaps a Japanese equivalent to Reuters. They were something I had to do *for* Reuters. I understood and had no reservations about that. But who to ask with them?

'And the date?'

'At once, at once. I mean, start telephoning at once.'

That was the hideous race that was now on. To catch the Important to meet the Important before the Important ran out.

I would have liked Desmond – but what was the good of that? And Margot... My head rang with the word 'Margot' – whose cutting lash of wit would flick over a table and by its very attack produce the intimacy of indignation. But if I used her up on the princes she might never come again.

I hated telephoning. I hated jumping into the morning life of any woman who wasn't a close friend. The other voice had no chance, I thought, to escape my invitation.

I knew pretty well what the guests should be like – to meet

* 'To Enid Bagnold' in Vita Sackville-West's *Collected Poems*. Volume One.

the princes. They should be faintly Foreign Office-ish, a touch of Admiralty.

And wait a minute... Arthur Waley! But one would have to know what kind of Japanese he would care about. The princes wouldn't look down on anyone. But he might look down on them.

(When the princes came, only one could speak English.)

I linger over this dinner party because it was always the same. The effect on me, I mean. I felt like a Show Jumper. – 'What? *Another* round? The Jump-Off? I *simply can't* do it again!'

When the guests were hooked and had accepted they had to be listed, their titles got right, and finally 'reminded'. The name-cards for the tables were actually printed.

The menus were handwritten because I remembered Grannie.

I was no delegator. If I had to do something against the grain the only fun was to do it well. It was I who moved the piano while Cutmore looked on. He would have done it but he would have done it wrong. That's the conceit of the non-delegator. And the flowers – my goodness and the fruit my goodness.

I had to decant the burgundy. It was Roderick's job but he never got home in time. Cutmore's standards were high but Roderick's were higher. I had to decant on his level. I became a perfectionist. Once started I couldn't compromise. I changed.

Roderick had no wish for convention. He didn't mind if I varied things. I had a large kitchen sieve passed round piled with dark chocolate – called 'caraque'.

(Mrs St Maugham, in *The Chalk Garden*, bemoaning the lost rituals of the past.

'We used to have celery with the Stilton...

... and the Bristol finger bowls and the épergne...

... and the sieve we served the caraque on...'

To puzzled questions from play-directors – say in New Zealand – about the meaning of the third line I answer 'It's an old English custom'.)

Harold Nicolson said – (he had been 'hooked' I suppose, to dazzle some guest: probably a French one) –

'Why do you give such large dinner parties?'

'To get it all over at once.'

'No. I believe you are afraid to be intimate so you cover yourself with twenty-eight.' (He had been silently counting.)

This wasn't true of the dinner parties.

But what was true was that I couldn't get on terms with Lady Jones. At thirty I had been marvellously integrated with Enid Bagnold. She hadn't been afraid on doorsteps, she held her own. But Lady Jones pushed ahead into rooms and sat in my chair. Who was I now? I had lost the crisp outline. One could say, looking back, that I had married a tycoon and that I took ill the job of being a tycooness. But I didn't think of myself like that; nor of him. That's one of those odd flat labels that people wear all their lives and never know it. And besides – those dinner parties were what any woman ought to do for her husband. Roderick wasn't asking something extraordinary from me.

And I did them: I put my neck into the collar and pulled. But I ought to have enjoyed them, and I didn't. I didn't because my days were too full.

When a woman with such a husband takes three hours out of her day for writing, has four children, and all those possessions, it makes her pant.

Roderick gave me a secretary. But that was no good. I couldn't manage her. I wasn't afraid of her but I gave her the slip. She added to the things I had to do, she lengthened my letters, 'reminded' me. And when she had gone in the evening there were all those letters to sign. I would rush instead into my writing-room and shut the door. Roderick's own secretary at Reuters took special delight in finding out on the telephone that mine was twiddling her thumbs. I begged to be rid of her. It was bad enough having a personal maid. I couldn't use her either. No one could help me. (Nor can. It's not a thing to be proud of. It's a stupidity.)

* * *

How did Reuters seem to me? Since I had to live at one remove from it. To so many young men it was a burning romance. Often I was asked eagerly what chance there was of getting into it. And it held for Roderick, and had always held, just that magic. He was Head of Reuters most of my married life and it was his nature, his duty, and certainly his pleasure to keep his finger on every department, commercial as well as editorial. Reuters' turnover was so huge that one could almost say, like a theatre, it could be ruined overnight. At that time its salaries were paid in thirty-eight different currencies. Its penalties for inaccuracies were frightening: its scoops so soon forgotten. If it didn't push its way into my life factually (for Roderick didn't talk about it) it pushed a throbbing strain over me as well as over him. If the telephone rang at night it was for misfortune. I don't think it was the custom to ring up for happy results.

When a pope lay dying in 1921 we had taken our first house in the country, a hired, mock-Tudor house near Tonbridge. All Reuter-crises happened at week-ends, with a week-end staff. The pope was dying through Saturday.

In the evening the young man in charge of the Editorial rang Roderick with the news that the pope was dead.

'Through what channel?' Roderick asked with quick anxiety.

'Through Berlin, Sir Roderick.'

'Good God . . . I left a note. Didn't you see it? *Not* through Berlin! *Has the news gone out?*'

'I rang Archbishop's House, Sir Roderick. I can hear the bells of Westminster Cathedral ringing.'

Despair. It wasn't true. He was sinking but not dead. We sat up all Saturday night in agony about the Sunday papers. Would he die in time for Reuters not to seem so desperately at fault? He did.

There were tight moments over the opening of the tomb of Tutankhamen. I find I can't remember enough: Reuters was like a roaring wind round the house and I must have shut my mind and memory to it. There were extremely sudden journeys. One for a week-end to New York with a burst of trouble over the Associated Press. We left so suddenly I only took two dresses; and both of them too hot: New York was snowed up but the hotel, from which I never budged, was like a furnace.

There was a journey to Pau to see Lord Northcliffe. I had to wean Laurian overnight. I didn't know then that that was wrong.

Lord Northcliffe had been round the world and was already deep in the illness-mania that was to kill him.

Eccentric all his newspaper life, his eccentricity couldn't now be distinguished from madness. An order had come from him violent, imperative, from Singapore, asking that the commissionaire from *The Times* should be put in as editor and the editor sent to mind the doors. This was at first taken as an angry joke – to ram home a rebuke.

Roderick knew some of this but not all. No one did then except those who travelled with him. Roderick, who knew him, wanted all the same for some special reason, to walk into him by accident. The accident was invented and we went to Pau.

Downstairs in the hall of the hotel I was standing alone among a crowd of men, all with a similarity, all speaking in low tones in English – Lord Northcliffe's staff. There had been a crisis. The lift had been rung up and kept up. It began to come down. It was of glass, supported by ornamental ironwork. The feet of a man, his stomach, and his head descended. A hush fell over the hall. The lift reached the ground and a furious Northcliffe stalked out in silence, and left.

That night he came from his suite to our suite. In the top newspaper world only suites were recognized. He was dressed in dark blue with a dark red tie, and he came straight over to me and talked about a novel in vogue then *If Winter Comes*. He stayed an hour and Roderick asked his particular question and got his particular and satisfactory answer and Northcliffe left. After his death I heard what happened when he was back in his rooms. His financial manager had just flown out from London and was waiting for him. Lord Northcliffe passed him without a word and went out on to his balcony.

'How many moons do you see?' he said over his shoulder.

'One, Lord Northcliffe.'

'I thought so. I see seven.'

The pills he took to bring him back to normality could only last one hour, the hour he had spent with us.

When Roderick later went round the world himself, he was invited by the Governor to stay at Government House, Singapore. He slept in a vast guest-room from which he could see the lawns and (I think he said) ravens on them. That night he found himself at the foot of the bed staring at Northcliffe's face on the pillow. Making the best of a strange situation he said: 'I hope you are better, Lord Northcliffe.' First one hand and then the other came out from under the sheets and there was menace from the face on the pillow. Roderick turned, opened the door, and fled down the corridor. Then, shaking himself awake, returned. The bed of course was empty. He got back into it, read for a while, and went to sleep. The same thing, in every detail, happened again. After that he sat in a large armchair till morning.

At breakfast the Governor asked him how he had slept. He told him. The Governor looked at him oddly.

'That's a strange thing,' he said at length. 'Lord Northcliffe had that room. He had one of his turns in it.'

I met the wives of the news-chiefs, not very often, but enough to wonder how they lived. How they lived spiritually, I mean. What calm they were able to achieve. Lady Northcliffe, Lady Burnham, Lady Camrose, Lady Kemsley. We met at Geneva at a Press Conference, or sometimes socially in London.

Lady Northcliffe had become Lady Hudson before I saw her at all intimately. And that, for her, was at a crisis.

Sir Robert Hudson had hiccoughs in Assouan. He had them to the point of death. The hiccoughing hadn't stopped for a week, day or night. Everything had been done, doctors, a nurse, medicines from Cairo. Nothing was any good. She was desperate.

There rode into the hotel on camels a tourist party of six German doctors, all friends. One of them was the world expert on hiccoughs. Roderick got him at once to see Sir Robert, and he spoke to him afterwards downstairs alone.

'He may die,' said the doctor. 'It's affecting his heart. I can't stay. We have to take the train tonight.'

'Can't you possibly stay?'

'No, I can't. All six of us have saved up for this holiday for years. It's all been mapped out. It's not possible.'

Roderick argued. Lady Hudson came down and pleaded. Nothing was any good: the train was to leave at eight.

At nine he was reading a book in the corner of the writing-room.

'You haven't *gone*!' exclaimed Roderick.

'I couldn't do it,' said the elderly man. He saved Sir Robert – for that time.

Lady Camrose was the sweetest, was the tops. But even so I never got to know her well. And of none of them did I ask how they did it. How they drew breath, I mean.

It was at Geneva, at another Press Conference, that we met the only Baron de Reuter still alive – Oliver de Reuter.* He was the son of the second baron's brother.

He was nearly stone-deaf, unmarried then, and had stayed in Geneva I don't know how long – always on the point of leaving for Paris. Roderick and he played chess. Oliver, at that time, loved to lay hold of a human being and keep him up all night. He had some kind of terrible loneliness, and his deafness isolated him. He was full of eccentricities, developed in his world of silence. He was always being rescued when he set up his camera tripod in the middle of a flow of traffic. Once in a restaurant, having ordered fried eggs, he tore off the whites and flung them in the air. To my surprise there stood a waiter with a plate ready to catch them. 'Since the womb,' said Oliver, 'I have not eaten albumen!'

A friend of his, Princess Pauline Duleep Singh, also played chess, so the four of us played in pairs. Once that started we never went to bed either.

We played at Maxim's, but it closed at eleven. The games weren't finished.

'Come with me,' said Oliver. He was so deaf we never argued. He walked out of Maxim's holding his board as though he expected to keep the pieces standing. Carrying the second board, we followed him. Oliver hailed a taxi and as we shook over the cobbles the pieces fell down. We drove to an address where they immediately gave us a bedroom; and on two beds, with bed-tables between to hold the chess boards, we played till dawn. Then on an order from Oliver they sent up champagne and eggs and bacon. It was a brothel.

One would think from this story that Roderick and I were brilliant chess players, but in fact we weren't very good, and though I played with him at home every night of my life we never got any better.

That night, in an illogical state, we went back to the hotel in a taxi, and I drove with the driver sitting inside. Outside the closed hotel door we stood half an hour wondering why it didn't open. Nobody had rung the bell.

Roderick made his speech on news-gathering next morning before the Assembly in tinted glasses to hide his eyes.

* Baron Oliver de Reuter, who died in January, 1969, at Lausanne.

Chapter Eight

*

AND now we bought that country house, the city that I live in. I wonder what the medieval ladies did, as they travelled between their several castles, about the forgotten engagement-book, the novel left by the bedside, the sleeping pills. Roderick at once duplicated everything. I never could.

The country house, which vaguely should have been an inland park with deer (at the rate we lived) was totally an accident. We stayed a week-end at Rottingdean with Sir George and Lady Lewis. Sir George – walking round in his pointed boots, twirling a London stick and needing a neighbour – got the better of Roderick and made him buy North End House. 'A mere cottage. You can easily sell it again.' (Sir George knowing well that nobody leaves Rottingdean. Here we keep what we've got, to defend, to consolidate, to put one's tongue out at Brighton.)

It's a wet and windy village full of rheumatism and beauty with a history of great men. Kipling, Burne-Jones, Poynter, Maurice Baring. And later the Beerbohm Trees, their gay daughters, the young Diana Manners, courted then by Duff Cooper, a sense of London revelry brought down among the old houses.

People wear a private look when they speak of this village – the assistant at Harrods, for instance, taking down my address.

'Do you live *there*?' (the sea in her eyes).

'It's just a village,' I say crossly. Not to run it down; but not to have to live up to it.

'Isn't it very built over?'

'Not at all.'

It is, but I don't notice it. Where I live it's still as it was because Roderick saw to it. He bought four houses on two sides of the Village Green. If he could he would have bought the church.

Burne-Jones, walking over the Downs from Brighton as a young man, bought the cottage which is the south end of North End House. Then, when richer, he bought the cottage next door. These he put together in an L-shape. Physically-attached to the side of the second cottage was a seaside boarding house – 'Gothic House'. This belonged to a very old lady, Mrs Elliott, who was soon to die.

The first Lord Reading, Viceroy of India, was staying a weekend with the Lewises. 'Mrs Elliott! Still alive!' he said. 'I must go and see her.'

As I walked back from lunch across the Green there was Mrs Elliott sunning her old self on the village seat.

'Do you remember,' I asked her, 'your first lodgers?'

'Yes, I do,' she said. 'A beautiful young man. Jewish. Mr and Mrs Isaacs, with a small baby. Very poor. They had one room, that top one.' (My Tower Room.) 'I charged them three and a half guineas a week for everything.'

'Do you know what became of them?'

'No. I don't remember. A lot of boarders began to come just then.'

I skipped the jumps.

'The Viceroy of India is coming to see you in half an hour.'

Lady Burne-Jones long survived Sir Edward Burne-Jones, and then Sir William Nicholson bought the L-shaped house while old Mrs Elliott was still alive. He had left it empty: Sir George walked us over the Green to see it.

Roderick, brought up in South Africa, hated flies. The house was buzzing with them. Gloomily we looked at the electric light pendants. The flexes were as thick as your thumb with slowly-crawling flies. 'It's just the manure,' said Sir George. He waved airily towards the garden. (Why the manure?)

*   *   *

Sir George and Lady Lewis, Elizabeth, Peggy and Georgie – how I enjoyed them. Especially Elizabeth. Strong, wilful, deep and gay, she would laugh at herself in a sudden explosion that burst direct from some tickle in her mind. It was Elizabeth's laugh that put situations into focus and made difficulties seem absurd. She stood out from her family like a rock on a hillside.

And what a family life it was. They hid nothing from their friends. Everything was discussed. To go to dine was to be in the middle of life, and even the butler responded. They did for me then what the Asquiths did for all of us later, made that double life which is at its richest in the country, when two families meet daily and share and swop and tell the comedies and small disasters of every day. They buzzed with week-end visitors, so that I could do what I loved, be entertained without the weight and trouble of doing it myself.

Marie Lewis was beautiful, with a pile of dark hair and a face full of light and life. She was musical, and from Munich, of the warm glowing stuff that opera singers are made of. And she had a most special taste in her garden. And knowledge to back it up.

Sir George was elegantly Jewish, witty, sharp, and wore a City look even in his bathing dress. Roderick rode with him on the Downs. Both men were punctual – Sir George in reality and Roderick only in his thoughts. So Roderick was late every day and Sir George waited on his horse on the Green with a fierce face. I bathed with Sir George. At each bathe he had a small legal war with the beach man, who had brought a length of canvas and had spread it over the cobbles to the water's edge.

'Not a foot on that unless you pay, Sir George!'

'You have no right to enclose the foreshore.'

'You put on one foot an' I'll push you offen!'

Sir George walked down it. 'Touch me and it'll be assault.'

In the sea he would ask me the time to see me raise my wrist. It nearly always worked.

When I dined with them at The Grange (which had once been the vicarage of a well-off hunting parson) Sir George saw me chivalrously to his gate.

But there came a day when he didn't. It was near the end of the Carnarvon case, Sir Edward Carson I think opposed him. I don't know what had worried him or gone wrong. But that night he sat very quiet at his table and never saw me out. Next day he left suddenly for Territet.

Two or three days later I asked Georgie, his son, whom he adored, to bathe with me. It was after tea.

'The danger flag's up.'

'What does that matter!' I taunted. 'They put it up for a ripple!'

But it so happened I didn't bathe.

That night I sat alone at dinner. The telephone rang. It was Marie Lewis.

'Georgie's dead,' she said.

I thought, '*I've drowned him!*' (I had jibed at the danger flag.)

I ran madly across the Green: she met me at the gate. 'George is dead,' she said, and held out a telegram. So it was Sir George. The telegram said it was a fatal accident on the railway and more news would come.

I sat with her in the room on the right of the door, his little room. All I could do was to ring the papers. I would start with Reuters, and then make the round. 'Any news?' 'No news.'

Elizabeth was upstairs in bed because she had had that day an operation on her foot, and there was a nurse in the house.

At two in the morning the *Daily Mail* rang.

'Are you the widow?' asked the Night Editor-in-Charge.

'No. A friend.'

'Sir George was run over by a train near the tunnel at Territet.'

I thanked him and told Marie, who seemed not to take it in.

'Come up to bed. Come and lie down.'

She obeyed me and we went upstairs. Elizabeth's nurse was there. Elizabeth herself had been long asleep as her operation had been in the late afternoon. I went downstairs to fetch something. When I got back the nurse said, 'She won't take off her stays.' Nor she would. Marie sat on the side of the bed rigid, so that one couldn't undo a snap.

'I'm going home,' I said, 'for half an hour. I'll be back.' In fact I was starving. I got home, ate something, and returned. There she sat on the edge of the bed with those stays on. 'Well, come into the garden then.' We went together, she with a light dress thrown over her.

Suddenly she linked her two hands through my arm and swung as a child does, so that her face was almost at my waist. We all but went over against a tree. 'Look out!' I said sharply,

Roderick and I (*Cecil Beaton*)

Myself with Timothy, Tucker (on my knee), Richard and Laurian (*Elwin Neame*)

for she was going to do it again. I looked down at her face: she laughed.

'If we'd never changed that fireplace from Montague Square to Bryanston Square this wouldn't have happened,' she said with a sort of glee. (They had been changing their house from one square to the other.)

From that moment she was mad. Her face was as beautiful as before, but wild. I couldn't believe it. I couldn't believe that someone I knew so well and saw every day could turn over in her brain in a second. I tried being sharp with her. It might have been hysterics. But it wasn't. I turned with her back to the house.

'Where are you going?'

'Only up to your room.'

'I'll stay here,' she said, and sat down on the grass. So did I. She looked at me and I looked at her. Then the nurse came out. 'I've got your breakfast,' she said. And Marie got up and went with her.

Elizabeth went to Switzerland to bring back her father's ashes. She had long been a Catholic – the loved convert of that group Belloc, Chesterton and Maurice Baring.

With her impetuous ardour she was set on burying her father as a Catholic, but his stubborn Jewish ashes defied her. It was another of those open – those funny – family rows. Lewis Verey, the Protestant clergyman of our village, said: 'You must ask the Rabbi in Brighton.'

She wouldn't. But she asked Mr Verey to conduct the burial of her father (as his very old friend) and this compromise worked.

The urn had stood overnight in the beautiful hall at the Grange. Marie had got away from another nurse they had engaged and nearly threw it over.

For years afterwards Marie was mad. Mad, and sometimes sane. Sometimes she had four nurses in shifts. Sometimes she went to a home at Ticehurst. Sometimes she could be asked to lunch. There was a little clique in London who whispered (but they were quite wrong) – 'If her daughters would let her come to London and hear music she'd be all right.'

Maurice Baring, who then lived in the village, was one of the whisperers, and having André Maurois to stay – 'I'll take you to tea to meet a beautiful, charming, musical woman,' he said. Marie was all this. But he had left out 'mad'. – Mad, with a sort of diablerie.

Maurois went to tea. I too. Elizabeth and Maurice walked up the garden to see the roses. Marie, who had been perfect till then, asked Maurois: 'Do you see that bush? Don't look too long at it because my husband is behind it.'

'He is there, Madame . . .' (Maurois made it very neutral.)

'Waiting to spring out at us,' said Marie, turning her dazzling eyes on him.

Even when you know English as well as Maurois did, it's possible to mix up eccentricity and insanity. For several sentences he didn't quite adjust. But soon I had to call Elizabeth.

Marie, when mad, had an impish knowledge that she was mad. She liked to startle. There was a kind of freedom in it.

When Violet Bonham Carter was staying with us, Marie insisted on coming to Sunday lunch.

She got the nurse to go up with her to London, where she bought an all-scarlet dress. She came to lunch in it, looking splendid and amazing.

She said to Violet (who hated embarrassment) –

'Do you know what this village is full of?'

Violet looked up.

'Jews and lunatics,' said Marie intensely.

Violet said nothing. There was nothing to say.

When I was on the point of having Tucker she asked me to tea, and met me in the garden with a large pair of shears. Opening and shutting the blades she said: 'There's a new way of doing a Caesarian now!' I went home. Then she sent me a note saying would I come back? Which I did. She lived, alas, for years like this, growing less beautiful. But oh how beautiful she was when I first saw her.

* * *

So Roderick bought the L-shape and I cried. He didn't buy it against my tears. They were lease-signing tears, dead-end tears. 'Here I am for life!' – And here I am.

Roderick bought (of course) the racing stable next door which caused the flies. And its cottage. He bought The Elms (the house Kipling had lived in) and all its circle of cobbled walls. It was there that Oc and Betty* came with their four little girls (and their ponies).

For years they took The Elms from us every summer, and for years the eight children, mine and Betty's, grew up and rode and were happy together. Cynthia Asquith too took a house or a cottage, with Michael and Simon. They extended a kind of golden cousinship.

When Mrs Elliott died, Roderick (of course) bought the boarding house next door. We broke through eight feet of cobbles and found every floor on a different level, and left them so. From then on there were thirty rooms. There are still. The front of the combined house-and-cottages still looks a reasonable size. But the back is a city.

Roderick adored building. I too. No occupation more quarrelsome. The village builders weren't out of the house for twenty years. The rooms ran out over the grass at the back forming pyramids – and balconies were put up to connect the pyramids. At last – my gift on his eightieth birthday – I gave him the thirty-first room. Facing south, very small, the floor a foot above the lawn to avoid rheumatism, yellow as a buttercup. He did the planning. The birthday present was a wild success. It brought him one more year's happiness before he began to die. He filled it with a writing-table so immense he could only just creep behind it. But writing was done. There was no more writing.

*   *   *

So from the buying of this second house we entertained both ends. Both ends of that journey up and down – Mondays and Fridays in my car. I drove the maids; the maids gave notice; the flowers never died in the vases. And inserted in this hurrying, stumbling, list-making life I wrote, and always wrote, those rigid hours. It had the effect that, like Pavlov's dogs, I salivered as I laid my hand on my door (at either end). Gone were the housemaids' troubles as I shut it. Once inside I tried not to dust, not to rearrange the books. All writers know this trembling delay, the fear of the impact of the want of talent.

I made money when I wrote. I made a lot of money. I didn't write to make it because I had enough. That is part of the 'luck'

* General the Honourable Arthur Asquith and his wife.

that has brought about the Image. I made perhaps twenty thousand pounds out of the first publishing of *National Velvet* in America and here (excluding the film). And much more. But I lost it.

Roderick had no time to advise me. The film when it was bought went three times round the world with the young Elizabeth Taylor. Paramount, who first bought it (and sold it later to MGM) gave me a cheque for eight thousand, less the things they cut off it. (They didn't cut enough.) I dined out and sat next to Israel Sieff.

'What do you do when you make a fortune in a day?'

'Put more money in your pocket,' he said, 'than you ever carry. Walk down Bond Street and spend it. Invest the rest carefully.'

I walked down Bond Street. 'What's the most expensive gold cigarette case you have? For a man?' I asked at Cartier. At that date, about 1936, it was a hundred pounds. I bought the case and gave it to Roderick. For a hundred and twenty I bought a silverish pony for Laurian. Then typewriters. For myself and for the others. The rest of the money was invested.

A year later I got a notice from Washington mentioning taxes. The words were complicated but unurgent. 'Back-dating of liability for taxes not sufficiently deducted.' I showed this to someone. He said: 'Oh that's for Americans! It's not for foreigners.'

'Not for me?'

'Pay no attention to it.' I threw it away. Next year it came again – same treatment. And the next.

At the third year the tone changed. New York now, no longer Washington. I owed...

I took a taxi to the Bankers Trust and asked to see the manager. I owed thousands.

'That's Pains and Penalties,' he said. 'They're snowballing at compound interest. Pay by cable. (I'll draft it.) If you don't you can never set foot in America again.' It was a crisis-year. My investments had dropped. I paid away all I had earned; plus two thousand borrowed from Roderick. The pony died: it was a bad buy. The typewriters wore out. The cigarette case remains: my eldest son now has it. All I made in the first years from *National Velvet* disappeared. The television and radio rights were slipped in gratis with the film. So when years later a bastardized version of *National Velvet* ran three years on radio in America, France and England I made nothing.

This is true but I don't know who'll believe it. Most of the money, however, that the Rich Old Image is living on was made by herself. Partly I suppose because she didn't need it. This making of money from a book is wildly accidental. I started *National Velvet* as a study in a girl's relationship with her pony. But it turned immediately and by itself into a story. All our gay life and its details, dogs, canaries, emotions of children, everything jumped into my hands. I had only to snatch and type on and all our full life was on the page. All the fantastic joy and fun.

Richard* said to a friend not long ago, 'My mother will tell you that her whole life was spent taking us from one gymkhana to another.' He is right but it wasn't a sacrificial life, it was utter bliss. There were *my* children . . . winning. *My* children . . . rosettes. *My* children cantering round with a silver cup. It was like having children on the stage. I enjoyed it so wildly that out tipped the book.

I asked Thayer Hobson† – I had had my appendix out and he sat by my bed – for an advance. I didn't personally care but I thought he should give it.

He said: 'This little story won't sell in America. It's charmingly written in its way, and one of the pleasures we publishers sometimes afford ourselves is to be able to publish an unfinancial bit of writing.'

BANG! . . . So you never can tell!

* * *

I was born impatient. I had been impatient enough to get at living. It had been complained of before – impatience. 'Can't you sit down when you come to see me?' asked the Ivor Wimborne of my day.

'But I'm just going!'

'*Go* – but don't *say* so! – It's very putting-off!'

But now I was in a wind of impatience. Now it was a fever. I ran and I mustn't be waylaid. This went very deep into our

* My second son.
† The then President of George Morrow, Inc. (Publishers U.S.A.)

married lives. I did everything at the fly-past. I became someone who couldn't listen.

'Can't you sit *down*?'

No I couldn't. The chair would burn me.

'Make lists,' Roderick said. 'All the things you have to do will then boil down to nothing.' I made lists. I changed. I became efficient. But it cost me my sleep.

'I can't sleep because you've remade me!'

'Then you oughtn't to have married.'

'But you *made* me marry!'

'Are you sorry you did?'

Sometimes I was sorry. But fundamentally I wasn't.

He too was impatient. But the quality was different. His impatiences were partly real and partly he set them free like terriers after rats. His tiny injustices were terrible (so I thought– so he wouldn't believe!). If he had trouble and delay getting through to me from London on the telephone it was with me he was angry.

'It's not my fault!' I was in a blaze at once.

He wouldn't accept blame. He could be furious with a footstool. It had got up and hit him.

Another time (people who live together repeat themselves) –

'You oughtn't to have married *me*!'

But that was said as a row was ebbing like a south-coast storm when suddenly the trees aren't moving any more (which have bent to the ground). It was said in exhausted tenderness, in wonder at the size of the storm.

'Ought I not?'

'Who would have looked after you? You couldn't have lived alone. Who would have brought you round when you cried about death at midnight?'

(For I could go to his room when I was unhappy. I could wake him any time in the night.)

– And the collisions of mistiming!

Away – coming back from London in the train I am seized with terror about the rooftree. Have I lost him? Is he dead? What has happened? I sit. I howl without a sound.

At the station I snatch the car from the garage, press forward, gallop – I get there – fit the key in the front door, run across the library to a far little room.

'*Roderick!*'

He lifts his head, from papers, calculations.

'*Don't bother me now.*'

'How can you say that when I . . .'

'When you what?'

But it's no good telling him (then) that I thought he was dead. That I had been running to the wreck of my life . . . 'If only . . .' (passionate, wiped clean of love) 'you wouldn't use the words "*bother me*", as though you were talking to a poodle!'

Words leapt out of my mouth like fireworks, no sooner uttered than bitterly deplored. He threw his spectacles on the floor (to break them). This was a desperation that ought to have produced murder. After such a storm the crust was broken and we could grow together again. But each personality snapped back into place as we moved away round the house. We could 'collide' – meeting round a corner!

It's hard to describe a man with whom one fights for three parts of forty-two years and explain that one so loves him. And that with his exactions, his insistence, his domination, his infuriating habits, not one of which would he change, that he had for me total loyalty, total admiration, and that while he was angry with me he too, like my father, thought me the Seventh Wonder.

This pride in me (it seems extraordinary but it's true) I only discovered some thirty years later; and through Diana. We were standing, she and I, in the stable yard at St Firmin when she was ambassadress in Paris. Roderick walked away from us to fetch something.

'How proud that man is of you,' she said as she watched him.

'Proud? Of *me*?'

'Yes. Didn't you know it?'

I hadn't known it. I had to be told it. After that I never forgot it. But how strange that I hadn't known till then.

He was complex, with layers of nationality, Scottish, Welsh, Irish. More Welsh perhaps than he knew. Like Churchill he could cry.

'Nobody has made me suffer like you do!' He would stand with his face in his hands, in front of what he called his Garderobe. Tears fell. One would have thought I had dealt him a deathblow. Yet it was only the climax of a choking argument about nothing, about an inexactitude. But they're not about nothing, these married arguments. They are fought by one against the other with all the foreignness of a man and a woman who have not the same blood. And if one of them wins it's not a triumph but a disaster. Why do they build so – these pyramid-rows?

For the breaking of the skin. When the blood runs it runs somewhere: it runs into the wound of the other.

'*Write about it*, darling! Write about *us*.'

(I couldn't. But now I am trying.)

And isn't this difficult to say? In my storms I have wished him dead. Who knows, in the wild angers with the beloved, what the heart will cry out before you can stop it? Did he wish me dead? I should think never.

He drove me mad. I drove him mad. He indulged, adored, admired. For my mending of a pocket of his jacket, for my writing a play, for my planting a rose.

* * *

And now we are somewhere in the middle of our lives. We have come together like the coupling of those trucks they shunt violently by hand without an engine – collide, recoil, collide again. We are snapping and slogging. Don't make a mistake by the words I use. This will be a good marriage.

There is nothing we don't know about each other. He was small. Beautifully dressed. We could neither of us bear the word 'dapper' but that's what he was. We bore that together.

He was vain. Not of his achievements, not of his brains. Of his slight figure. He loved to look at his outline full length in the glass. He had great charm. His charm didn't work for me. What worked for me was his rock-nature, the bed of loyalty and belief on which I lay. I hardly knew its strength and comfort, and yet I always knew it.

I noted – when I cut his hair – how good was the shape of his head; but I was more occupied (entranced) with my own skill as I snipped the 'fan' he brushed back from his ears. I cut him once. At his rage I thought I had lost a customer but the customer remained. (I cut my eldest son's ear on the Fourth of

June in the ladies room at Eton and he never let me cut it again.)

He had endless suits, cupboards of shoes, battalions of hunting boots, with trees, and cared-for leather. Once, very ill, before precipitating himself into the unknowable for ever, he said wistfully, 'What will become of my boots?' Because of that remark I can't touch them. They lie in a box in the hall covered with a dustsheet. I got half-way to taking them to Brighton and then stopped. Now they have become invisible. I pass them too often.

He was 'never late'. He altered time to suit himself. He was never in time. He said he kept his punctuality for Reuters.

What was startling living with Roderick was his use of his own point of view – unexpected, unassailable, and often wrong. This he kept in a watertight box. The power of seeing others' he kept for Reuters. Inside his family, with indignation and affection, he was mocked and contradicted. Sometimes he laughed. You couldn't depend on it.

'If I can't be myself at home, where can I be!' But what was himself? Not easily got at. It closed and opened with the tides, like a sea anemone.

But in Reuter-negotiation, renewals of contracts, etc., with opponents abroad of every conceivable angle of mind – with a brilliancy of patience his powers of persuasion were almost mystic.

His exploration of the opposing terrain was so sympathetic, his reasonable assents so quietening, that when he began to get his own way, no point seemed to have been turned. This, of course, he didn't tell me. Nor, of course, was I there, but it was told me, with his dry humour, by Frank Noyes, then President of the Associated Press. At the end of a long day, a long conference-battle in New York, he said to me in the evening – 'Nobody knows when Roderick takes off his coat or when *we* put it on.'

He had been brought up by aunts. Strong Scottish ones. He wasn't afraid of women. Perhaps that's why he married me. He liked a woman to stand up for herself. So then he bowled at her.

I was well dressed, good-looking, rough. I swore when angry. I got that from my father. I exaggerated, laid down the law, then broke like an egg. I was 'soft inside'. Nobody knew that but Roderick.

He didn't know he had been loved as a child. It took quite a time to get down to his vulnerability. *I* knew he had been loved. I knew the last of his aunts. She was a pillar of silent pride in him, with nothing showing.

They had been poor. In that terrible way gentlefolk are poor who have once been rich. (Everything lost in a bank-failure.) They were poor resentfully. He told me it had shown at every moment of the day, the anger and humiliation of not having money. To the day he died he would hardly speak of his youth. It wasn't unhappy but the air was second-rate with deprivement.

'First make money!' he swore to himself. And then forgot all about it in the magic of meeting Reuters.

He was born in England and brought up by his Scottish grandfather, William Gibb (a cousin of Queen Victoria's favourite Archbishop of Canterbury, Archibald Campbell Tait). Roderick went to Pretoria to join a married aunt when he was sixteen or seventeen. She was the aunt, Mrs Faulkner, whom I knew as Tanta. Going to school in Pretoria he learnt Dutch easily and, still before the Boer War, he became sub-editor of *The Press*, the principal Pretoria newspaper, and personal assistant to Leo Weinthal who was then Reuter's Chief Correspondent in the Transvaal.

Through Weinthal he met President Kruger and he tells in his own book of a night when he was summoned to read the Bible in Dutch aloud to Kruger who lay in bed. It was at that time, I think, that he met Smuts and formed a lasting friendship with him, came into contact with Botha, and knew, more intimately, Dr Leander Starr Jameson. At the outbreak of the Boer War (when I was a child in Jamaica) he and Leo Amery conceived separately the extraordinary idea of going with the Boer Commandos so that (in Roderick's words) they 'might give exclusively to the world an Englishman's day-to-day account, from the inside, of England's foes at war'. Neither knew the other was going, they met – at first rather jealously – made friends, and for their lives, and were both sent back to the English armies: Roderick via jail as a Transvaal spy for three days.

The story of his career is in his own book, *A Life in Reuters*. He came back to London to Reuters, and worked in Old Jewry under Baron Herbert de Reuter, the second baron, by whom he was eventually sent back to take full charge in South Africa at the age of twenty-seven.

On the baron's suicide in April 1915, after alarms, delays, frustrations and a prolonged fight, he returned to London in July of that year.

In 1916 after happenings which don't belong to my book for they are in his, he and the Honble Mark Napier, the then Chairman, borrowed £550,000 from the Union Bank of Scotland, and some time in November 1916, standing in the rain waiting for a taxi to take them to lunch from the City, Mark Napier turned to Roderick and said:

'You realize, my dear Roderick, that there stand on this kerb the two sole and absolute owners of the world-famous Reuters! Who would think it?'

Chapter Nine

✻

So now, guests in both houses, there was a kind of ferocity of living. Roderick made me perfectionist about the Rottingdean bedrooms. He had Government-House-standards from South Africa. Not only flowers, bath salts, soaps, matches, rows of tiny towels (all sizes), scribbling pads by every bed, Evian water (glistening tumblers), but on the populated writing-tables of each room there were 'Government-House' folding leather blotters with brass or silver spines, most difficult to polish; and castellated inkstands (wedding presents), and many kinds and shapes of writing paper. And – with the writing paper – *pencils had to be sharpened*.

After we had stayed with Paul Cravath on Long Island, things got worse. The guest-suites there had a replica-chemist-shop in the bathrooms. Spare everything in case you came without. I struck at that. 'People don't come "without"! It's as though we were preparing for tramps.' But there had to be stamps on the writing-table. These were wolfed by the Monday-morning housemaid, who also took the pencils for the laundry book so that Fridays saw me sharpening again.

This enormous trouble, which I could never delegate to anyone (– my private character –) put me off guests. But we had them. And chosen pretty haphazard. I became a good cook-mistress, and much later on a cook.

My first cook, a young ex-kitchenmaid, hero-worshipped me (none since). She stayed three years, but the 'worship' grew into an insane jealousy. She dropped strange hints about the other maids and at first I believed them. One day she said the head housemaid had syphilis. This brought me up short. It would be slanderous to ask her, I didn't believe it, and a light was shed backwards over earlier tales. One didn't think so easily then of neuroses, but it occurred to me.

Immediately following this there was a crisis.

I was in the dining-room (at Rottingdean) over the cellar. Like cattle stampeding, two bodies raced down the stairs below my feet. I, too, after them, great with child. The stoking boy had picked up the coke broom. The cook knocked him down and threw a kitten into the boiler.

'It's alive!' yelled the boy.

'It's dead!' she screamed.

'Yes it's dead now!' said the boy, and the smell of burning fur came out. She packed and rang a taxi and left – in a white silence, pushing her wages aside. I wrote to her home but no one answered. I drove to the little house in Kent where her sister sold fruit. It had been sold six months before.

My second cook stole on a big scale by placing orders with several butchers and reselling the joints. This couldn't have happened if I had paid my bills weekly, but I paid sometimes only at the end of two months out of lack of method.

My third cook came from an asylum. She was high class at her art. I have still a mortar like a Christening Font and a pestle six foot high. She would only cook in copper, so everything had to be bought anew. She made bi-weekly stock with two boiling fowls and a pound of veal; then disappeared leaving a note that she was being poisoned. After a lot of tracing I got right back to her steady address, the asylum. Her obsession, they said, was poison.

The attempt to get servants at the last ditch of servanthood pierced my happiness and filtered through my sleep. They were a dying class. Mine too. Treacherous courtiers round a paper queen on a paper throne. (With exceptions.)

In those first years guests in the country were a load and a cloud. In London nobody stayed and dinner parties didn't press so heavily. But here in the country I and the guests were shut up for the day. I didn't so much become exhausted as dilapidated, cross and empty. It wasn't fair of me because Roderick upheld that I continue writing in the mornings. But the afternoons became unbearable by tea-time, and somehow I had to get recharged for the evening.

I would go through the garden as though picking flowers, but there's a gate that leads to the garage. The children's ears were cocked for the self-starter, and it was possible in a rush to catch me and stop me as I passed the front door.

But gradually (I look at the old, long-empty Visitors' Book) I see what happened to make it all different. I got a Dolly again. The huge, whale-like Albrecht Bernstorff* floated into my life. Floated as a fat man floats, light as laughter, indulgent, amused, a Proustian, pre-second war, society man, Counsellor at the German Embassy; at that time under von Neurach and later under von Hoesch. By appearance alone he was cut out to be a figure. By size alone he could not be missed. He was nearly a giant, perhaps six foot six, certainly at one time weighing twenty stone, younger than in young middle-age, blond as a baby, bald, but with the remains of curling tendrils above his ear. He had been a Rhodes Scholar. His Anglophilia dated from those Oxford days and was held in his heart like the flavour of a lost love. England he adored. It was his romance and his 'library' from which he could take down any book. I saw him at London parties, often shaking with blond laughter, wit and observation on that flat Dürer face. I didn't personally know him for years, but at last, at a party given in the country – one of those parties given 'for fun', effortlessly, grandly, richly, gaily – in a ruined castle which behind its ruin had the latest tap and the sweetest bath salts – I sat next him at dinner and we became friends. After that he came a great deal to Rottingdean. He was a weaver of intimacies. He was forever saying, 'You must know . . . I'll bring him.' He did not suppose one had to like everyone with fervour: his really close friendships were few. But he could not imagine why anyone shrank from contact. He loved talk even if it was chatter, he loved meetings, he loved to bring friends to other friends. Men came here on a basis of intimacy already made. He always painted people better or stranger than they were.

He brought down Donald Strathcona because he prayed on his knees at night by his bed. He found that eccentric in a peer.

* Count Albrecht Bernstorff: then Counsellor of Embassy. Killed in prison by the Nazis.

And Donald brought Geoffrey Eastwood: old-fashionedly-handsome, dryly witty, and Clerk to the House of Lords. 'My old Lords . . .' as though they were Clumber spaniels – and the House of Lords jumped domestically alive.

Ustinov came, Peter's father. I think just as funny as his son.

Albrecht laughed over treasures of discovery. And I suppose, though I never knew how, I was in reverse a treasure too.

He made my social life much lighter in texture. If he had been alive now he would have done the same for my grown-up children: he would have made a difference, all the time, to all of us. That is a lot to say of any man.

I trace in the Visitors' Book my first clique. I had never had one before. Not even in Dolly's time. I had taken part then but it had never been mine. Suddenly I had people around me who liked me. Desmond, Antoine, Albrecht, coming and going: Albrecht every week all through the summers. Roderick enjoyed it too. The Government House standards and the house-proud troubles grew less.

What one wants out of life is known to one; but what one wants out of people is very obscure. I suppose one's relationship to people round one (quite excluding love, wanting honour) is only half faced-up-to all one's first forty years. As a little girl I wanted with violence to be popular. Then I set myself complicated standards socially. Some people can manage crowds around them, superficially: others want a lover – something close. What I like best is to be known. Known like a village or a near field, known without bothering, and not got wrong.

That was the difference in all the years I knew Vita and Harold.* Vita knew me. With Harold I had each time to wriggle out of being got wrong.

By Desmond, Antoine, Albrecht it was marvellously comfortable not to be got wrong. If I had married one of them I should never have fought as I did. But Roderick loved me better. Best.

I wonder whether it was the Welsh in him (which he despised and loathed) that made him so original and so indulgent: so odiously furious about unpolished brass; so capable of love.

Marriage makes the greatest social change in a life. Par-

* Vita Sackville-West and Harold Nicolson.

ticularly in a man's. Old friendships grow thin, and though new ones are formed they are seldom on such intimate lines.

After years of married life Roderick said to me:

'You don't like my friends.' Not in anger, simply wondering. I was furious with myself that he had seen it. It wasn't jealousy: it was arrogance. After they had gone, try as I would, I picked holes in them. What had happened was that he had been for years crossing over to me and they had remained behind. When they came I felt something call him like a hunting horn. It called from South Africa.

Smuts, for instance.

Roderick had known General Smuts from his youth and loved him. I thought him a showy old hypocrite. I don't say this lightly; I saw him often, either at the Cape or in our own house in London. I have been on picnics with him all day long, to the Hottentot Hollands, those blue mountains opposite the shore near Capetown. I tried hard not to criticize, even to myself, but I was irritated by the front he put on. All men in power use a skin for their public life, but his he never took off. His was 'holy'. He was highminded; and while his beautiful blue eyes watched you to catch you out he was lowminded. God knows he wasn't cosy. In his dry way he was theatrical, a stage saint; and very affronted if the stage robes were tweaked.

He was my eldest son's godfather and very kind to him.

Very few married couples are really integrated as host and hostess. How extraordinary I thought Virginia and Leonard Woolf the first time I went to see them. (Leonard says it wasn't the first time; he may be right; but the mind rearranges itself.)

The reason I went was because I had to laugh with somebody, but it was a bold gesture to go and laugh with them.

Having come up from a rung just below I had never shared youth with the people I was now meeting. One became, often, on Christian-name terms, but that didn't mean they were the Christian names of childhood. Sir Matthew Wilson – Scatters Wilson – for instance. I knew that that was what his friends called him.

One morning in summer (a book had just been finished so I didn't feel guilty) I had given myself a morning off. Roderick was in London for the week; I was gardening, nails full of earth, when the telephone rang.

Timothy (author of *The Small Hours of the Night* and *Mr Twining and the God Pan*

urian – now mtesse Pierre Harcourt – author a novel *Prince Leopold and Anna*

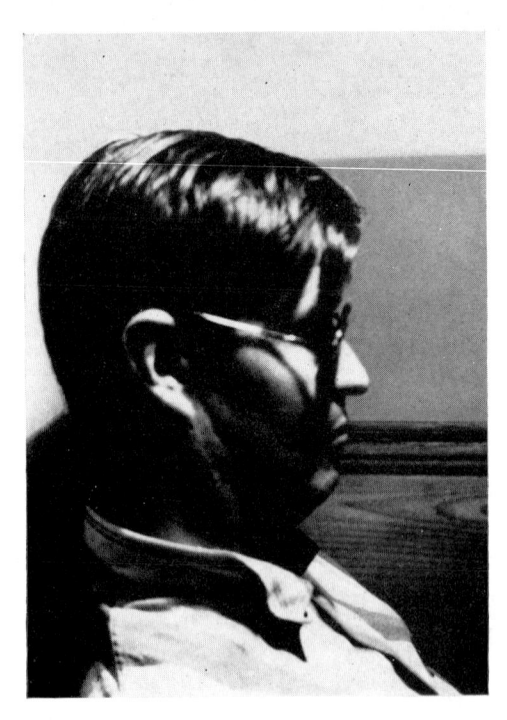

Richard, by himself. Richard Bagnold Jones, author of *British Narrow Gauge Railways*

Dominick (Tucker)

'Is that you, Enid? It's Scatters.' – *Never* had we been on those terms! I was dazed and flattered.

'What about coming to Goodwood? We could be there by lunch-time. I'm at the Metropole. Come in your car and we'll leave it here and go on in mine.'

As he spoke the pro-con thoughts zigzagged like lightning. Odious and quite terrible to go. Smart to go. I didn't race. *Why* go? But upstairs I had a new Paris dress, navy blue, and a Reboux hat, a huge, smart-casual panama, never yet worn. ('What an idiot you are always to back out of things . . .')

'I'd *love* to.'

'Right. Be at the Metropole at twelve.'

There was no money in the house. I could have gone down to the bank but there wasn't time. There was ten shillings. Wouldn't that do?

I dressed, drove to the Metropole, changed into his hired car, and between us sat another man who slept all the way and had no name.

Half-way to Goodwood Scatters said: 'Of course you belong.'

'Belong where?'

'You're a Member, aren't you?'

'Goodwood? No.'

'Good God, I shall have to pay for you!'

I felt shame. But immediately rebellion. It was his look-out: he oughtn't to have asked me. All the same there was gloomy silence till we got there.

It seems to me there was a raised platform on the right of the Entrance as we turned on which stood the Duke.* Scatters called up to him and tried to pass me in free, but the Duke wasn't having any so he had to fork out.

The same trouble with the champagne luncheon.

Cardie Montague, the friend of the man I got engaged to and whose name I can't remember, ran the luncheon. Cardie Montague was firm. Sir Matthew paid again.

I had already explained to him I had only snatched up ten shillings. I could have said I'd write a cheque and refund him, but I didn't. Perhaps I didn't think of it.

After lunch, before the first race, we went down near the door of the Jockeys' Changing Room.

* The Duke of Richmond and Gordon.

Sir Matthew – Scatters – buttonholed them outside as they came out. Advices were exchanged. He arranged his money on the first race.

We stood right beside the Start – by the tape. There were no starting stalls then. The horses were hard to line up, fretting backwards and forwards. At last they were fractionally lined. A sea wind burst over the Downs. Up went the tape. My panama bowled between their legs, everything in the betting went wrong, including Scatters' bets.

We drove back gloomy as we came, the sleeping man always in the middle. I got my own car out and went home to Rottingdean.

And there in the hall of the house, in my Paris clothes, I wanted to laugh with someone. With whom? –

– The Woolfs.

I barely knew them (though Leonard said I did). I rang them.

'Something funny's happened. Can I come and tell you?'

I was at Rodmell in twenty minutes.

How they listened! Perhaps this was a life they hardly knew (nor I). The social disaster, the racing disaster, the mistimings, the misunderstandings – by the quality of their questions they made it funnier than it was. Not that they spoke on a single wavelength, but as one enriching the other and both enriching the guest.

If I went through my address book and put ticks against couples who could so make themselves at one with an intruder I think I should find none. If you like the wife you feel you are boring the husband. If you like *only* the husband.... But that isn't what I mean.

Roderick and I were not in the least integrated. Both liked to talk: and on quite different subjects. It was like taking turns, and where did the guest come in? One could make a skimming joke of this difficulty, but sometimes the joke plunged. Alas, I know we both out-talked the children as they grew. And I suppose out-talked the guests.

But not when Albrecht took over. Every standard changed. He took away from us the 'host and hostess' aspect. He came down here with the comic side of his London world sparkling on his fingers like rings. He had enormous secrets which musn't be told and which he told at once. At last, at last Roderick and I began to enjoy the same people.

Albrecht he preferred. Albrecht alive with gaiety, while Desmond, sweet Desmond, innerly lined with gloom – 'Age I abhor thee – youth I adore thee' – Desmond watched for age, trying to forestall it by assuming it, quivered under its approach. Antoine, though so different, though his wife's ex-lover, Roderick truly liked. Antoine, with his gift for intimacy, not a good talker, never holding a table, yet inserting a sharp wit that shone with flattering knowledge of the speaker. So different, so very opposite, from his sister-in-law, Violet Bonham Carter, who while brilliantly talking was quite unaware to whom.

When Desmond came alone to stay, as he often did, I kept an eye on Roderick in case he should be bored. He was, each time, delighted to see Desmond, heartfeltly-welcoming, but I knew quite well he got tired of the manipulation of words. It went against his life-training for Reuters. He liked thought undecorated, unsubtilized, clear and short. Also he liked to talk himself. His welcome evaporated when Desmond coiled and spun.

For my sake, at a moment when Desmond was in some financial difficulty, he put him on the staff of Reuters as a liaison between Reuters and the Foreign Office. But Desmond only paid one small visit to each, and it lapsed.

Outside Reuters, and deeply connected with it, Roderick's interest was the politics, the interrelationships, of the world. He read, on this subject, more and more as he grew older. He was extraordinarily well-informed. This left Desmond a little out. But Albrecht and Antoine in.

As one can't tell, looking back, whether it was raining when we quarrelled, so I can't tell whether things that happened were 'in' or 'out' of war. War went on like weather.

In the Visitors' Book the summers before the war are full of Albrecht. He was recalled to Germany late in 1933 but he made many visits after that. When the Nazi cloud was swelling he laughed: he found them idiotic. He laughed from the start and he laughed from his prison near the end. There is a bedroom here, with a label on the door – 'The Bernstorff Room'.

* * *

It's here that I should tell about that journey I made so strangely to Hamburg; and why I went.

I lay awake one very early morning in 1933 and thought that something curious was happening in Germany, something I wanted to see. It was May and very light and I kept thinking, 'I must go. I must go and *see*.' I was fascinated by the storm cloud and the dust raised and the sense that one single man was making history, even if it was terrible history. I wanted to be there to see.

At any rate when Roderick came in in his dressing-gown to say good morning I asked him at once – could I take the car and go to Hamburg? That was the sort of question to which he always answered yes. And besides, except in efficiency, he thought I could do no wrong. Albrecht too said, 'Go if you want to. Go and see.' He knew of course how things stood. It was odd he said so little to me. People have said since that everybody knew in 1933 what was going on behind the open surface. Others that they didn't know – at that date. I was one of those who didn't know. Why, if it was all so clear, did Albrecht not tell me? He didn't. And I went.

It would have made no difference to my going if I had known. But it would have made a difference to what I wrote afterwards. I would not have looked at things so naïvely, nor taken that shining surface so for granted, although I was no more naïve over Hitler's Germany than the Left were over Stalin's Russia.

I sent the car by ship to Hamburg and I was there standing at the dock as it hung over my head. I looked for a Nazi and met one in the street. He was a merchant and also a writer; and spoke English. My recollection is that though he may have joined the Party he was a limited Nazi and on the whole reasonable. He guided me a little, but once started I looked about for myself and drove from town to town.

What I wrote was written in good faith. The impression of each day was undone the next and it was impossible to arrive at any conclusion. All I could do was to hold my mind up like a looking glass. I stayed ten days and when I got home I found Roderick in bed recovering from influenza. I started there and then to tell him everything, and he said, 'You'll never tell it twice. Go and write it.' So I did.

I took it down myself to *The Times* and it was published on a Friday. It was either on that night or on Saturday night that Roderick took me to supper at the Savoy Grill.

As we left, Violet Bonham Carter sprang up from her table and asked me with bitter indignation how I had dared write what I had written. I was taken aback. I thought I had been 'observing'; and I thought I had got it down right.

Brilliant Violet, scalding Violet (of whom Desmond said 'at one time she was the best speaker – man or woman – in England'). All this I had to take, while she pursued me with that curious pecking action too close to the face, as I backed across the Savoy Grill, through the door into the foyer, and, dumbfounded, joined Roderick in the car outside.

Years later I find in a letter I had written – this:

> I saw Violet the other night and she was so funny. It was at the Astors' party and I said to her just by the buffet: 'You can't think how often I think of you.'
>
> On this she looked inquiring but guarded.
>
> 'Whenever anything international happens I immediately measure my arguments by what I know yours would be and see if I can sharpen mine up.'
>
> At this she laughed and leant forward and said 'Whenever a million Jews are scourged through Europe, or half a million suicides appear in the paper, you say to yourself: "Wouldn't Violet make a song and dance about this."'

I was tremendously attacked. And very surprised. Letters poured in – some for me and some against. Rebecca West, for whom I have enormous respect, rounded on me at the head of some stairs leading away from a party. I never had an answer. It was too difficult. Something had made me go to Germany, and it wasn't just curiosity. Roderick stood absolutely steady. It may be wondered how, as Head of Reuters, he let me go. But his training as a journalist all through the troubles in South Africa, from the Boer War onwards, had taught him before everything to 'go and see'. Albrecht twinkled at me philosophically: he even laughed.

As the years closed in and the danger closed in, particularly on him, he defied that danger with a stream of jokes, his social weapon. No joke against Hitler, Göring, Goebbels, but did not find its way first to Albrecht, then to ring through the Savoy

Grill. There was always a joke rolling from Germany and rolling out again from his supper-tables. There came a moment when his friends said, 'Albrecht will get into trouble.' He had no notion of avoiding such trouble. He flaunted his brilliant, gallant disgust in his own way.

When Ribbentrop first came to London, Albrecht's spirit was gay with laughter; Ribbentrop who thought an Under Secretary of State was an 'under' Secretary, and was offended because he had not been approached by an Upper; Ribbentrop who thought the English played games from Friday to Monday because when he rang their offices on Saturday afternoons he got no answer; Ribbentrop who made the social mistakes that gave Albrecht the most exquisite pleasure.

We were in London when Albrecht first heard The Greeting. His Ambassador, Herr von Hoesch, could hardly take his new bosses seriously. Not at first.

Albrecht was with von Hoesch after breakfast when a messenger from Berchtesgarten arrived. He leapt like Massine through the opened door, his arm raised high, crying 'Heil Hitler!' Von Hoesch looked at him (for him too it was the first time) and gravely said 'Good morning'.

Albrecht was constantly sorry for his Ambassador and the fix he was in, but for himself he was in no fix; Counsellor though he was he made not the slightest compromise. He ignored the doom warnings and went on telling his tales about London.

There is one I borrow from Harold Nicolson.

'Who could we send,' a group of English were asking, 'to convince Hitler that our patience is not inexhaustible?'

'Send a sergeant-major of the Grenadier Guards,' said Albrecht. 'He could say "Stand up, corporal, when I address you." And Hitler would stand up.'

Soon of course he had to go. What he was doing wasn't, by his enemies, forgivable. He was recalled in July 1933 and was succeeded as Counsellor of Embassy by Prince Otto von Bismarck.

We gave a luncheon of farewell for him at Hyde Park Gate. H. G. Wells and Harold made goodbye speeches, and Albrecht, for once serious, replied. He came back several times to England after his recall, until finally he could come back no more.

In Germany he became a junior in a Jewish bank. The bank

made a cover for him for all the help he could strain to give to the Jews. For them he had a natural affection. They represented to him something classless, bohemian, oppressed, witty, sad. Perhaps it was that like children they love pleasure. In every country there have always been certain aristocratic natures who love Jews as kings used to love their jesters.

'As the bosses are picked off and sent to prison I float upwards. I shall soon be boss.' This he wrote to me on an open postcard. He feared nothing. He knew he would go, and he jeered his way to death.

His portrait is in the dining-room here, and often as we walk into dinner one or other of us has longed to feel again the stimulus of that delicious personality, and to see lower himself cautiously into a chair that huge rosy man, for whom every meal was a party, and every talk a game of skill with man's relationship to man.

It took years to be certain that Albrecht was dead. It was said that he was taken from a prison in Berlin when the Russians were very near, and shot in a square with many others. His body was never found.

* * *

Because of my article on my visit to Germany Hitler invited Roderick to one of his Rallies. Of course he refused. And also because of that ill-starred article when Ribbentrop came to London he came to see me.

I asked Roderick if I could ask him to lunch and he said, 'Well ask someone also who can tackle him.' I asked Austen Chamberlain and Bernard Shaw. They came; and in an alcove in the drawing-room they cross-questioned him. Ribbentrop, pale, puffy, semi-goodlooking, stood there, I remember, out-talked, out-flanked. He seemed to be whispering The Greeting to himself for comfort as an Arab tells his beads.

Later on he came as some kind of floating ambassador and he and Herr von Hoesch dined with us. It was a largish dinner party. I couldn't think who to put on my right – the Ambassador or the Ambassador-Extraordinary. I settled on Ribbentrop; but for me it was a dull meal. He was as pasty as ever, and made intermittent small speeches instead of talking.

Thirty hours after the dinner, Herr von Hoesch was dead,

supposedly from a heart attack. We must narrowly have escaped suspicions of food poisoning.

After his death, Prince Otto von Bismarck carried on for a time. It was then that I advertised for a head housemaid who could also valet. A tall, solid woman applied. She had been valet-housemaid to Hoesch in Paris and in London, she said. I rang up Princess Bismarck and it was so. She had been devoted to Hoesch and as I too had liked him (and Albrecht had liked him) I took her. Little as she looked a 'Mimi' that was what she was called. She came with us to look after the packing and the clothes on a voyage to South Africa.

We had anchored in that shining bay off Madeira. Roderick as usual wasn't dressed, was late. Mimi and I stood together near the cabin looking out of the gang doorway at the boatload-market (of lace and toys) on the water.

In a kind of hypnosis, in a sense of being separated from life as she watched the foreign sea and mountain, she unrolled, in a hard, inexorable way as though impelled, this story. It began unheralded. Except that I have told it to other people I was then, and am, the only person in the world to know it.

Hoesch walked every morning early in the Park with his dog (which I think Diana had given him). When he returned he had a bath and rang for his breakfast. On the morning of his death he rang as usual. The old butler, who had been with him as long as Mimi, and was equally fond of him, came on to the landing. Instantly one of the Secretaries slipped out of another room to intercept him.

'His Excellency's breakfast...' said the old man.

'*I'll* go to him.'

The Secretary went into Hoesch's bedroom, didn't come out for some time, then called the butler on the landing.

'Put me on to the doctor at the German Hospital in Islington.'

'If His Excellency's ill there's a doctor quite close whom we have in urgency....'

'Do as I say. And I'll take the call in his room.' The call was put through to him.

Mimi talked woodenly on. She had made up her mind. I knew by now (but not before we left England) that she belonged to the Party. Why did she tell me?

'When the German doctor came – it was quite a long time – as long as it takes to come from Islington, he carried a large black bag with him, bulging. He was taken up to the bedroom.

'After a time I was called to the door and told to bring two buckets, a basin and towels. I was told to go into the bathroom and fill them with hot water. I never saw His Excellency; the bed curtain was half drawn.

'In the bathroom there were coils of black rubber tubes. I was to stay in the bathroom and pass the buckets backwards and forwards. When they came back to be refilled there was blood. It seems to me there was more than a bucket of blood.'

'What do you mean, Mimi?'
'I think they were embalming him.'
'Then if the doctor arrived with all that. . . .'
'Yes. He must have been dead when they called him.'
'But why should they want to embalm him?'
'To get what was inside His Excellency out.'

The story came to an end. Roderick called from the cabin. She turned and went to him. She left us when we got back from South Africa.

It was possible that it had been arranged in the Embassy that she should apply to us because of Reuters. The result however wasn't what they had expected.

* * *

How personal the things that matter. The first bomb wasn't as important to me as that my troubles domestically were over. That the staff we had collected – the 'nine indoors' – were gone.

They were there for the first siren. The siren with a magic like the Last Trump. As galvanizing. 'Get ready quick, dears! They're all coming out of their graves!'

They were there for the Battle of Britain. The village builders dug a long trench in the orchard of the other house. At the entrance an old fractured apple tree got in the way of the moon. In the light of a hurricane lamp we slept with astonished worms, in dampness listening. There was room for everyone and it was pressed on the 'nine', but they minded rheumatism more.

Suddenly Hitler was going to land on the Downs. After the fall of France every unnecessary person was cleared from around Brighton and all along the Downs. The area became prohibited and passes had to be got to go to London. If 'they' came, we were told, we must bow before the wind and remain.

No roads were to be cluttered.

So the women went to factories and the men to war: or if they didn't they weren't allowed here any more. We moved across to the other house. Easier to run. I started to cook – walking from Mrs Beeton to the stove. ('Six ounces' – did she say? And back again.) Nothing mattered. What was heaven was the peace at the opening of the war.

I won't talk of the war; it was everybody's war. All England, and every countryside has its stories. All I prayed and hoped was that it wouldn't come near Timothy, the son who was nearest it. But it did. And it took off his leg. He wrote to me as soon as it was off: 'I never liked walking. And now I shan't have to.' But he was wrong. He re-learnt everything, walking, riding, dancing. If he has managed again to ski he has hidden it from me; but I shouldn't be surprised.

Chapter Ten

※

AFTER I married (and free of Daddy's interdiction) there was an explosion of dogs. I saw very soon what he had meant. One might have had sheep they became so rowdily impersonal, always thinking of each other, never putting me first.

If a dog doesn't put you first where are you both? In what relation? A dog needs God. It lives by your glances, your wishes. It even shares your humour. This happens about the fifth year. If it doesn't happen you are only keeping an animal.

So we settled down to the one-dog theory, except later on when the children wanted a nursery dog. In and out of our long lives went Pekineses, a labrador, a fox terrier; famous in his own right. It was not I who made him so. As Jacob in *National Velvet* he wrote himself on the page.

He had a vast sex life. He was absent as often as he was present, and when he came back it was in circles, curving to avoid McHardy's boot. 'They bitches . . .' snarled McHardy. And Jacob's louche smile was full of insult.

Certain people like dogs. Kipling liked dogs.

After Laurian's birth Kipling, who was her godfather, wrote an advice, almost a plea, that we should get a bulldog for the baby. So we got Mary, a bulldog bitch, who had red mange. Cured of that she seemed very bad tempered. At the christening, as Kipling was coming, I felt nervous. Sure enough he swooped on her.

'Be *careful*!'

'No dog ever bites me.' But she did. Luckily only on his sleeve.

Later on he gave his goddaughter a field at Rottingdean, but it had slipped into the sea. He gave her at her christening a necklace of real pearls.

When you sit remembering your life – even the dogs – the mind flickers. Things turn up out of place. So thinking of the bulldog bitch I think of Kipling.

He was a little man whom nobody knew very well. The traces of Kipling in this village are on the whole pro-Carrie and anti-Rudyard. There are few people who remember him. I would have said, but nobody knows, that he and his wife had a hard time together. She seemed to feel herself the guardian of his genius, the governess of his working hours, even his hour for bed. They had death-battles on the subject of his dogs. He loved his dogs in a claustrophobic way as though he was short on friends. He didn't seem clever. He was obstinate and reiterative on politics.

Roderick had known him for years in South Africa; they were old friends. On the subject of South Africa he would talk violently, but I, listening, could never detect anything that marked him out from other men. He had so long ago made up his mind and went always on the old trail. He had nothing new to say. That was what was so extraordinary. That the wonderful thing he possessed within was there – a prisoner – either by his own wish or by his inability to use it in the common change of conversation.

'Can there be . . .' (I remember thinking) '. . . *is* there such a thing as a second-class mind inhabited by a first-class genius?'

I took Laurian and Timothy to lunch at Bateman's. Timothy was eight and had just gone to Summerfields.

At Bateman's they were so kind but the lunch didn't go very well. Kipling kept up a charade at all times. He had a special one for boys.

'Do they give you extra chu?'

Timothy went scarlet. He had no idea what was asked. We were so few at such a large table that I couldn't whisper, 'prep'. Kipling said it again with the same result and the subject dropped. After lunch he made Timothy fire a revolver and the thing kicked. He used his Kipling-talk as a defence, as though painfully wounded or painfully shy. Lonely, contradictory, cut off from life, he had had this marvellous gift quite separate from himself, like a bird singing on a fence.

Once, at Sybil's,* sitting next to him (and he was glad I was there, I was as near as he could get, at that luncheon, to cosy), he began a story. 'Once there was a man who had a baby.' I turned my head to listen: we were off.

'As always when new things happen in the world they never happen singly, so there were other men in the world who gave birth at the same time. One in China and one in Lapland. But they were so far apart they didn't realize they weren't unique. My man in England when he had his baby was overcome with shame....'

'What are you two talking about? Come over here, Ruddy. What are you telling Enid?'

So Sybil broke it up. I would have thought it would have been quite a story. Did he ever write it? Or was he trying out on me whether that bird would sing again? He was heroic and stoic. He ploughed through a dull second part of his life to its end with the ghost of that enormous cake of success he had eaten too young.

He adored brave deeds, machinery, big men, tough soldiers. It used to cross my mind that he had the misery also of being a quite unconscious homosexual. This would have horrified him deeply. I just make the remark.

So – dogs.

When Annabel my granddaughter, was at the age of the play pen we had Zoë, a bull-mastiff, with a wooden face and abrupt hard manners, who loved to make Annabel scream. She made grim jokes but she would never have bitten her. She spent her time dragging the toys out through the bars of the play pen, munching them as Annabel yelled. Catching Annabel on the stairs going up to my bedroom she would curve her body and pin the little girl, screaming, against the wall.

And during Zoë's life we went against the Principle and had Edward as well. He was the first of two toy Manchester terriers, black and tan, whose combined span was twenty-five years. No dog so hardy, so little trouble, so amused with so little. Edward lived ten years till his death by an accident; Henry fifteen.

* Lady Colefax.

Annabel, at four, came with me to the station to fetch the puppy Henry. I ought to remember with shame, saying crossly: 'Don't look at him first when I open the box! He's *mine*!' She remembers it too because she was surprised we were both the same age.

If I try to count how the years went and who came to see us and what friends were closest, I can count by the dogs. Desmond was a Zoë-ite. He despised Edward and called him 'Little Misery'.

'Molly won't let me have a dog,' he said sadly.

He and Molly didn't go about together. He liked to leave her at home. That was a little blot on Desmond. On his courage. She was bitterly, angrily deaf. She, who loved social life, was so suited for it, by her wit and intelligence and her love of people, was so cut off that it made a barrier between them. I think (she thought too) he could have helped her more. It was owing to this that she kept up her bickering while Desmond sat back and pretended not to hear. She would attack him but he leant back. He was for being the indulgent one. It wasn't quite fair, but it couldn't be cured. They spent a week-end here like this. There was nothing she wouldn't come out with. If you are as deaf as she was it insulates you.

Once I asked Desmond to lunch alone with me in London, but he rang up and said he was bringing Molly. 'We're in the middle of a row and we can't finish.'

We sat down to lunch. Molly attacked without embarrassment.

'I've come back from Devonshire this morning and I find Desmond has engaged a *valet*. From a prison.' The word 'valet' fairly scorched. It couldn't be true. It was so obvious just to look at Desmond that he hadn't a valet.

Desmond sat back, far back, in one of those deep Regency chairs we had then. 'Not a valet,' he murmured, 'and not from prison.' He knew she couldn't hear.

Molly's indignation never stopped. It seemed to have no basis and no reason. (But all married troubles have reasons.) Luckily lunch had only two courses. It was soon over.

At the front door she said bitterly, 'Take Desmond in your *car*. I'll take a *bus*.'

✱ 196 ✱

It hadn't worked, the lunch. You can't shout delicately on marriage.

But he loved her and she loved him. It was the deafness that was such a savage cruelty. Far worse than any infidelity. So while Desmond shone abroad she, capable of shining, sat at home. But she had her adherents.

Desmond was on the whole readily sad. There was a sad river flowing underneath. Like Kipling, in a less gigantic way, he had had his cake young. He had had a magical Oxford. He had a golden wizardry at luncheons. And when I say luncheons I mean Wharf-quality.*

'I was rather young when I went to Oxford,' he said once. 'They were afraid (perhaps his mother) I would sit up too late.' 'Sit up!' He sat up all night, he told me, talking. 'It never did me any harm, dear.' No, I should think it was his private reefer. (He had that curious way of saying 'dear' – as on the stage they say 'darling' – which he intended to be avuncular, somehow setting our relationship, forestalling the hated 'elderly' by adopting it. Thus he tried too to forestall age by pressing towards it. He stroked and caressed death as one who hates a cat tries to show he doesn't.)

When Desmond was old Roderick was older. Though he liked Desmond's arrival he grudged my attention. Once when they were both ill Roderick from his bed turned an irritated face:

'Where have you been all this time?'

'With Desmond. He's ill too.'

(Fretfully) 'Ring for an ambulance.'

With us Desmond wasn't brilliant. It was better that way. He was dear and comfortable, and sad and gay. He was a shameless repeater of his own jokes. When he came to the word that made the joke he lingered on it. When it was a new word he slid it out, like handing a sweet, with a look of delight. He was a fowler with words.

Desmond slept badly all his life. From guilt, he said. And it was true. It was the guilt of always being behindhand, of never catching up. He was late with his articles for his newspaper, late for his trains, late for his luncheons (Lady Horner, impatiently

---

* That famous country house of the Prime Minister and Margot Tennant, where Desmond likened Mr Asquith to a tree whose branches whirled with flying parrots.

waiting: 'Desmond lives up to the very edge of his charm!'), late, too late, for the novel he so wanted to write. Late, late, and never with carelessness, always with guilt.

When I, edging away from the hated idea of a secretary, 'Don't be a fool, Virgilia,' he said. 'Learn to use one. Don't lead *my* life!'

When Cutmore drew his curtains in the morning, bringing him his tea, he would turn his face to the wall, saying – 'What's the weather like?'

'Not good, sir.'

'Oh *more* than that! Go on. Describe it. Which way is the wind blowing? From left to right? What about the clouds? Go *on*, Cutmore . . .'

He wanted, he said, a human voice while he was recovering. And at night, prowling round the Garden Room –

'Have you a detective story, dear? . . . A *kind* one. Not a cruel one! Just come and look . . . Oh no, not that one! That's a cruel one. I can't sleep with a cruel one . . .' He couldn't sleep anyway.

He was asked to Buckingham Palace. He stayed with us in London and brought tails, dress-shirt, links, everything he needed. Six months later I found the whole lot stuffed in a roll in the po cupboard.

One day – in London –

'Can you *imagine* it – I've nothing to do today. I think – I *think* – I will walk out and just take a bus.'

'Where to?'

'Westward,' he said solemnly, as though he was going into the setting sun.

He went. The telephone rang. The B.B.C.

'Is Mr Desmond MacCarthy with you?'

'He's just gone.'

'Gone where?'

'Gone westward.'

'*Westward* – my God! In five minutes he's on *live*.'

He had felt so talented and had wanted so much more. Above everything he had wanted to write a novel. And he was fitted for it. He could have done it, except for a weak will. I should take into account that he had to earn his living, and by journalism, a profession that leaves you guilty and exhausted with its waste and its everlasting hurry. Journalism is a dragon that eats you and nothing is left. But he could have done his novel. Others have, in worse circumstances. But on top of the journalism he had those lunches, those small and brilliant audiences, the rapt faces as he talked, and the wine. It wasn't three when he left his tables. It was four. As he said goodbye and departed one could see in his modest way how he had enjoyed himself. True he was late for his office again.

One can't call back that stroking, meandering voice, so sure of its words, or if it hesitated it was for a word as tipped with phosphorus as a match, to set the table alight.

I suppose there are records of his broadcasts. But I heard Kathleen Ferrier singing last night and I hate a dead voice. He could listen. Not quite enough perhaps, but what did it matter. Laurian and Timothy asked him once when he was staying here how it was done to break into a conversation – (their great difficulty then).

'You have to choose,' he said, pleased at the question, 'whether to go under or over. It's an affair of pitch. Interruption is an art. I didn't always have it. I asked Henry James a question when I was young. I thought he had got to a pause. He hadn't. That vast machine, hearing something, stopped, changed gear, put itself into reverse and clanked back to where the question might be answered. "I think you asked me something."' Desmond was so appalled he had forgotten what it was he had asked him.

As I have said, he was in love when I first met him. He couldn't have his way with the lady. She later became as near to being a judge as a woman can be. She was then, I think, a barrister. I listened to his grievance. He was more annoyed than sad. It was funny to think of Desmond in love with a lady who was in love with the law. She was beautiful, a little stern, with a low, quiet debating voice, debating with herself about what was right. The right word, the right action, the right course to pursue. Desmond hadn't a chance. I don't think (but I don't know) that he was cut out for a successful lover.

When Desmond was literary editor of the *New Statesman* he printed a story I wrote called 'Vivien, the Spinster'. I was somewhere about twenty-four and he was a great Light and Power. He took me into a pub. 'Let's correct it.' I watched his pencil for a little, rather pleased. Then the fight came into me. He was really beginning to rewrite. I said so.

He smiled his Desmond-smile, recognizing himself, recognizing his trouble.

'I love correcting,' he admitted. 'You're right to stop me.'

It wasn't that Desmond couldn't invent, but he never caught up with his mislaid power to do it. He could do so much else, but to invent was what he wanted. And if you were such a fool as to give him the mapped-out course he took it over and galloped on it. I never showed him anything again, except, oddly enough, perhaps twenty years later, *The Squire* – a novel about birth.

'Where's Papa?' he kept saying.

'There isn't one. – He's gone to India.'

'Better put Papa in.'

'Desmond! The whole point is that *she* is 'The Squire' – the woman. I've got rid of the man. That's the point.'

'I'd prefer Papa,' he sighed. He went up to his bedroom taking the book, and wrote in pencil four dense pages of praise of it. Not only did he never print it as a review ('I can't review my friends') – (and he had so *many*!) but I lost it.

Both Desmond and Antoine treated me as a rather gifted child, found on a doorstep, but who had to be kept in her place.

'You're not a lion,' Desmond had said to me when my first little book came out. And he bought me a little glass lion with its toe off.

Somewhere in the middle of my life (and later on in his) he rang me up one morning in London.

'I've been through my desk and thrown away everything.'

'What things?'

'First acts. Second acts. If a play isn't finished, Virgilia, it hasn't begun. Unfinished stories. It's been a sad morning. I sat and thought' (with his little laugh) 'how well I wrote!'

It went in a circle. He couldn't get up in the morning because he couldn't sleep. And he couldn't sleep because of this writing-guilt. He worked so hard and in a way he did so little: but it shocks me how soon and how much he has been forgotten.

* * *

> Drawing by Desmond MacCarthy
>
> Lionetta, by means of pendant paws and an expressive eye, almost succeeds in persuading Desmond that the ~~creature~~ feeling he inspires falls little short of REVERENCE.
>
> May 19th 1918

'Lionetta', by Desmond MacCarthy, 19 May 1918

Antoine . . .

One wants to know how people's loves turn out. What's the end?

I had loved Antoine desperately. But it got mopped up in marriage. I became too busy to love.

During most of the war Antoine was in Roumania. Elizabeth died there. After the war he came often to Rottingdean, and we had gone back to North End House by then.

When he came I was proud he had once been mine. I was

proud that my daughter and my sons should see my past, undated, witty and alive. He had grumbled about them as babies. That I should have four seemed to him a monstrous waste of my time. But as they grew up he noticed them as persons, gave them his shafts of abrupt intimacy, made them laugh, put his mark on them as though he had stamped his linen. The 'joke' was that he still governed my life, but I noticed in his jokes that there was something gone. He was poor. I didn't know this. He had so loathed poverty. Like all those of the top layer who had been tipped out of Russia and Roumania he had never dreamt of it for himself. His estates in Roumania had been over-run, and wherever he and Emmanuel kept their cave of gold – perhaps America – got cut off too. Or emptied.

He borrowed five hundred pounds from me once, and I was astonished, but so proud I had it. He often referred to it. 'I love you so much I haven't paid you back.' That this was a joke didn't hurt. He had loved me three days but given his friendship for life.

I was so used to the image of the golden prince with emeralds in his pockets I never dreamt that five hundred could be badly needed.

After Margot's death he was left something. Valuables or silver.

When Diana was ambassadress in Paris I often went over to stay with her – by Newhaven; and often she drove down to Dieppe to fetch me. Suddenly one evening Antoine, whom I hadn't heard from for months, rang me up.

'When are you next going to Paris?'

'As it happens tomorrow morning.'

With a mocking tenderness not meant to be believed – 'Ah, dear Virgilia, I'll come down and say goodbye to you!'

'Oh, Antoine – *NO*! I'm leaving at half past nine . . .'

'I'll be there.'

'*Please* don't . . . it's such a rush to get away . . .'

'Don't you love me?'

'Not at nine.'

Of course he came. He was there, laughing, in the porch. Roderick was seeing me off in his dressing-gown.

'Will you do me a favour, dear Virgilia . . .' He had a sack of dark canvas, strapped and tied.

'What is it?'

'I have a friend, a poor priest in Paris. These are things – sweets, tins, two tongues from Fortnum's and a ham.'

'Dutiable?'

'No no no of course not!'

Of course I took it. I had never refused him anything.

'Come in and have some breakfast.' (Roderick.)

'No no, I have a friend in Brighton . . .'

After saddling me with the canvas bag he wanted to be off.

There's always a last time. This was the last time. What a poor last time it was.

They knew me on the boat. And the Harbour Master and his officials, they too knew me from my constant crossings. Diana met me.

'What's that sack?'

'Antoine's. Something he wanted me to bring.' She was busy madly driving (those marvellous eyes always, it seemed, half blind, but the speed of her reaction caught up on it). She said nothing, but she marked the sack in her mind.

How they laughed next morning in my bedroom – she and Nancy Mitford – 'She's got a sack. From Antoine. Full of food for a priest.'

'Do you believe it?'

'Of course not.'

'Open it and see.'

'No, no!' (from me).

They opened it. Some acid drops in paper fell out from the top. Underneath was old silver: candlesticks, sauce boats, cream jugs, worth several hundred pounds.

'Put it all back. Carefully. It's here now and I'll leave it with the priest.' So I did. Or at least I took it to a doorway where a shadowy man accepted it.

But Diana and Nancy concocted a telegram of torture and sent it to Antoine.

'Poor Virgilia, much upset, left sack in restaurant on Dieppe quay.'

Antoine, frenzied, crossed to Dieppe, and hunted up and down the little eating places on the quay. Distraught, reckless with anxiety, giving himself away – 'A sack of silver! A sack of silver!' Returning by the next boat he almost wept his story to the purser. '*Lady Jones* took it over' (as though I was a local character. Which I was). When I went back I had the same purser, whom I knew well. He was grave. 'That prince,' he said, 'upset those men who keep the restaurants. They were all in the Resistance and they're jumpy.' Though I disdained to say it the purser knew I hadn't known. I could see in my mind's eye: 'Knight's wife caught with sack of silver.' It wouldn't have looked a joke.

Able to live again (other journeys by other mugs?) in his beautiful flat (actually his house) Quai Bourbon, he was always about to come to England but he never did. Or if he did he didn't ring me. Everything for him got duller and duller. He had had such a life so long before I met him. Just as Emmanuel had decided that certain churches were too beautiful for me to look at and turned me back from the very doors, so Antoine had decided Proust was too special a part of his life to share with me. But I got the showers of sparks after the fire: and when I quote his sayings (many in the mouth of the butler in *Serena*) I never know – since I met George Painter* – which are Antoine's and which came down from Proust. When he died his daughter Priscilla was with him. I dared to write his Obituary. It's a good portrait of how he was as he *seemed* then. How he really was he had again forbidden me to know.

It would have made him neigh with laughter that so many women wrote to me. They wanted to meet me, thinking they had found the hub of the wheel, the real repository. Not I! It was my pen. But the guesses of literature are often as good as life.

'*You!*' – '*You* write my Obituary!' The typewriter should have fallen in pieces. But here it is:†

THE TIMES TUESDAY SEPTEMBER 11 1951
PRINCE ANTOINE BIBESCO

Prince Antoine Bibesco, who has just died in Paris, was for nearly 40 years my friend. I saw him in London in May and he said: 'I think I shall be dead this year.' That was his joke,

* Author of *Marcel Proust: A Biography*.
† Reprinted from *The Times*, by permission.

which he had made before. But all the same he changed his parlourmaid whom he did not like, that she should not be at his deathbed.

Immensely intelligent (and much else besides as I shall try to show), he was so private a man that in his latter years he had become impenetrable behind a patter which earned him a sort of title of prince-buffoon. In life, stammers, mannerisms, relationship-gadgets are snatched up haphazard, often for defence (as in a fire people pick up odd clothes to run through the flames). Antoine's gadget was a fountain of questions, used long ago to stave off prying, to keep the 'lead'; but as he grew older, and finally a little deaf, the fountain swelled to the noise of a fireman's hose. On his rare revisits into Paris society he would set out, walking intolerantly fast, already infinitely impatient. He hated to be bored. Arrived at the party he would not listen; knowing how on each mouth every sentence would end. Then he would return through Paris, perhaps on foot, shuffling a little in thought, buttonholing a friend near his own Quarter, to give him, in one of his bursts of loud laughter, the ribald or intimate conclusions to which he had come.

If he could not be intimate he wanted no other relationship. Anything unintimate made him yawn. He avoided those from whom he could strike nothing. But he could tease a laundry woman or the barman round the corner from his house as the Good Lord might tease his sheep – because he knew them – because he had probably already routed out an oddity, knew that a small pearl would show in the reply. Unique, advisory, mocking, staccato, affectionate and impatient, swept by sudden depressions and as sudden laughter (against life or himself), he would sit in these last years quite unchanged in his wisdom to his few old friends, in the tarnished silver quiet of his house by the Seine (two branches of the river flowing reflected in mirrors through his rooms), just as he had done when he lived beside another river with his brother Emmanuel in London. . . .

He was extremely vintage, but the ghostly cellar of a man's mind fades, and in the end how we are looked on by our friends is all we have.

From a Paris paper unknown:
Antoine Bibesco

La mort de cet homme délicat qui avait pour la France et pour les Lettres françaises un tel amour qu'il disait: 'Si, brusquement, j'étais transplanté loin de Paris, je vieillirais tout de suite de vingt ans!', a passé presque inaperçue.

C'est à peine si deux ou trois quotidiens – et avec une discrétion qu'ils n'ont pas quand il s'agit des 'moustaches' de M. Adolphe Menjou, ou du sourire de telle autre vedette de cinéma – ont mentionné la disparition d'une figure inséparable de la vie parisienne.

Il était d'ailleurs d'une indulgence si souriante que lui-même eût excusé une telle indifférence consécutive aux moeurs actuelles. Avant d'être terrassé par la paralysie, un jour de grande lassitude, il dit à un de ses intimes:

... Je perds la mémoire, peu à peu ... vous voyez ... j'oublie même de mourir. ...

My legacy from both Bibescos was their cousin Marthe. She is now an old princess but she was once a young princess. Before her first arrival into my life, when I was perhaps twenty-four, both brothers talked about her as though I wasn't in the room. They made intimate allusions to each other that built her up from inside out – one of the ways of writing a first act. So I knew a lot about her, but all in a muddle. (Rather like sex.)

At sixteen she had married, at seventeen had had a daughter. She had a mother-in-law who wouldn't let her read; for fear she should become more clever than her husband (which she was).

The brothers tied up books, she let down a rope and pulled up the books at night.

She was beautiful. Emmanuel was angry with her. (Why?) They dealt out these fascinating cards from only half a pack.

Though curious I was rather jealously against her disturbing arrival. But when I met her in Catherine d'Erlanger's garden, and she was walking up and down with distinguished men, very beautiful and dignified, she had a large hole in the back of her stocking. I was mollified.

We talked. And to my great surprise (breathlessly so, since neither brother would ever let on that I counted for anything),

I gathered she had heard of me in as great detail as I had heard of her. She laughed about the hole in her stocking and said the perfect, to be perfect, must always be imperfect.

Her intricate wit is period. But so is Henry James's. She has been all my life loyal to me: more loyal than I, with my selfish dislike of being disturbed.

She is not only a great writer, in that French so-professional way, but she has physical courage and great kindness, and an embroidered mind that puts faith in pulling wires. She would be at her best in a court or in a concentration camp.

At eighteen she had written a little book called *Alexandre Asiatique*, which fact she hid at that time, for fear it would spoil her young married success in Paris. Antoine badgered me for years to translate it. It took ten years of badgering but at last I did it.

It was she and not Hitler who caused my long estrangement from Violet Bonham Carter.

We gave a summer garden party in the garden of Hyde Park Gate.

'Marthe' – said Violet, with too much drama – 'has been put under house-arrest at Mogosoea.'

I didn't doubt it but I laughed. I meant that the Germans might find Marthe a handful. But the wretched joke went wrong. Violet was in an immediate flame of indignation. She had never put herself out for Marthe as I had done (when I had her and her maid, Blanche, to stay – which was always a little royal but worth it). Violet had never done as much. I would have said so but I didn't get the chance. I was scolded around my own garden, so that, after a storm of pursuing words, choked and frustrated, I burst out: 'The trouble with you, Violet, is that you talk too much!' – I had said the unforgivable! She gathered up Bongie and marched out of the house. I ran after her into the street, hands out, crying how sorry I was. It was no good. I wrote. I wrote to Bongie. Nothing was any good. And it was no good for twenty years.

Suddenly the other day it was all forgotten. I hope not because of age.

When Marthe comes to stay at Rottingdean she changes the furniture round. I don't mind that: it's endearing. I used to do it myself. She has extraordinary tiny meals of strange substances, but as Blanche is there to carry them up and down it doesn't matter. She writes all the morning; as I do. Her 'staying' when I look back on it is rich and fruity; she is some kind of glorious nuisance, but worth while.

Yet when she suggests coming I shrink. This is my secret sin, this guest-shrinking. I know she will want to meet eminent people all over Sussex and either I shan't know them or I shan't like it. There will be a disruption.

When she wants something big she is direct, as when she asked if she could come for Christmas. I said no. She took it with simplicity. Christmas, even without a single guest, gets more of a nightmare each year. There is this terrible sense that one must give pleasure. And more and more pleasure. Nothing will make Christmas big enough, rich enough. So I said no to Marthe.

My attitude to Marthe's arrival is my attitude to all visitors, a relic of 'Government-House-trouble', a dread of being disarranged, a knowledge that it is I alone who must introduce and conduct and make a success of this strange element, the new arrival. And Marthe, in my imagination, before arriving, is like an elephant stuck with rubies, needing a gold couch, needing my 'brilliance' so that hers can quench it. But I am quite wrong. When she comes she settles in and becomes cosy.

She used to be beautiful in a dark, intelligent way. But now she is much more. She is tremendous. She has veils, and a white stick like the Blind, and Napoleonic jewels. She is a whale to meet, a whale for anyone I ask. Why do I make such a fuss and throw away so much that I would enjoy?

All my life I have had this tendency to isolate myself and now when I need them I have few friends. I am back to the pre-Dolly, pre-Albrecht time. I love people but it's too late to get them to come. I'm afraid of making a date lest the Muse should want a drink at the same time.

Chapter Eleven

*

I EXCLAIMED, when I started all this, that I wouldn't tell stories of people I'd known. I wanted to talk about ME.

But you can't do that. People turn the corners of doors, the doors of living. You can't leave them out; they are hinges.

When Maurice Baring came to live in Rottingdean some time before the war, Desmond had the impudence to say he wouldn't like me. But there was mischief in his voice.

'Why shouldn't he like me?'

'Because you have no charm, dear.'

That was a facer, said like that. I brooded. 'Well, I've got vitality! Won't that do?'

But I got to know what he meant. He meant I wasn't like Laura Lovat. I had no relation to that kind of Henry James charm.

Maurice asked me to dine with him alone. It was a nightmare. He was so alarmingly shy himself that he made me as tongue-tied. If I said anything 'clever' he instantly asked his butler to bring some bread. I couldn't repeat it: I couldn't go again. I didn't.

A year or two later Laura Lovat came to see me; stopping her car for a second at the front door.

'Maurice wants you to go and see him.'

'Oh I *couldn't*!' (I didn't even have the grace to say why.)

'He's very ill. Did you know that? He *wants* you to go.'

'Then I will.'

'Tonight. At six,' she said firmly, and drove off.

So that night at six I found him in his back garden, in a wheelchair, his hard straw hat crammed on his red face, and a chair put ready for me. He had been feeding the birds in the garden. We opened on that. It didn't go very far and we were back on jerks of talk, irrelevant subjects caught up in desperation. At half past six (which was all I could manage) I got up, mumbling '. . . goodnight to the children . . .' He didn't detain me but looked up from his chair with his curious smile.

'Come again.'

'When?'

'*Tomorrow night. Same time.*'

I went every night for years; till he left to die at Beaufort Castle. I had never known him in his larky brilliant days. He was now not brilliant so much as wise. His understanding took what you had said, contemplated it, burnished it, then gave it back as your own, but gilded. I never knew what side of his mind the talk would run down. He gave it a twist in his head so that it meant more. He shook all over like a jelly. He had paralysis agitans. He had a particularly desperate gesture which wasn't desperate at all; lifting his clasped hands, and wringing them together as they bumped on his forehead. I wanted to give him a dog but he said he was past a dog. Then I tried him on a black and white rat, such as I had had in my girlhood; a creature as trainable as a dog, and with a sort of humour. I had had such a rat again with my children and we would build a wooden bridge with bricks over a tray full of water, leaving a trap in the middle so that the rat would fall in. He did once, then shook off the few drops, and whenever I set him again to cross the bridge he looked at me over his shoulder, twitching his whiskers, jumped the weak place on the bridge, and sat on his hindquarters at the far end, gay and mocking. We had him for years till he finally died of a stroke.

'The nurses would hate it,' said Maurice, so I ended on a budgerigar. It was a jealous creature and screamed as we talked, like a wife who tries to lead the conversation. I gave him an electric blanket but he thought he would be burnt. I never have luck with this present. I gave Cuthbert one and he won't use it either.

But we found, as a family, a present which enchanted him. During a skiing month in Switzerland we all, including

Roderick, embroidered in black thread on white linen squares the names of his forty-three books. The squares were sewn together and Laurian worked galloping horses in black all round the margin. It became a counterpane. (Who has it now?)

He enjoyed the children. Before Tucker was eight he was very happy with Maurice. Then all of a sudden he grew shy. 'Never mind a silence,' Maurice told him. 'Sit still and let the talk trickle back.'

Timothy, then about fourteen, was much more shy with him. Maurice loved to tip him (nostalgically) before he went back each Half to Eton. Timothy minded that desperate movement of the hands to the forehead and would have given the coming pound to get out of it.

'Give me my coat that's hanging on that chair. There's something in the pocket.' Timothy knew what was in the pocket but didn't know how he was going to get out of the room.

Like Emmanuel after his stroke, Maurice liked seeing me because I hadn't known him in his well days. When Margot or Ethel Smyth wanted to come he tried to put them off. They were old friends but he saw in their eyes how he had changed. I took him as he was. Besides, I went every night. That makes it easier for a man who is ill.

Belloc came. Maurice enjoyed that; though it was all the same an ordeal. As he wouldn't eat in front of anyone because of the shaking, he arranged a separate little dinner of perfection for Belloc downstairs. He insisted I must join him when he arrived at seven (by train and village car).

'If he likes you he won't stand up when you come in. He'll laugh and say that his legs are too old. If he doesn't like you he'll keep his cloak on and get to his feet.'

He kept his cloak on and got to his feet.

What Maurice didn't know was that Belloc also couldn't eat in front of people. His false teeth wouldn't stay in. He liked me enough eventually to tell me that. I told him to keep them in all night.

I was reading to Maurice one tea-time winter evening (in a great bank-up of snow) when they rang me from the Theatre Royal in Brighton to come in and read a Prologue at the opening of a play *Heil Cinderella*. It was an amateur company brought by Cecil Beaton and Olga Lynn to Brighton (in aid of a war charity). Juliet Duff* was to read the Prologue but she had fallen ill. She was tall and slim and I wore her dress, safety-pinned in places across the back as in the day of mourning for Napoleon.

To find myself on the boards behind footlights was such an ecstasy that I spent all night learning the words of the Prologue. Juliet, however, got up and came on on the following night (though twenty years later, through someone who had been her temporary maid, I learned she had had measles).

'I could kill her!' I said in baulked fury to Maurice.

'Make a play of it.'

So I wrote *Lottie Dundass*. As far as I can remember it ran at the Vaudeville in the Strand, with Dame Sybil and Ann Todd, for five months.

In a 'blockade' part of the war, I met Diana again – with Maurice. Met her for good.

It was when we kept rabbits and thought (almost with pleasure) that we should starve. It was so gay to circumvent it. I watched my six khaki Campbells chase the tip of my spade for worms. '*Protein!* – That's what I'll do if it gets really bad. There are acres of worms: nobody could come to the end of them. I'll simmer them down and use them for stock and never tell the children.'

Diana was at Bognor then, with a Jersey cow, making six-pound Cheddar cheeses; with a pig, and the usual hens, and rabbits. She made the cheeses in a completely professional way, taught by Conrad Russell. I then bought a Jersey cow and she taught me.

Over this farmery the intimacy sprang up as though there had never been anything else. I went to Bognor or she came to me. We slid along the coast in a train that took forty-seven minutes. We went to market at Barnham. She always talked too clearly or too loud. Her voice carried.

'Don't buy that rabbit! It's got mange.' She was faced by a gypsy as angry as an arched cat.

It's true of course that with everyone she cares about Diana is on skin-similar terms. So I hesitate to say (or claim) that, putting aside the beauty, we are rather alike. Or perhaps we act in

* Lady Juliet Duff.

adventure alike. If I had had a former life I think there might have been some sort of cousinship.

Maurice grew worse and at last he left Rottingdean and went to Beaufort Castle to be with Laura.

Diana and I journeyed up to see him. It was to say goodbye. She wore her porter's clothes: navy blue trousers and a peaked cap. We each had a small knapsack. No food on the war trains. For some reason we sat in a sort of long saloon; perhaps a restaurant car that had no restaurant. She told me the fabulous stories of touring America in *The Miracle*. Some of the tales (to do with millionaires and glass floors) were hair-raising. Twenty soldiers and sailors and their wives were riveted. Who was this perfectly beautiful woman-porter who was saying these things? I could see 'tart' in one eye, 'actress' in another; but most of the eyes were baffled.

Diana had laid it on very grandly in Edinburgh. Lord Rosebery met us with two cars, a Rolls for us and a Ford Estate for the knapsacks.

That night we slept at Dalmeny House and dined on lobster and brandy.

At five in the morning Diana came into my room. 'I have to wake you because I think I'm dying.'

I took her pulse. It was running. She could hardly get her breath.

I hesitated. I had to know. 'Is there anything serious that you know is the matter with you?'

'No, darling. But why shouldn't it begin tonight?'

I tried the medicine cupboard. Nothing. So I read Trollope aloud to her as she lay still.

At six I got a housemaid who got a doctor who gave her a sedative. We were to catch a train at eight-fifteen for Perth but that of course now wasn't possible.

But it was. At seven-forty-five she was dressed and ready, curlers pushed inside the peak cap, and we went down to the car. Once on the train – 'We never asked for sandwiches,' I said. 'No food all day!' She drew out of her pockets two kippers wrapped in handkerchiefs.

'Where did you get them?'

'Off Harry's tray. On the floor outside his bedroom.'

One would think it an ordeal to say goodbye to a dying man,

but it wasn't. Once past that shymaking outer fence – with Maurice all was natural.

'What's it like at dinner?' he asked from his bed. 'All priests and nurses?' He saw us separately.

When he died Laura wrote in a Memoir she sent me (I quote from memory, I can't find it) –

'We pray to God for you, Maurice, night and day.'

'*Shout* it.'

* * *

At one time I collected Diana's sayings but I've lost them.

But it isn't the sayings I want to keep of her as the depths of the plunge they take. She says things like Voltaire in the light tones of Noël,* and one is kidded. That has been the reason for the accusations all through her youth (and life) of frivol. They have to find something wrong with a beauty (and a duke's daughter). She speaks lightly because she is shy, to minimize the discoveries, to say things and let them lie. No caps, no underlinings.

Desmond always said that when Diana saw herself in the glass she looked astonished because she expected to be dark.

What is unbelievable is that legendary beauty can belong to a woman of character. It's so often only gummed on. And her character, like her beauty, is often got wrong. She photographs badly. She gives offence unwittingly. Something abrupt and intimate panics the stranger. Too much passes in her head between question and answer.

A young Frenchman – in the big drawing-room in Paris – (stiff with formality) – '*Vous partez en vacances, Madame?*'

The whole predicament of their careers, hers and Duff's, raced through her mind. She rested her eyes on the questioner it seemed for ever. Catching hold of the mantelpiece – 'Going *away*!' she said with horror. 'If I don't hold on with both hands they'll take it from us!' (It was an Ernest-Bevin-anxiety-moment.) The young man, who didn't know what 'they' would take, was sweating.

There was a ball that night. Driving in the car with her in the morning:

'Where are you going?'

* Noël Coward.

'To the dentist.'

'Have you got toothache?'

'No, but Cartier's can't mend Louise's* ring in time for tonight.' To Diana this didn't seem elliptical.

She talked fluent French in English (her own method). Duff spoke beautiful French but was shyer.

'Don't you *mind*?' said Lady Cunard when Duff was in love with a passing fancy.

'*Mind!*' said Diana's blazing common sense, 'I only mind when Duffie has a cold.'

But it's no use. Stories don't do it. It would be better to say that she puts friendship above everything, that that is her gift of gifts. No catastrophe so black but she wouldn't tackle it. Go to prison and she'd have you out. Shame doesn't upset her. You could have an affair with a goose it would make her laugh. When you are her friend you are socially made, but no one would be her friend who thought it.

Though Duff would never allow that the character in my novel *The Loved and Envied* had any likeness to Diana, I don't admit that husbands always know best. I think when I wrote:

> No one liked to be excluded. No one could afford to leave alone such a dispenser of life: everyone fed at the spring. She seemed to develop, when in the company of those who enjoyed life as she did, a baker's yeast. . . .

. . . . I didn't do badly.

So well do I think I caught her that I shall go on:

> When she came into a room it was plain it was a spirited person who entered, a person with an extra dose of life. It was apparent on all sides how people were affected. They had a tendency to rise to their feet to be nearer her, not of course in her honour, but to be at the source of amusement, to be sure not to miss the exclamation, the personal comedy she might make of the moment of life just left behind.

As I quote from *The Loved and Envied* I would like to say that this book took me ten years to write and began in a curious way. I was asked by MGM to write a script whose heroine would be a woman between forty and fifty. I can see now that they would

* Louise de Vilmorin.

have liked to have put one of their older Stars back on to the map. I was offered a sum so big that I blush to say it. The whole thing was tied up before a notary public with red ribbons and seals.

But I couldn't do it. I tried; I was haunted; I had this miserable sealed promise weighing me down night and day. Then suddenly I sent all the papers back to them, admitted defeat, and began to write *The Loved and Envied*.

* * *

There had come a day in 1941 when Roderick resigned from Reuters. It has been lately said that he was 'pressed to resign'. Well, in a way he was. He was pressed by his own temperament and by a self control which though of iron had got to melting point. Every successful man is surrounded by ambitious men. So was he. There were men around him waiting to misinterpret a letter or a slip of speech. He was not democratic. Far from it. Nor was Churchill. Nor was Lord Reith. You can't abate a man who has learnt through twenty-five years to run the immensely complicated machine which is Reuters. The 'slowness' of democracy (of constant consultation) doesn't suit it. I have no doubt my husband sometimes stung his Board.

How well I remember that afternoon when he came back to me at Hyde Park Gate, sat on my bed and told me what had happened. He was a man who wouldn't lie, because he was able to smell a lie a mile off.

I had shared with him for a year and more every stab of his strain and difficulties. He had been goaded for months, and, baited again on that day, he had suddenly done what he had said no man should do: he had said 'I will leave it!'

There was nothing much to be said (of comfort) then. It was a time when life, which had been filled for him with one thing from the age of seventeen, was suddenly empty. He was startled at the emptiness.

My comfort (later) was that he wouldn't have stayed alive if he had stayed at the helm. There was the full war to come.

He had often told me that to sleep badly could be conquered by will. Now he too had sleepless nights. He was like a man who has lost a rib – a biblical rib. I was bewildered to look at him How could I help him?

He set about to help himself.

It was summer and the war got going. No one could get a carpenter easily. He bought a bag for tools (and tools for the bag) and at sixty-four he called back his boyhood's carpentry. He looked for the cure-by-hands. Sun on his shoulders, the concentrated effort to learn – it was morphia for an hour, two hours. Several times that summer he took the coast train to Bognor to help Diana with her rabbit hutches. These seem small things. But they were homeopathic.

As his misery was fought down so his human astonishment opened – on life, our lives, my life. In his older age – it's never too late – he lived as a farmer lives, with his wife and children.

When the war was over and we were back in North End House, Laurian fell in love. Complicatedly. It wasn't a mother she needed. It was this new man, her father, who helped her. I went away (to America) and the enormous aggravation of a too-intimate mother was removed from the two of them. His fatherhood began before seventy.

I had written a play – *Gertie*. Herman Shumlin had flown from New York to get it, and to cast it with Glynis.*

He asked me to fly at once to New York, my first long flight. I agreed, with terror.

The flight was as horrible as I had thought it would be. There would have been an empty seat beside me but Death sat in it. Once or twice he tapped a forefinger on my knee. At Gander he turned sharply and looked at me. The descent seemed vertical. I can see how public opinion can keep one quiet at the end.†

I flew with my little talent locked like a goldfish in my breast, for that was my part, my offering to the hard work to come and the reason for my going.

I had brought him with me but he had never been out in the open. Whenever I faced him up to the icy water of rewriting he began to turn on his back and show his pale belly.

My director was a man of great experience, great integrity, kindness and rage. Just before the first rehearsal he made me a

---

* Glynis Johns.
† This and other brief extracts from 'The Flop' published in *The Atlantic Monthly*, are reprinted by courtesy of Edward Weeks, its editor. Copyright © 1952, by The Atlantic Monthly Company, Boston, Mass.

striking speech. 'I want to tell you,' he said 'though I shall hate it to happen, that you and I will end in dreadful battle, that you may leave America loathing me.'

'Why?'

'Because from tomorrow. . . . But you'll see.' I saw – in time. He was right about the battle, but not right about my leaving America loathing him.

We opened. Terrible lapses were perceived. The play seemed long and frail. I had rewritten it until it was nearly empty. The little goldfish had been no traveller.

We opened in New York on a Wednesday and came off on the Saturday. But something important happened to me at the party given for the failure. I was introduced to a woman who altered my playwriting future. She had seen, I think, in my play what had once been there.

She was elegant. Her eyes were grey-green, black-edged, carved eyes – used to domination, risks, secret decisions; used to men, women, and money. She had a floating, prowling way of moving. Turning, seeming about to speak: not speaking. She seemed a thinking-machine, making intermittent contact, brimful of resolves, rather silent, dressed as a woman. I had just time to notice these things. She was Irene Mayer Selznick, daughter of Louis B. Mayer, brought up a princess of Hollywood, married to and parted from David Selznick.

I came back here (after *Gertie*) to Rottingdean and continued a play I had long begun. One doesn't start one play after another, as it may seem. There is so much pain, wasted life, time lost after the written word CURTAIN, and while the script, clean as laundry, goes out to seek its fortune. The only sanity is to be half-armed at least, with the roots or seeds of another, to have something up one's sleeve against the coming agony. There's the agony of being refused. I've had that from London, but there has always been New York. There's the agony of being taken, and mangled. In my plays there is something that always seduces the director, star or management into turning author.

I was well on, I thought, with *The Chalk Garden*. It took all the same three more years. Then I sent it to Harold Freedman. In some weed-burning month, perhaps November, I was on an upper deck of this garden, blinking in smoke, near the stables.

The bell rang down below that I was wanted on the telephone. It was Harold, from New York.

I remember the praise, and the prickling smoke in my nostrils. In his slow way, using plain words he made my head swim. He said: 'This play makes it worth while my being an agent.'

As I couldn't speak for the glory of it, he went on:
'Have you shown it to Binkie?'*
'Not till you say so.'
'Well, send it.'

I sent it. Binkie refused it over a week-end. He sent me a letter, in his handwriting, that he couldn't stand 'these allegorical things'. I had no idea it was an allegory. (Chalk soil – dry heart.) I had never dreamt of such a theme. It took the critics to pull that out of a hat. But Binkie knew. Binkie – that strange mixture of dramatic flair and bafflement at the written word; a name, a power for forty years to make a playwright's heart flutter.

Years ago at the Savoy Grill, after some First Night, he had come suddenly to me from his table – squatting down at mine so that his eyes were level with me, and said (about a book I had just published – *The Squire*): '*Write a play like that!*' Such an odd subject to catch his fancy – a novel about childbirth.

But yet, he had meant it. And how he had startled me, and almost precipitated me to try. But I couldn't do it.

Since then I have known him through three plays. But not known him better. 'Binkie.' How the little name suits him: suits his ungrandness (he for so long master of the London theatre), his charm, his matey gossip – as he tells all and never tells a thing. The subtlest giggle is in his eyes, but it's secret. That giggle will never put you right. You can say anything. There's no frown. But ask him too intimate a question (as I asked him once for what cherished reason he had made money) and there's a cloud, a bat's wing. You can almost hear the fortress close.

He is gallant. He doesn't rub it in when you've cost him half a fortune and the play's failed. I know what's called in money-dealing 'handsome'. Binkie is just that. But hidden in his breast there's the old standard – the 'vehicle' served up for a Star. He

* Hugh Beaumont, of H. M. Tennent.

doesn't tell you so, but you get to learn it. You get to learn that it's the Star that matters.

Harold rang up.

'What did he say?'

I told him (though I expect he knew. Those two were always on the telephone bargaining gaily with each other. An old friendship). Harold could be gay almost wordlessly, with grunts and implications; his heavy tone could twinkle from New York to London. Like a father he could make the practical and even the scolding both funny and loving.

'Do you think,' he said once to me, 'that I pay five pounds for three minutes to hear you cry?'

'I could put it on,' he said (of *The Chalk Garden*), '*off*-Broadway, right now.' (Pause.) 'Unless you want to go through a harder hoop.'

I choose the 'harder hoop'. Who wouldn't?

The Management who would do my play – *on* Broadway – was 'Irene Mayer Selznick'. And the 'harder hoop' was Irene. She would do it only on *her* terms – what's called 'working on it with the author'.

That's what I'm going to describe.

But first let me say that Harold came to London on his summer visit. He and Binkie. . . . Naturally they asked each other about plays.

'I've one . . .' said Harold carelessly.

Binkie waited.

'Irene's doing it.'

Binkie waited.

'*The Chalk Garden* by Enid Bagnold.'

On Binkie's face, Harold said, 'not a muscle moved.'

* * *

I have many afflictions in writing. Well, that's all right. So does everybody. 'Art isn't easy,' said Albee. I'm always remembering that. I dive after pennies as they do at Madeira. And when I'm under water I can't see straight. Then (dropping that image) I'm afflicted by images. They gang up at the mind's exit, and block. My thoughts come so quickly that I 'jump' the story. I think I've told it but I've not. When Irene came to England to sort out my tapestry it was like a battle of the dumb and the deaf. She couldn't create – but so nearly. I could: but in what a muddle. As I write forwards I have flashes backwards, afterthoughts and enricheners, on what's written two pages behind. Irene marked in red pencil the misplaced passages. These had to be unhooked and put where they belonged. Hooks, in plays, are little aids that turn the corner of a thought. They won't serve twice. How to undo them? How to make new ones? A desperate difficulty. I had no reserve of hooks. Then when the drama should be rising like a mountain I was apt to make comments on the situation – and cause a valley. This was pointed out.

When one has been alone so long with the white page, criticism is a burning shock. She had no tact and I no patience.

'What's your theme?' (Irene.)

As none of her questions was as simple as it looked I remained guarded. There was secret below secret. I had worked so long on the play that themes had crossed each other. If an act is written too fast it goes thin. If too slow you get these cross-currents. New lights flash in at the sides.

'What's your theme?' (insisting). She wanted the main one. She wanted to – what she called – 'pull a thread straight'.

'Thread?' It was a rope! She pulled and pulled, and I was a woman drowning in a coil of rope and liking it.

'Is it a mother-daughter relationship?' (about the play).

'It's *NOT!*' – I was very emphatic because I knew early on that this would be very near her heart.

'Try and tell it plainly. Try and think.'

I didn't need to think. I knew. But I couldn't hold it. It came and went like a bright fish among weeds. Irene – on a play – it's not like taking advice, it's not like being guided – it's a whole, an impregnation, a violence. On first impact she was awful. But so was I awful.

This distraught, gifted, raging personality undertook the clearing of me to myself. Fascinated, repelled, I wouldn't submit. I didn't mind discarding, but I wouldn't alter. And when I threw away the gilded things that led nowhere I ceased to love them. Irene took my waste-paper basket to bed at night. By the morning I had filled the empty spaces with better 'plums'. There was a new war over that.

She was nervous (from her upbringing). It had been 'royal',

and she was as nervous as the Duke of Windsor. I was tough and weak, hysterical and obstinate.

She had infallible logic for sequences: but there were ideas she wouldn't brook. There was a line in which I said there was no love in heaven.

She put the script down on her lap. The carved eyes were level.

'If there isn't love in your imagined heaven,' she said, 'I go back to New York tomorrow.'

'It's always been there – that line!' I lied.

'It hasn't. You've put it in since I read the script.'

'It's fundamental to the play...'

'It isn't. There are enough "ideas" already.'

I debated. There was silence. I knew I needed pruning. Grudgingly I gave a nod.

Imagine the contentions! The two strange languages, used like misdirected weapons. Irene so clear, but now and then mistaken. I in my overplanted garden crossly defending every bush and twig of thought.

* * *

I said that Desmond used to say 'Never be afraid to bore'.

If I'm Samuel Johnson, standing before the open fire, emptying the Garrick, whoever reads can skip. But I go on. I won't believe it's boring.

If I'm fascinated by myself one must be fascinated by me. The panorama within the brain-chamber – *not* confined to writers – everybody's property – then why are some people writers and others not?

For me it's because I fear the boatload going down, the things I have noticed from the very beginning (from 'Look, Mummy – look, Mummy...!' 'I'm busy').

The wish to share, to record, to pass on the discovery. And if the human being's busy there's the page to write it on.

'How wonderful to be a writer!' – This is said sometimes by such unlikely people. As though of a 'hobby' (entrancing) that the speaker hasn't got. But in fact the world is full of writers – broken off short. What *is* wonderful is what happens. And why. Who knows about invention? Or in what cavern of the mind it lies? We can handle memory, shape and reshape it, like plasticine. But when the 'story' starts (if there *is* a story) do we lead it, or run by its side? Inside the brain there's a kind of instrument, never quite learnt, and most *un*fully played.

And last (daft) question. But not so daft. The best things come out of nowhere. How do they come? Are there certain levels where the warder sleeps and the prisoners slip out? 'Clear-minded' reduces everything to sea-level. 'Fuddle-minded' goes nearer to the bottom of the sea. That's where the riches are but often what you bring up the play can't digest.

No time for these thoughts when Irene came. No time for explanations. When she said 'What's your theme?' I could have gone on (if not interrupted) (but always interrupted) digging, for my fun, for seed corms. Did I say when I saw her in New York she was silent? She was now a torrent. Everything I said reminded her of something. Here, in a foreign countryside, her past loosened. She shook it out like dice upon the table.

I, a talker too, was for the first time nearly silenced – fascinated at the upbringing (not so easy, not so painless) of this once-shy Hollywood child.

My writing-room is five floors up, though I have had to move down now. It's a kind of Gothic tower stuck on to the side of this house.

Irene sat up reading or working in her bed half the night and slept late. I could write (and do my rewrites) while she was sleeping. Mid-morning I could hear her begin the climb from the bottom. That was always an immediate, burning moment when at last I thought of 'treasures', pushed the block out of my mind, and banged the typewriter as she climbed. Then the door opened. We settled. Discussions began.

Her marvellous New York dresses hung in her cupboard. When at work she wore always the same one. Or a red dressing-gown and a big diamond.

We began. But in five minutes we broke off over the question of warmth. She had snapped the electric fire on. My face began to burn. She said (with less and less pleasure) she admired my circulation. In a few days she discovered the truth. Unknown to her, and hidden by that same long table (with two vices) that stretched between us, I sat in a woollen bag up to my waist and at my feet was an electric pad. We rearranged ourselves on lines of greater justice.

She wouldn't let me eat. Or a tray came up. Sometimes we sucked chicken bones. Sometimes I hated her, but it didn't last.

Roderick was amazed by her. And she, in a way, by him. They were to know each other better as time went on. He admired her. But all the same he kept thinking his wife was away too much and the home floundering. So it was. One night – and she wore so short a fluffy skirt that I remember it exactly (she looked like a baby doll with a barrister's face) she made a small speech to my children just before dinner. They were far beyond being children then, down for the week-end, embedded in their own careers. She told them I was 'immeasurably important'. That was nice to hear. And that they must do the cooking and leave me upstairs. They didn't (couldn't) – but somehow by immense planning and cold food the meals got done. I liked hot lunch and tea and drinks at six. I didn't get them.

It was an extraordinary job she took on; away from home, often uncomfortable, always opposed. Two tigresses growling over moving words. Yet I think she liked the terrible fight. She sent to New York for her secretary and 'cut and paste' was handed through the door for a clean type.

She never wrote one word of the play, and this was her pride. And it was true. She pushed and poked me into rearrangements, into doing things I thought I couldn't do. Nobody has ever got so near writing without writing. Out of the heart of the play, and always from what I wrote, she kept her hand on what she called the theme (we never mentioned it because I got cross at the very word). She was like a stalking Indian who (through the forest) knew the only track.

This went on for two years, here and in New York.

I went twice to New York. The first time I can't say that she was affable. She was oddly changed. I think she felt, out of the tradition of her upbringing, that I was a writer-on-approval. A *script*-writer.

She wondered, I don't doubt, whether I could work away from home and keep faith.

Also she had something on her mind. It took a week before it showed.

'You have to do a new scene.'

'A NEW SCENE!' I felt capable of going back to England. But not quite.

'In the third act. Between the Judge and Madrigal. When they are alone.'

I couldn't speak.

'It has to be the heart of the play.'

'Oh my God, *now*, after four years. A *heart*!'

'She has to say why she's where she is, and defend herself.'

'I can't.'

'You must.'

'I won't.'

'Let me tell you this. There'll be nobody in the audience (when we get to having an audience) that won't want it. When there's something everybody wants then it's got to be there.'

I remembered Archer's '*scène á faire*'.

'Nothing's any good,' she said, 'that's done on tour. People write and write in those hotel bedrooms' (I remembered Gertie) 'and they hardly ever make the play any better. It's got to be *now* that we tighten and finish everything. And then we have to stand side by side over every word.'

So we did.

My letters home to Roderick at that time before the new scene was written are full of baffled anger; but once it was done it was the last thing she asked of me – and from then on there were *two* people who believed in every word and its position – and one was the 'Management'.

The second time I went out to New York I was her own playwright. I was stamped 'passed'. I was to be totally defended. (But my arrival all the same had its Irene-flavour.)

Her secretary, her own chauffeur, her car, met me at the Docks. I was driven to an hotel where several alternate suites had been reserved for my choosing. Irene was there, standing in a 'suite' (bedroom, sitting-room, kitchen); but there was a preoccupation in her eye. Her eye, for some reason, was in California. The telephone rang that moment by my bed. My luggage was not yet in the room, but on the floor was a tightly strung carton of bottles.

Irene sat on the bed and spoke. I mean into the telephone. It was five o'clock – it was continuous. Anyone who has ever heard Irene truly telephone will understand what I mean. No muscle moved, except of her mouth, till seven.

Once the luggage had tried to come in but she had waved it out.

Once she turned slightly and indicated the bottles (her present to me). I deduced we might have a drink. No opener, no glass, no scissors because no luggage. There was nothing: just a desert and the bottles. She indicated the door. I went through it. Corridor, emptiness, no human being. No drinks.

At seven she said into the telephone:

'Have the call transferred to my apartment at the Pierre. I'll be there' (looking at her watch) 'seven-thirty.' She didn't think it strange that she had been speaking for two hours.

No luggage, no comb, no powder, we went to the Pierre. There we took up where we had left off – California.

At eight-thirty she ordered dinner. – This is not told in the slightest blame. In *wonder*.

Chapter Twelve

*

Between my being On Appro and her Playwright, Irene had come to London – casting (for New York). Gladys Cooper agreed to do Mrs St Maugham. She was shown the lines where she mislays her false teeth but she didn't mind.

For Madrigal, Irene decided on Siobhan McKenna. I had the power of veto. But I didn't want to veto. I trusted Irene, and I knew too little.

Siobhan was on an island off Ireland. The island couldn't be found, hadn't a post office, hadn't a telephone, and to a telegram Siobhan made no answer.

If Irene had wanted a dead actress she would have fished her out of the grave and put her in working condition. So Irene got Siobhan.

The girl 'Laurel' was difficult because young teenagers in the theatre are typed and the mothers send the applicants to be auditioned in the equivalent of pigtails and white socks. It seems they can't live down that effect.

At that age (from twelve to fourteen) it's possible to be as witty, as barbed, as dangerously concealed in intention as the young Margot Tennant, and that's what I had meant. But White Socks prevailed.

Cecil did the Set – a beauty. Black and white, intricately simple, like the ironwork round the stables of a Queen Anne house.

Irene had asked me whom I wanted. I had said Cecil. He and Irene were enemies from the start. They had known each other before but there was an instant renewal of dislike. Each had pride a mile high. Cecil had the whip hand of invective but Irene was Management. She asked him to 'submit' sketches (Cecil not used to that word). He brought a few washes for her to see (reserving his liberty behind the vagueness). She conveyed to him that he 'wasn't professional'. Dynamite after that.

'What about measurements?'

'Get a man in New York to do that.'

Irene simmered: Cecil flashed. Both had the same carved eyes. His missed no personal eccentricity (Irene had a million) that he could mock. Their tension was like a bright wire pulled tight across the sun.

In Claridges, one hot summer day, she ordered a luncheon of lobsters upstairs in the sitting-room. He happened to be there. As the white table was being wheeled in – without a touch of invitation – she bowed him away.

They arrived in New York at white heat – wild cats of insult.

'Where's that bitch' – I heard his high, complaining voice – 'before I blow my top?'

It was a vibrating atmosphere, starry with annoyance. Squibs went off if you sneezed. I loved them both, and I don't use the word easily. But the play was my life and I stuck by Irene.

George Cukor was to direct. He was Irene's old friend since the time of her marriage; godfather also to one of her sons.

In his room at the Savoy he had previously got me to do a recording of the play; so that my intention – not of acting but of the inflection which conveys the mood, should come through.

Short of having ten weeks' rehearsals, such a recording or (but this is an explosive subject) my reading of the play upon the stage myself – either is a short cut. A short cut needed in the three weeks now allowed.

I don't speak for others' plays. I speak for mine. To get the good out of them the complications have to be understood. And the words heard. The intended 'fun' depends on a sly awareness of two levels, the matter of fact, and what floats beneath: on juxtapositions of meanings, a polite, small battle, an implied watchfulness between the characters. They know more than they say. It's a sure rule that there's the barest allowance of emotion. At all events until one has found one's way through the trees.

All this is hard to come by. Time is lost. Sometimes there is an oh-so-slow discovery at the last ditch. And the last ditch is too late. There's no time for sitting pretty on what's been found overnight.

The point I am making now, and want to make, is that since *The Chalk Garden* these 'curiosities' have never been insisted upon, worked hard upon, perhaps not seen by any director.

The same technique of dialogue is in all my plays, but only Irene, with her drive, her passion, her involvement, her disregard of battles, has brought it out. She impinged and invaded everywhere, heel and toe on holy ground which fizzed as she walked on it. The play had to be played as I had worked on it; she saw to that. She got herself hated. But she only cared for the play.

Now in New York we are set for rehearsals. Was it August? I can't remember. If it was August it was pre-cooked in an Aga. It was tin-plate-hot. It was sizzling.

George asked me to read the play to the company on the stage. He *asked* me. I swear it. I didn't suggest it.

It alienated, alas, my Star.

At the end of the Reading I asked Gladys (sitting next me) if she was tired.

'*Tired!*' (and the laugh told me all). 'I haven't heard a word!' – So then we have to live down this. But we never did. It started up something like a live serpent. You never knew where it was going to glide.

If I am to give the tang of these rehearsals, the whole adventure, I must temporarily blacken Gladys. If she'll have patience and indulgence as she reads she'll find she comes out more than all right.

Before the Reading she had called me Enid. After it, Miss Bagnold. Later, Lady Jones. As I ascended in social position and went down in contempt I realized she had classed me as a social character who by luck (and possibly ghosted) had got some fool to put on my play. And as my oddly-contrived words were appalling to memorize, I believe she said on the telephone to New York (from Boston or Philadelphia), 'We're out here in a lot of nonsense!' (I forgive her.)

Now Gladys is an old hand. She had owned her own theatre: she had been in management. We were about the same age but I was inexperienced. We were both positive characters and I annoyed her from the start. Having put my foot in over the Reading I wasn't allowed to take it out.

Irene and I stood together. Irene did the fighting, but we were tarred with the same brush. Having pitched her battle with me about the text over two years it was a glory to see now what protection I got. We had word-trouble (text trouble) with Gladys from the start. She said she was going to 'approximate'. Irene didn't budge an inch. As an enemy she doesn't avoid scenes. There was Gladys on the stage approximating and Irene in the stalls in a white heat. At the close of each patch of rehearsal she lit bonfires.

George was in a difficult position. He adored Gladys and her beauty and loved Irene as an old friend. He hadn't directed on the stage for twenty-five years, and his film-habit was to concentrate on the Star. That put him in a spot. Siobhan sat neglected. The rest were on chairs like schoolchildren 'overhearing' the Headmaster. George, whispering counsel to Gladys, finally took to asking me (for Gladys's sake) what certain speeches meant. As he went to Gladys I heard, 'Enid says'. After 'Enid says' there was no hope any longer.

Before I knew it, Irene sacked George at the back of the stalls at eleven o'clock in the morning.

It meant a lot to her. She was deeply fond of him. She looked as though eagles had attacked her and she had fought back. Instead of her rehearsal-dress she was particularly grand that morning. Perhaps she had dressed to help her nerves. As she talked sables slipped to the floor, dark hair came down, she dropped a bracelet.

George said softly: 'Irene – I never saw anyone get up so smart in the morning go to pieces so quick.'

He was full of chivalry and offered to 'see us into Boston'. In the end he was full of forgiveness too.

That day he had been going back to Hollywood anyway for four days, by arrangement, for 'cutting' on a film. Now there we were with no director.

I was put on the stage. 'Lady Jones' – God help me. I eyed Gladys. For the moment she didn't speak. What I knew I could do was what I had longed to do – point out meanings mislaid here and there. Deep things not said lightly.

I was surprised at the response I got. Siobhan understood half an indication. How quick they are, actors, once they have got over the muddle of the first week.

But suddenly (Gladys's voice), 'Goodbye!' (from the wings). 'See you on the First Night!'

I could believe my ears all right. But could I grapple with it? I went over to her. I don't remember what I said. It was soothing and I was smiling. What a smile! It was like a false moustache. The thing blew over. I suppose she had meant to say it but hardly do it.

I know now (not so much then) what it's like for an actress to be nervous – to what lengths she will go. I write my part of a play in safe secrecy, but an actress has to come out on the stage in her bare skin. I think now that Gladys was at that moment really frenzied.

Arrived in Boston (was it Boston?) what a row there was over Cecil's Set. It was too white. Even he sat in the stalls in black glasses though he wouldn't admit it was for that reason.

Irene had it sprayed down. I think she started by asking his permission, but whether she got it or not I forget. Anyway she did it, and he never forgave her. And alas for many years hasn't forgiven me. Not for the spraying of the Set, but because Binkie, urged on by Irene, who was his partner in the London production of the play, got another designer to do the London Set. That I didn't know, though Cecil thought I did. I didn't know until almost the last ditch.

Cecil thought I should have laid down tools and cancelled the production of the play. Perhaps I should. But would he have done so if he had had to make such a decision about his play *The Gainsborough Girls*? I don't know. I have missed his friendship tremendously. I have suffered – if that's any joy to him. I have lost, all these years, his delicious companionship, the iron fun, the barbed comments that spring so effortlessly from him, the relentless eye – like a gardener's noting ground-elder in the social world. Long ago, some time in the war, he had my cottage here for a summer and we wrote plays, not together, but simultaneously. How patiently Diana listened to them as we read them aloud to her at Bognor (two plays on one night!). She shook her head. 'Not very good, darlings.' Mine was called 'The Long Grass' and was terrible. His was about India.

All these years that he has wiped me out of his life (until the other day when it ceased) Cecil bowed when he met me (at a party, at a First Night). A deep bow, very startling, out of Dickens. It made me laugh though my heart ached.

After George Cukor's departure it was hard to get another director. Our aura was not so good. Irene got Albert Marre. He read the script in an hour or two, handed it back and said it was Oblique (rhyming with 'bike') – accepted to do it, continued to dislike it, disliked me, disliked Irene, and loathed the words.

His name is on the programme for ever. Like an Augustus John signed by Landseer.

Dilapidated, slowed-down by the 'approximating', scenes at every scene, divided by schisms, we stumbled into Boston, hobbled into Philadelphia, took less and less money, and it was said we'd never make New York. Gladys didn't learn the words. All the comedy-replies and couplets-woven-for-laughter failed to get a laugh. It was shame-making every night.

While we were at Boston Roderick came out to join me. He came by boat. Carol* met him at the Docks, took him to her house for the night and put him on the train next day for Boston.

Roderick, of course, knew Irene, at dinner, but not in action. The moment of his arrival was at a crisis-point. Marre had taken over and was at daggers drawn with Irene and 'the author' (he hardly ever met me) over his hatred of the words. We were about to move on to Philadelphia. Carol, knowing the high, trembling heated peak of an 'Out-of-Town', arranged for Roderick to drive with them next day to stay with Samuel Hopkins Adams. This took him away for three days. On his return we were in Philadelphia.

I had a bedroom and a sitting-room. (The sitting-room for conferences.)

They were conferences of two – Irene and me. If Marre had come she would have locked the door. He had tried each day to make me write 'sensible words'.

On this particular day Roderick was expected back in the

* Carol Brandt of Brandt and Brandt, my friend and agent.

afternoon. I was on tenterhooks about Irene's cigarette-butts. There were hundreds, tipped scarlet, in bedroom and sitting-room.

'Do let's clearup,' I said, one eye on the clock.

Roderick came. We hadn't tidied. There was a strange little scene – (when Irene sees it she will cross it out – she is so secret).

I had wanted her to go away before he came. She didn't. She lingered. Our meeting, Roderick's and mine, was a clasp – never mind what age we were – of excited love. It was a clasp of the husband, the home-coming schoolboy, the lover – all in one. Irene burst into bitter tears. She fled into the next room.

'Go to her – *quick*.'

'What's the matter?'

'Never mind. *Go quick*.' He went.

Suddenly that forest-tiger (flaming, fierce, exhausted) was in pieces about her life. She sobbed. He comforted. She half-recovered and left us. I've never forgotten the forlorn, the tidal misery. She wasn't thinking of the theatre. Oh not at all.

It's not worth while describing Philadelphia – two weeks – the probable prelude to failure. I've had it since, I'd had it before. The immense hotel we were in had a man-Conference. Men filled the lifts, names pinned to their breasts as though that was the only way they had a name. Loud-speakers played hymns at the crossroads below the hotel. All that – and failure coming, and Roderick seeing it come. (He never had as yet.)

Day after day he prowled round to the Box Office. That made no difference. You can be down to nothing and yet win. Then we moved off. The elephants came and the mammoths. Giant men, giant trailers, machines with ramps. The scenery was to go into its last stand, New York and its destruction.

We too went. I suppose Marre too. I never saw him again.

* * *

Americans don't like failure. Well, I don't either. Perhaps in New York it shows up as more final, a bruise that won't go.

We went to the First Night of *The Chalk Garden*, Roderick and I, braced, holding spiritual hands. We could take it.

The Curtain went up – and *who* had written that dancing play? That play I hadn't seen yet. Gladys 'knew her words'. But oh so much more than that! It was a gay, enjoying Gladys, the difficult, halting words running like liquid amber, her timing magical, with a golden authority for laughter, the right laughter. The chuckle that says to itself: 'I know, I know!' It was a balloon of a play. It rose in the warm air to the ceiling.

At one of the intervals I heard Noël Coward get up in the stalls and say to a woman with him: 'For those who love *words*, darling! For those who love *words*....'

Success, success – but how short a time one can taste it! Is it shorter than despair?

It was Gladys's evening. Did I get to her dressing-room? I can't remember. I think I didn't: I was afraid she'd throw me out.

Someone asked me, reading this, how could this happen 'overnight'?

It happened because in comedy you must know the words so *incorporatedly* (with yourself) that you no longer think of them. You live and laugh inside them. You 'make' them yourself; you play with them, according to your capacity. And Gladys's was great. Somehow she had got to know the words in time. She never had before. It was a near thing because she mightn't have obtained the flash of responses around her, she mightn't have been able to 'play the others' as fast as a piano. But she did. And they did. I suppose there was the week-end before the Opening in which the miracle was done.

There was no party at the end. Irene went to one given by Truman Capote. Roderick and I, Harold and his wife May, went to a pub and had scrambled eggs and gin. Then back to the little hotel on Fifty-Eighth. It had an old-fashioned telephone on a stalk between our beds.

At one a.m. Harold rang and said the reviews, the famous four butchers, had dealt me a packet of glory.

'I must ring Irene! Where's Irene?'

He gave me the number of the restaurant where Capote's party was being held. After a time I managed to get her on the telephone.

'Irene....'

Sobs.

'But *Irene*...'

Sobs.

'Irene! It's a *success*.'
Then in the excessively deep voice, made deeper by tears –
'I know. I was all geared up for failure . . .
. . . and I just can't *take* success.'
We went to sleep.
At seven in the morning I woke and the other bed was empty. Oh my God EMPTY! Where was he?
'God has paid me out for success!' I cried to myself. 'He's jumped out of the window . . .' (Roderick, the last person in the world to do it.)
I twiddled the telephone on its stem for the night-clerk.
'Is there a gentleman downstairs?'
Some sort of Czech-ish ejaculation.
'A *MAN*!'
'Yes.'
'*Send him up – at once!*'
For all I knew it might have been a stranger. I heard the lift wobbling up and my door opened. In walked Roderick with a Bonwit Teller box in his hand, which he had hidden the evening before in the night-clerk's desk. (I'd forgotten! – I remembered. My birthday, my sixty-sixth birthday. An exquisite night-gown.)

Oddly enough no flowers, no parties. We sailed for England. In the months following I was given the Award of Merit for Drama by the American Academy of Arts and Letters for *The Chalk Garden*. A thousand dollars went with it and I built the little canal that crosses my garden.

Binkie couldn't have been more welcoming. There was the red carpet down, Dame Edith, Sir John Gielgud to direct, the Haymarket, the lot. Plus twenty-three months' run.

Edith was wonderful, and John made the rehearsals smooth and easy and allowed me to give him notes each night on the path we had picked our way through in America. What gave me as much pleasure in London as the Award of Merit had done in New York was Kenneth Tynan's review in *The Observer*:

On Wednesday night a wonder happened: The West End Theatre justified its existence. . . . One has thought it an anachronism, wilfully preserving a formal, patrician acting style for which the modern drama has no use, a style as remote from reality as a troop of cavalry in an age of turbojets. One was shamefully wrong. On Wednesday night, superbly caparisoned, the cavalry went into action and gave a display of theatrical equitation which silenced all grumblers. . . . The occasion of its triumph was Enid Bagnold's *The Chalk Garden* (Haymarket) which may well be the finest artificial comedy to have flowed from an English (as opposed to an Irish) pen since the death of Congreve. . . . We eavesdrop on a group of thoroughbred minds, expressing themselves in speech of an exquisite candour, building ornamental bridges of metaphor, tiptoeing across frail causeways of simile, and vaulting over gorges impassable to the rational soul.

I have given this length of description to *The Chalk Garden* because of all that's happened since.

The Chinese Prime Minister is a better play than *The Chalk Garden* but it didn't get the works.

Irene wouldn't do another play with me. And I thought then (I was wrong) that I wouldn't with her. We had both given that play too much of our lives.

* * *

It was when I got back home that I caught sight of my face (like a stranger) one day on the stairs. I felt I hadn't seen it for years and I much disliked it. I wrote a poem.

Dear Sir Archibald McIndoe,

I wish I could have a face lift
Not for anybody else but for me.
Or it might be for my husband (who loves me
But thinks I still look as I used to be). . . .

It's out of delicacy that I write to you in rhyme.
Would it be unreasonable . . . would it be out of place . . .
If I asked you to take a stitch in my face?
Its tiresome to be immortalised
By the last appearance.
I should like a sort of clearance
To antiquity.
Before I go back into the ages varnished by Time.

I don't want to be young again! I wouldn't undertake
Two such risky journeys! But it would be agreeable
In the foreseeable
Fifteen years that's left me
Not to look disagreeable....

Months, it seemed to me, went by. I had almost forgotten it. And then came a poem by Sir Archibald. He had been away on his farm in Kenya.

> 149 Harley Street.
> Sept. 17. 56.

Dear Lady Jones,

> In reply to your rhyme
> Re Old Father Time
> You've reached the Canal Turn in life;
> Just come and see me
> And your husband will see
> Mary Rose instead of his wife.
>> Yours sincerely
>> Archibald McIndoe.

He told me when I saw him that to write it had cost him sleepless nights.

By that time I had almost lost the wish to have anything done. But I went. I remember thinking in the waiting-room that it was all a lot of nonsense and that I should be able to refuse. However, I wasn't able. His certainty and his charm and my confidence in him, the whole adventure of it led me on.

'What name will you come in under?' he asked.

'What name! Why – my own.'

'Do you want everyone to know?'

'*Everyone.* So that if it isn't good it will be a sort of blackmail!' He laughed, and had me photographed.

It was to be done in the late afternoon in the London Clinic. In the early afternoon he bounded in and said, 'Let me see – it's your *nose* you want altering, isn't it?'

'NO. *My whole face!*' Out he went laughing; he had mixed me up.

I took a large pair of cutting-out scissors with me because I knew that for three days my eyes would be bound up and my head enclosed in a helmet of bandages, and I get claustrophobia. There was no pain at all after the operation, except that I imagined my ears had been cut off. The first and second days passed happily, slightly drugged, but on the third morning (still blind) a sister came in with the menu for breakfast and just as she said 'Would you like eggs or haddock?' I knew that the claustrophobia was going to jump on me like a cat. I could hardly wait for her to be gone before I felt my way to the cupboard near the bed. With the cutting-out scissors I cut through all the bandages, then held them together with my hand. The sense of bondage had gone and its terror. I rang the bell and asked for Sir Archibald's assistant, and when she came and I told her of course she was as furious with me as I deserved. But he forgave me and no harm was done.

Before I left the Clinic I asked him if I should need to have the operation done again.

'Not for ten years,' he said rather strangely, 'and then you won't want it.' Well, it's ten years and it's true I don't want it: I care too little how I look. Did he mean that?

I asked to see him again when I was trying to write a play that involved just such an operation but for different reasons.

'I'll be operating all morning but come and see me.'

I went, and he came out of the theatre covered with blood down his white overall, and blood on his white rubber boots.

'I've time. I've finished her,' nodding back at the door of the theatre. 'Sit down, and tell me what you want to know.'

'Did you take off my ears?'

'No, I just lifted them a little and tucked everything in behind.'

'How much skin did you take off?'

'Enough to cover a handbag.'

'Could you do it alone and without an assistant and with only a local anaesthetic?'

'Yes.'

He gave me every detail for my act, which was to change the features of a criminal. I wrote the act not badly, but I couldn't finish the play.

The play, if it had ever been finished, would have been for Charles Laughton, who came into my life while I was struggling with another play *The Last Joke*.

His wife, Elsa Lanchester, brought him; it was the summer of 1958.

I was bathing Timothy's daughter Annabel in the old nursery bathroom when I heard the front door bell. Down in the porch they stood, he and Elsa, he with a bunch of Downs' flowers in his hand.

I was immediately hooked with excitement, entranced; wanting Annabel disposed of in bed and simultaneously wanting to fetch ice cubes. I left them with Annabel in her bath while I fetched the cubes.

They were made shy by the child but the child was up to it (beautiful and social from four years old). I bribed her with toys and books to go straight to bed, and we sat with drinks on the lawn. This was the only time that we three talked together. Or nearly. Why? Did Elsa decide that Charles got on better with women alone? (Or better with writers?)

I instantly fell in love with the whole machinery; the electricity, the experience, the reputation, the vitality and power to charm of this ugly man. (But it was the theatre I fell in love with.) Nevertheless, at sixty-eight, it was very like love. I leave this remark on the page as a gift to women – that the incandescence can appear again in winter like a hibernated moth.

He concentrated on me. Charles's concentration was like having the car recharged. He concentrated the whole summer; perhaps even the next one. I suspected him; I was enchanted by him. He enchanted, for that matter, the whole family. I don't think he liked any corner to escape the spell. It comes to me now as I write that he was not unlike Frank Harris. The mesmerism was the same. Frank Harris's passion for 'greatness' was a bit used-up when I met him (though I was too young to know it). Charles's passion for 'greatness' (in any art, in any sphere) was real. He revived my lost understanding of painting. God knows how far he went in that. Very far. He could cross to Paris and sit among the latest of the painters, talking as an equal. He had that burning curiosity, that nimble intelligence, that recognition of beauty and wonder (not excluding science – a friend of Henry Moore and Sir Solly Zuckerman) – so that he spoke 'in the language' without an accent.

He understood to the point of involvement. But he was not a creator.

Charles Laughton was acting all that summer in a moderate little play in London (in which was the young, hardly-discovered, Albert Finney) but living in Brighton at the Royal Crescent Hotel, six minutes from Rottingdean. He became a total visitor: lunching every day except matinée days, and on Sundays he lunched and dined.

Here, all that summer, or perhaps it was the next, he rehearsed himself for 'Lear', which he was to do at Stratford. In the library his voice thundered against the low ceiling. At Stratford it seemed much smaller.

He gave us his magic, his private theatre, willingly. He was used to people under that spell. Once, when Timothy, full of unspoken criticism, came for the first time Charles whispered to me 'I feel a draught'. And set out specially to capture him.

He told stories. He inflicted the Bible and it was not an infliction. To hear him (unwarningly) change places with Bottom, having played his thickness with hanging lips and idiot delight – change places and become the Wooer (startling, unbelievable) – the Fabergé jewelled voice placed ventriloquistly high on his harp ... commending her fairies ...

> Sleep thou, and I will wind thee in my arms
> Fairies, begone, and be all ways away.
> So doth the woodbine the sweet honey-suckle
> Gently entwist; the female ivy so
> Enrings the barky fingers of the elm.
> Oh, how I love thee! how I dote on thee!

– was to believe you heard Titania.

Then glance at him, cumbersome, in his dark suit, his glasses on the end of his nose, and it was a miracle of deceit, the loveliest confidence-trick.

He had tricks. Who hasn't tricks? Art isn't all an invasion of inspiration. He was a brilliant and intellectual actor (with none of the maiming limits of the intellectual). And that was part of the charm; one was hypnotized at such a high level.

He wasn't the tops, as Laurence Olivier and John Gielgud are the tops. His glamour included a touch of the conjuror: an element that (like the now Richard Burton) needed police cohorts to protect him from crowd-adoration.

His 'fame' fascinated me. I know one or two great actors, but they are protected in the street by a quality of invisibility. Laurence Olivier especially. Charles's fame in a mob would take the Duke of Windsor at the height of the Abdication to equal it.

His unique ugliness plus the film of *Henry the Eighth* got him spotted. Spotted in a way that gave him claustrophobia. Old ladies swarmed, holding out pencils for autographs. Women pushing prams swivelled the front wheels towards him. Here on the Village Green tourists nudged each other and walked nearer, as he hurried into the car. It frightened him, he hated it, but he wouldn't have been without it. It was his honey and his cross.

When I drove him to Brighton Station to catch his 5 p.m. for his evening performance in London, I secretly tried to get him there a quarter of an hour early so that I could snatch up a joint at Sainsbury on the way home. But this he wouldn't have. '*Don't* get me to that station so early! *Don't!* I can't bear it! They mob me! Elsa always protects me.'

At first I thought he was putting it on; I watched, leaving the car in the station yard. It was true. People glanced, then looked again. 'Charles Laughton.' They clustered and closed in. It wasn't for the best in him. He was doomed and blest with it. We discussed it, I had never seen it close before. I had never seen a human being unable to lead a private life in public. It was then I tried to write the play with the face-lift in it. It would have been called 'The Monsters' (the sacred monsters). But there are plays which come on a traffic hold-up and get stopped.

Chapter Thirteen

*

'DON'T SPEAK OF THIS EVER. AND DON'T SPEAK OF YOUR SILENCE.'

On and off over six years I had been writing that play I called *At the Top of his Form*, but which was finally called *The Last Joke*. It was the play I spoke of earlier, the forbidden *Bibesco* play, which the dead Antoine inhabited with malignance, and broke up from the skies.

Whatever its weaknesses it was still a play I would have wanted to see myself; it had ideas which would have excited me if I saw it. It's very strange, and wrong, that in the theatre you have to be a 'total' success. It cheapens the inner matter.

The musicians really have collared it – fame. Nobody sits reading Keats, reading literature, as the music-public sit rapt by a Nocturne of Chopin's. Music enters more easily; it by-passes the brain. And when critics write of music they are essentially musical, and for their own musical sake they recognize what has been attempted as well as what has failed.

But in the theatre when the crash is a crash nothing constructive is said. 'This playwright might, in spite of his vile play, have it in him. . . .' No, no one says that. And the critics are not always experts on drama.

Glen Byam-Shaw directed the play. Nobody could have been kinder. He had just given up his term of directorship at Stratford. As he had had chiefly to work with Shakespeare he wasn't used to discussing points with the author. I, on the other hand, automatically expected another Irene.

However, we started. With the play as it was.

Everyone seemed pleased. Binkie was so sure of its success that he spent a great deal of money on it. The Sets, beautiful and complicated, were by Felix Kelly. I had wanted very much that Sir John Gielgud should play the part of the Tycoon. The only part he would consider, however, was the other male part – the Prince. And he would hardly consider that either. And no persuading him absolutely because he was in New York.

The point of the play was that the Prince had (mathematically) discovered God. He had worked Him out. He wanted proof. So he wanted to die. His brother, treating him as an ordinary suicide, tried to prevent him. To do so – to watch him, to devote every moment to this object, he was ready to put aside love. Of course, it being me, there were other complications: so many perhaps that the Prince-God-total-drive was obscured.

But what *was* essential to the end of the play was that the suicide should be by poison. I had my eye on Socrates. Death by the raising of a cup can be a fascinating secret between the playwright and the audience. Not 'Will he die?' but 'When?' The audience, allowed the privilege of knowledge, is agog: the peopled stage in ignorance. Also (Socrates) one can talk while dying. And in parables that the audience alone can understand. This was my carefully-worked-out drama for the play's end.

John Gielgud wanted to shoot himself. And amid fireworks. This is what he said on the telephone to Binkie from New York. The dead Antoine with a potion must have made him mad.

For so great, so beautiful, so perfect an actor he was being silly. Stars are sometimes silly, but very seldom he. *Why* shoot himself? But without a revolver he wouldn't take the part. Binkie said, 'I'm afraid it's take it or leave it.' I was weak. I ought to have said, 'Leave it.' But I sat down and dragged in the revolver, and Glen said that as there was a ball the fireworks would be easy.

John consented. Then suddenly there was a new development. Unasked and uninvited, Sir Ralph Richardson wanted to be in the play. He wanted the part of the Tycoon-Art-Collector. Glen arrived one morning here in Rottingdean and told me of this.

'But he isn't . . . he hasn't. . . . I just don't see him . . .'

'You'll find it's Box Office to have him. It'll be madness to refuse.'

'But can you manage *both* of them?' (The two Knights, I meant.)

Glen considered. He smiled (at the situation, at himself).

'No.'

And it was true. Ralph Richardson was as unmanageable as a roadblock. He thought the part suited him. It didn't. He had seen the script somewhere – probably in Binkie's office – and something in it set him on fire. Something that wasn't there.

As he wasn't in the first act, and was finishing a film in Cyprus, we started rehearsals without him.

After the first Reading, Rupert Marsh, then Binkie's stage director, said to Binkie, 'If ever a play's pretty certain of success it's this one!'

We rehearsed a week without Ralph Richardson – the first act only, the one he wasn't in. John Gielgud was brilliant. Sweet-tempered (as he always is), amusedly adaptable – 'Would you like it this way? Or that way?' – (and *all* ways he was my prince that I had written). He had the ironic authority, the grand unreason, the arrogant self-certainty that I wanted: he was not only a prince but a prince of the mind.

'I don't understand a word, darling!' He laughed. That maybe, but he understood as an actor.

Ernest Thesiger, then very old, and almost immediately to die, wove in the opening exposition, and the word-scenery which produced the atmosphere. Bit by bit this was taken from him. Glen thought his voice had lost projection.

At the end of the first week Ralph Richardson arrived, tough as oak and looking like wood. While in Cyprus he had decided his movements and at what place on the stage he would say certain lines. He began about some long gloves (in the second act) counting out his steps as he spoke. He walked, driven by his own pre-imagining, about the stage. He walked over all Glen's planning. Glen looked aghast.

Silence.

'Aren't you going to . . . *say* something. . . ?' I whispered, also aghast – for him. He walked up to Ralph, Ralph turned his empty pipe upside down and began to look like Priestley. Glen said his polite say. Ralph smiled across his pipe-bowl and said nothing. Nothing was achieved. That was the beginning of the end. That, and the fact that he had 'heard' himself beforehand delivering a certain speech so that the flesh crept. It didn't creep because of the situation: it crept because of him.

When I protested he put an arm round my shoulder (lovingmanly), smiled at Johnnie – 'We must save her from herself!'

The speech was in the third act and it had a kind of terrible contagion. Even John was not quite himself after this. He was shaken. For the first time uncertain (of himself or of me) he became 'romantic'. He blew up the lines. At rehearsal one morning he called out from the glare of the footlights, shading his eyes, 'Is Enid there?' At an assenting nod from Glen I walked up under where he stood.

'Is that how you want it?' he asked.

'No. It's too Shakespeare.'

'You don't want it Noël Coward!'

'Yes, that's just what I *do* want! I want it played against my words!'

Glen was angry with me. John never shook off 'romantic'.

In the now sick-making third act the two Knights galloped in different directions, tearing the body apart as in the Middle Ages.

Glen telephoned from, I think, Edinburgh. (I had been unable to face more of the tour.)

'Is it any better?'

'No, it's worse,' he said.

The Knights turned author on their way to London. They were my words, but sorted out and re-jammed together.

The play's end made no sense. There was some bare effect like a hound howling in the moonlight on his master's grave. John shot himself in a long cloak each night.

I bought pink taffeta for the Opening.

Roderick, my brother, my daughter and my sons, who knew the script well, couldn't recognize it. The third act was unforgivable. The critics forgot any merits there might have been in the two previous acts.

'Miss Bagnold, looking like a strawberry mash. . . .' It was a disaster.

A young man rang me up for his paper: 'What does failure feel like, Miss Bagnold?'

'Like calomel,' I said. 'If you take too much it goes right through you.'

Roderick said: 'You aimed high and you were shot down. Too much was given you and too much expected of you.' He wouldn't show that he too suffered.

The theatre and the newspaper world are alike dangerous and ruthless. Roderick knew what it was like to look down the throats of savage jaws. Northcliffe knew it. Cecil King now knows it.

I then started to write *The Chinese Prime Minister*.

* * *

Before he died I had read Roderick the first draft. He was tireless in listening. I had never known that he understood so much what I was after. As I read he knew exactly where I had heaped on 'plums' that didn't help the drama. He saw what I saw. And he saw where I kept overlaying what I saw.

He said once: 'I'm out of it now. *You* keep the flag flying! What does it matter which one of us does it!'

A first version of the play went to Harold in New York.

In the autumn of 1961 (Roderick frail, but not, I then thought, threatened) there came to Rottingdean the lawyer of the Lunts. Quite why, or how the contact was made, I don't remember. Perhaps Harold had shown him an early version of my play. He wasn't a direct emissary, yet he spoke almost as an emissary. Just as he was leaving he said: 'You ought to go and stay with them.'

'The Lunts?'

'I think they would like it.'

'But I've never . . . I've only met them once . . .' But his taxi was leaving.

I rang up Binkie.

'I can't – can I – go and stay with them without a direct invitation?'

'No. Of course you can't.'

'Might they . . . Might it be a question of *The Chinese Prime Minister*?'

'I'm going to New York tomorrow. I'll ring them and see.'

We made the autumn move up to London. There we spent our mornings as we had always done, I buried with my typewriter: he drowsily, reading the newspapers, growing older. We met at lunch – each with our minds full to bursting with separate interests – flared a little in the old way on meeting – subsided, melted, grew always closer.

Now began the long fight of the little illnesses which seem to have nothing to do with each other, and which precede death. One thing after another gets tired of its function. Each slight Unworking is a surprise.

There is no adding up. Not at first.

(I got a letter from Lynn inviting me. Of course I couldn't think of it then.)

When my father died he lay there. Everything in his room, on his body, his fingernails, was no more hidden. There was nothing private. I had power over him for which I wept. The little drawer drawn out, the fond rubbish. I took my father's brush-holder. I took his old check duster. It was the first time I had dared.

For those who have been in authority I have such bitter pity.

When my father died – he was older than Roderick, he was ninety – everything in the house stopped too. The clocks, the locks, the things he had watched and attended to. The house gave up.

Now I had another man beside me, faltering. My husband (but again my father). His clothes grew old. He wouldn't buy new ones. The little contrivances in his room broke, I was always mending them.

And so we live, after forty-two years, till everything drops away, and the hooks of friends slip, and, two in a boat, there are only we who understand each other.

I thought I knew everything about him. A week before his death I helped him with his boiled egg for breakfast.

'Do you like the top cut off? Or cracked and peeled away?'

'Don't you know?'

'No.' It was true. I didn't know. He was always alone at breakfast. We had arranged it so.

But from now on to his dying I knew at last to what a point he needed me. It was a kind of crown of wifehood, a reward every day, every hour. Everything was summed up. It was as though the 'sum' stood, and the way it was arrived at was wiped away.

There is a link below love that gets you to where you hardly see eyes or nose but the heart beating. There is a pinnacle of married life, the end.

I am a victim of remorses. They keep me awake at night. But about Roderick and about being his wife I never had self blame. All the hundreds of hours I had taken from marriage and marriage-duties were approved by him. He had never grumbled about them, never tried to withdraw them. Hadn't wanted to. And now I saw that even though he had always demanded everything from me, had let me off nothing, had made me live a double life of the highest pressure, he knew that I was equal to it, and that he had never taken my ambitious, desiring life – my happiness – from me.

It became Christmas. I seemed to be slipping between nurses – always at a tap, always in the kitchen. I didn't know what he knew. He would never have said 'I am going'. We had faced all his illnesses together all the years. They had never been really grave. He was a nervous man. But now he wasn't nervous.

Once he said, after a long silence, 'I shall never get away from this bed.' I saw with horror that one could be 'caught' in a place not chosen – the sea, a railway, a shop, a hospital bed. He would rather have died in Rottingdean. But so soon one doesn't care.

And once he said (to no one) 'I wish I was a man again.'

Why speak of the death of my husband? Is it particular? Yes it is. Nothing more wildly unlike life can be imagined than the death of one person.

Often we had spoken about death when for him it got very late on. Now it came. We had never known of that death before dying, that dividing, preoccupied silence when one is going and the other watches.

'Where?'

The face on the pillow reflects but does not answer. He is testing the last seconds of himself. The last breath is not good-bye. It comes earlier. The preoccupation with Self becomes overmastering. He had not known he would lose her. Now he felt her going.

Don't disturb the silence of that shocking parting, don't speak to the bent face, its curves hollow, its eyeballs protruded with the starvation of dying. A face like a moon's scimitar – the tissue-paper of dying.

I say (of a liquid), 'A little sip . . . darling?' The head barely shakes the refusal. Why eat? The cow and the sheep and the corn and the fruit have not died to nourish the dying.

In that stony silence I lost him. Once, with a strong, human voice for the last time he cried out (not to me, not to any living person – there was none in that landscape) –

'*Get me out of this!*'

* * *

Then you were laid back and arranged for eternal lying. Through the night the arrangement obediently took for ever the dictated position. There was severe silence. I slept.

* * *

I have been a widow three months. That sour word. Carrying with it the ancient uselessness of women deprived of men. I am one with the black-clothed women wailing in the Sudan, the quiet women in Kensington hotels, the bouncing women thriving unrighteously in bars and bridge clubs. But I can't belittle the inventions of life, even if one of them is death. It's hard to surpass this brilliance we live in. The extraordinary jungle fronded on the face of the revolving earth, waterfalls, earthquakes, deserts, cities, coloured people, coloured birds, lions roaring, and the clogged chain of buses down Oxford Street.

He is gone, and what is shocking is that after the indissoluble has dissolved I go on living. Not only living but enjoying. But the terrible warning has taken place. From now on I am poisoned.

From now on I am poisoned and I still desire fame. I can't bear to be lost with my boatload of eccentricities – things that I have picked and prised from the rocks and pockets of life. I row my boat like a demented creature to get them to the shore.

It's harder now. In my conceit, while Roderick lived, I thought I could do anything. Roderick thought so too. We grew old together he dispensing this marvellous belief. What a kindling for a writer. I don't have it any more.

This is the end of my marriage.

I say, with care, with observation, that there is a picking up of personal life in a woman after her husband's death. There has been love. There has also been a burden. There is always a burden in love. One bears two pains, two responsibilities.

In the middle years, after midnight, when Roderick said I became melodramatically melancholy, I used to cry out to him: '*What* shall I do without you....'

'You'll do very well.'

He answered carelessly, but out of his common sense. My youngest son (who so loved him) said to me after his father had gone – ' I used to wonder whether Daddy would die in time.' It was said with the same tender common sense as his father. 'In time' for me to recreate myself. To live again.

Some people are 'lit' at night. But for me – and this is just the same in age – 'perception' comes in the very early morning. Extra strong. Extra-sensory may be the word, but I don't like it. It is for this that I set my alarm clock at six-forty-five. It is for this that I go to bed when other people are still talking.

It is responsibility that is the death of this perception. Responsibility, inside a house, is specially a woman's problem. Food, dust, clothes, letters, answers to questions.

I swore to myself when Roderick died that I'd manage non-responsibility. It's not so easy after a lifetime. I said I would live like a watchful hermit; watching myself, flowers, a dog; things that don't ask questions. That I would get out of bed (dress or dressing-gown) carrying my 'perception' undamaged into the day. Freshness and solitude are vital. I must have written a lot of this into *The Chinese Prime Minister* in the long period after Roderick died and before it was produced; for this 'resolve' comes into it constantly. I gave lines to one character (a butler over a hundred):

> 'Five months,' (he says with strange joy) 'Five months of my own – what I never had before! – the sun and the moon passing over me ... And nobody saying to me the dinner's ready – nor the morning's come! – And it isn't being alone that makes the difference! – It's being alone – *without Time*!'

But habit is strong. Like an idiot I fabricate duties. And then too there has to be someone to look after me; the least possible. The house, not me. And a human being in the house takes something; a fraction, hardly noticeable. But noticeable! I have to give; pour something into a cup held out. It's a little wine, taken from myself. I mustn't grudge it. And then (the habit of a woman) indignation for work not done must be suppressed. It's a destroyer – indignation! So we live. With the minimum of battle. Plus that little glass of wine.

I catch myself talking like a young poet; not an old woman.

Why not? At present I imagine myself timeless.

Chapter Fourteen

*

So all that spring and early summer of 1962 I went on with *The Chinese Prime Minister*.

Harold then rang me from New York. A director who 'loved my play' would be coming to London.

How do you know what to feel, except grateful pleasure, when a man arrives mad about your play? We talked and set to work. I forgot that those who love my plays want to change them. – Alas – this wasn't Irene.

'Pick out that character, put her further on. In fact – keep her for the third act entirely.'

'Do you think so. . . .'

'I'm certain. And write in a new scene just in front of the third act.' A new scene? I felt astonished, but in my newfound conceit at being 'loved' I felt I could do anything!

You can sit and play with a finished work and move its pieces here and there, but in some curious way it will leak at the corners. Suddenly one doesn't know how to do any better. And – does *he* – the man to whom you are listening? You can't share the personal shine of your thoughts. They're your own. You can't tell what mirage other eyes take off the page and put into that unknown place – the Other's Brain.

What I knew, but I never can learn, because the loneliness of writing is so great and the first praise so intoxicating, is that one can sit beforehand with a man all love and understanding – love of the play, the script lying in his hands – but when it comes to rehearsal it's not the same love. The inner conception of neither has discerned the other. The man in rehearsal is not the man by the fire reading. He is affected by the troops under him. He is pulled about and changed.

The Chinese Prime Minister has a very long part for a woman. One must think about casting. This woman is nearing seventy (warning to playwrights: never name the age).

Just at that moment, as we talked of it, there came another letter from Wisconsin, from Lynn Fontanne. Wouldn't I come and stay? Couldn't I now come?

So I went. Oh with such flashing and paling excitement.

Afraid (terrified) as always by the plane – by the long way to fall, by the noise like a beast, I yet got to Chicago. Alfred (not 'Alfred' then) met me in his car with chicken sandwiches and whisky; immensely elegant, looking thirty. We drove the hundred miles to where their home is buried in wooded countryside, past villages where every clapboard house seems to stand on the grassy grave of an Indian.

That night it was later than late because of the usual time-reasons. But I was euphoric and visiting the gods. I didn't need sleep.

There, waiting for me – a summery late dinner in the garden – dressed as for a First Night at the opera – sat Lynn and Cathleen.* The impression of two women kept aside from wear and tear, in some age where there was no age, has never left me. You couldn't tell, and didn't want to know, whether they were two hundred years or twenty. The vitality, gaiety of eyes, the *flashing* came from within; not from additions. If both wore applied lashes it was as one wears gloves, a polite habit.

Alfred, seventy that year, was the baby.

(I switch into the present.)

Whenever I have been there (every summer since) nobody younger has been near us. Our level is never interfered with; no doubts come. So, nested in our timelessness, we are all young. Or – youth has nothing to do with it. Alfred and Lynn in their total success choose to live alone. They have exhausted fame. They don't want it any more. At least one of them doesn't. The other very nearly hides it.

The house rests on an orchard slope. The rooms open on different levels. The 'silver' (of a meal), candlesticks, salts,

* Cathleen Nesbitt.

peppers, are in a basket. Lynn picks it up and says, 'Where shall we dine tonight?'

There could be seven answers. Everything to do with eating is 'finished'. Nothing is picnic. Jules* is now the delicate, cherished, easily-broken artist who for thirty-seven years has cooked for them. Long ago he was Alfred's dresser. Then he and Alfred together got their Cordon Bleu in Paris.

The house, inside, is as gay as a birthday. Every strangely-ruffled, inventedly-pleated, fobment of chintz, of muslin, has been made by Lynn's fingers. She has a private sewing balcony and an electric sewing machine as complicated as a lathe; and uses all the sewing 'feet'. It practically makes up her face for her.

A swimming pool, a studio across the orchard, the sound of an apple falling. A fringe of trees and the rest silence. Lakes, scrub, forest, Lynn and Alfred have bought the land for miles around.

(Letter to Georgina)

Remember this when you are 77 (it's as a gift to you that I say it) that nothing has lessened the ecstasy of walking with bare feet over the dew, between the shades of apple trees, down a slope to write in a little wooden studio at 8.45 in the morning. They say people can't feel as much when they are old. They can.

Inside this fastness endless visitors at every meal – their Past. Nobody comes: they invent them. We dress expressly for this each night. Alfred talking, Lynn correcting, Alfred stopping with a smile, Lynn proceeding, Alfred interrupting. These are not memories that most married couples could manage without flames – communal, personal, pre-marriage, post-marriage.

'No! It was *not* like that! *Not* like that!' But this makes a double level to the picture: the music of the past every night has a bass and a treble.

Early days at Alfred's local school, characters, schoolmates, I still see them in the village. 'How's Alfred?' – (the policeman, the barber); his past in Finland on his mother's second marriage, his step-father's strange death in a Finnish hotel when

* Jules Johnson.

the boy shared his bedroom, the black, behorsed, be-draped funeral, the Finnish step-aunts, the coming strain of, 'How shall we live?' The anxieties, the lack of money, the daring steps taken – Alfred's more frightening than Lynn's for he had his mother and sisters and brother to keep alive.

Lynn says, 'Tell Enid' . . . and rushes in to rearrange the story's angle.

Alfred's mother, Harriet . . . (they both take up the tale) lived in this house, and for long after they were married; irresponsible, flamboyant, a dresser-up each night (from old trunks and cupboards of 'play' clothes such as children use), living the 'actress-life' that Lynn didn't live, singing Temperance songs (Lynn sang them to show me), living very long, very old, and always a handful.

Photographs of her are everywhere. The Tales of Harriet light up the room. More brilliantly and less infuriatingly because now she isn't here.

It must have been odd to be Queen of the American stage and to have a mother-in-law who was queen of a stage in a dream.

This is the setting. But when I got there nothing was said about *The Chinese Prime Minister*. Nothing next night. Nothing next. I had supposed I should stay two or three days, and for this special purpose. I don't know what had been originally meant, nor exactly why I was there, nor what Binkie had said on the telephone, nor what had happened since.

After three enchanted evenings and not a word about the play, I burst out and asked them. There was smiling inscrutability. I was to fetch it downstairs and read it aloud.

True, Lynn liked reading to herself, but Alfred liked listening. His eye hurt him.

The little reading that took place would break out at the edges into theatrical discussions, and run down long alleys and give rise to the past. It was a deliberate mist raised by long experience. In the hall outside the drawing-room there were piles of unopened envelopes with scripts. In the gentle arrogance of such a royal lifetime they toyed with scripts they would never read but which might prove wonderful. Looking back on it now I understand perfectly that they didn't deal in yes or no. But they liked me. And I adored them. We talked of my play but bit by bit I let the subject drop. Bit by bit I found this experience of the

Lunts more important than a play that was finished. *They* were a play, a new one. Ah, if I could only do that!

I shall never quite understand how I got there. But I know why I went on going. It was for the enraptured fastness of that magic garden, for the weeding of the one and the sewing of the other inside the play they were always playing... 'When we get the right script...' (What hope – what torture.)

That was the first visit.

The next time I met them was in New York in 1963. I had come out to work again with my director.

When I got there he said: 'We are to go to the Lunts.'

(New hope? New hope?)

'Why?'

'I don't know, but Roger Stevens* also will be there.'

The Lunts' New York house is a doll's box on the East River. Squirrels look in at the windows. Since then I have stayed there.

Tea was in the drawing-room.

Alfred said: 'You know – if we *were* doing this play I would want to play Bent, not the husband.' He was on his feet, 'drawing on' the part, amused at himself, his eyes twinkling.

Lynn whispered to me: 'Don't build hopes, darling. He'll reverse it in the morning.'

Reversed it was. Not in the morning but three days later. They had done the first day's televising of *The Old Lady Shows her Medals*. Alfred was in a state. Alfred's states have always been Lynn's preoccupation. Before a play he all but makes himself ill, grows fevered. Would 'it' come – that living thing he gives to a play? He wasn't going to risk it again! No, no! – He'd rather go gardening!

(So Alfred always tells me when I stay in Genesee that he has 'had such a perfect day weeding'. He wants to rub it in that he no longer wants the theatre. Lynn listens to this and makes no comment.)

* * *

The refusal was definite: the chance gone. So what? So Ina Claire?

Superb comedienne, no longer needing money, a married,

* The Management.

happy woman, who only toyed with a return to the stage. (But always there's the chance. Once they've had it they may want it again.)

She came to New York from California (it can't have been for me, she must have wanted her hair waved). A meeting was arranged. I took to her: I think she took to me. She talked and talked. She was famous for never stopping. I asked her to stop.

'Why?'

'I want to talk about my play.' She took this as it was meant – ('Let's get down to it.')

'All right,' she said aloud, 'dine with me and read it aloud to me after dinner. My eyes ache.' She had the directness of Diana. I wasn't afraid of her, I knew where I was. It might have worked.

My director at once intervened. It was *his* job! *He* would read it to her. The light went out of the faint chance. He was no reader.

She toyed with him as she toyed with her return to the stage. She kept him dining while she talked, and wouldn't listen to a word till near midnight. They got through one act.

He lost her. He was relieved to lose her. He knew she would have been too much for him. She wouldn't have been for me.

* * *

So back to London. Then Maggie* came into my life. But not at first securely! No one comes into one's life securely when it's a play. It's like fishing. It's like a mayfly with trout . . . 'Are the fish feeding?'

(Edith had wanted to play Madrigal instead of Mrs St Maugham. Peggy† didn't want to play anything but she did. John Gielgud. . . . So it goes on! A seesaw of agony.)

With a thousand yesses and noes – with persuasion from my friends who were also hers, with heart-shaking anxiety, finally Maggie came to rest – a most beautiful fish.

This extraordinary and shining woman, not seventy by thirty years, humble as a dog, nervous as a cat, made of moonshine and talent and deep self-distrust, astonished at success, sure it must be an accident – yes – she would do it.

* * *

* Margaret Leighton. † Dame Peggy Ashcroft.

Before I went to America I wrote inside the cover of my working script – 'Don't try to be popular'.

It's fine to be popular. You've only to say nothing and you're liked. I love being liked. But who would suffer longest if you barter your play to be popular? The warm group dissolves, the director gets new work and you're left with the failure. It's you who get the blame.

* * *

I had Maggie. I had Alan Webb. We three went to New York determined to be well-behaved, not to interfere, not to be clannish, not to be English.

I was not in time to stop a fabulous sum being spent on the Set. It had all the faults of the Set of a play that you look at and don't hear. It was done by the most expensive designer.

I was told only the other day (by the Set-designer of *Call Me Jacky*): 'Oh I never look at the author's directions for the Set!'

Why not? Am I not the author who wrote them? I looked across some forty-eight years at this boy of thirty and contemplated his confidence. It will fade, of course. He has not in him what I have. But none of them have, the workers in the Court Circle of the Theatre – the Set Designers, the Management, and I include the Director. One isn't dealing with artists, but with Adaptors. The imaginative levels are poles apart. This is the great difficulty of writing for the theatre. The actors, searching in what I have written for the thing that is living, without which they will fail, *they* are my countrymen. (Except a Star who has become unmanageable; since too much glory is too strong a meal.)

On that first day in an empty theatre on Broadway, meeting together – the Company and the Play – my play's 'lover' made a speech about his love. For the first time I knew that he loved the wrong woman.

I want to say here that this was a man of honour, a concerned and kind man, a man of loyal enthusiasms. But when one steps out of the world into the theatre there are different levels of truth. He was to face me with his career at stake. I was to face him with my 'findings'; things drawn and concluded from living; in some way too my own portrait. I faced him with a play that I had partly written before Roderick died, and that had a new depth (for me) of experience. If this was threatened with disaster sharp and deadly things would be done in battle.

For the first time he was speaking, not to me, but about his professional business, and there ran out a landscape I had never caught sight of before. It was a strange lyric speech (no mention of comedy) that told the actors nothing, and told me that everything was wrong. After all the adjusted talk between us he had come out on the wrong side of the page. It wasn't like that – the play. It couldn't work like that. I didn't say so. But without a word from me he knew I knew it. He asked me to go and sit in a dark box near the footlights, from where my face, eyes, expression, would not show.

The Casting had been half done before I reached New York. The younger son in the play was written as being very intimate with his mother. In ancient Greece that would be incestuous. Since Freud it's homosexual. I only meant that the son got along well with his mother.

Fearing the Freud-implication they had cast a shaggy manly fellow. They threw a sort of labrador into poor Maggie's lap. I wouldn't accept him. I had a Veto. I said he must go.

The Management (Roger Stevens, a strong and gentle character) was specially got down to rehearsal to reason with me.

I watched his big figure angling among the empty stalls towards my cage. Leaning over the parapet he said, preparedly casual, 'Not so bad – that boy – don't you think?'

I was alone, immovable, afraid (but none showing) and the old sea captains spoke up from the space before I was born.

'Get rid of the bastard.'

Roger went quietly back. 'I see what you mean' (I was told he said), 'you'd better get rid of him.'

In that box, like a prison, and dirty with crumbs and old programmes, I sat for days – for the three weeks' rehearsals, and watched the time being used up in debating where the actors should stand!

It was the *play* that needed all the time in the world – three weeks! – Not 'Where shall we stand?' 'Break it up' – 'Make the move to the window'.

I set my teeth and swore to myself that I would have patience, that I would keep my mouth shut, that I would remember every moment that the director has to speak a different language, that the play I had written would presently come through. It showed no signs of it.

He told me he would prefer I never spoke to the actors. All right, I never spoke to the actors.

I had one major ally, Alan Webb.

But I knew what the play was about. Alan didn't care what the play was about because he could do it. No one could ever be nearer the perfection of comedy.

Maggie was in deep distress. She had all the weight of the words on her shoulders. There was so much in this odd, elliptical play that she didn't understand as yet. Intense, intelligent, anxious, nervous as a violin string, she tried to cope. I could have helped her with the meanings in the speeches; but then she knew already that what I would tell her was not what she was getting from her director. She knew she would be divided with a quarrel on her hands. Her beautiful eyes pleaded with me: 'Don't speak! Don't speak!' And I didn't.

But she was like an imprisoned bird of paradise among us, liable to go mad.

There was Toronto just ahead. Toronto with a play like a flattened-out poem, not a comedy! Not pointed up, not fit to get a murmur. Maggie was faithfully trying to act as though she was in reality seventy. Was no one going to relieve her of this harness of age? I had written of age as a special landscape; age as known to me, curious, not devoid of pleasure; a time for adventure (when the duties got less). So what was Maggie doing getting out of chairs with stiff knees?

Through Alan I got the message over to her that it was all against my meaning, and left her to work it out for herself.

But when she spoke to him my director knew at once where that had come from! He and I had had these arguments in London. He was furious. It was the swift, offended fury of a man who had been wounded before in his life. His scars flushed easily. It took on the guise of vanity, but it wasn't vanity. You have to be married to a man or make a play with a man to know these things. He had wanted to be a writer. Then an actor. Thus he became a director.

The first review in Toronto said that there was too much movement, so more time was spent in undoing that. Maggie, after Toronto, would have got out of the play if there was any way of doing so. But there wasn't – luckily for me.

She rightly (theatrically speaking) depended on her director. But she was getting nothing from him; and she was moving into the jaws of death.

Thus we went to Boston.

In Boston, the snow, new dropped, piled to the skies, was dramatic. The cars round The Common were buried. Twenty-seven people were in the theatre, scattered separately: you couldn't try yourself out against that. We got the first (terrible) review.

A taxi-driver, carving his way through the soft fabulous stuff, said, pointing to the theatre: 'You bin to that?' I lied. 'No.'

'Kind of a tacky show, they say.'

What Herman Shumlin had said ten years before when we started *Gertie* was true again. 'You and I will end in dreadful battle. You may leave America loathing me.' I don't, and didn't, loathe my director. But in the end he loathed me.

I had, up till then, done anything that could be done through him. That is the accepted way, though, God knows, I think there should be a better one. How can you keep the very fount of the material you are working with under your thumb?

But now, with New York to come, I cared no longer about manners, discretion, usage. I fought openly, to the extent that it now should be known that I would talk to Maggie. My director from then on wouldn't speak to me. I got used to his back. And Maggie herself was panicked, distraught, unsure. Who was she to listen to? She was so afraid of the torture of double-direction.

It was Alan who soothed her. This beautiful actor – this acid, doubly-gifted, contemptuous, witty man – believed in me, believed I could blow away the fog that was settling over the play. At long last, Maggie and I talked about the script together. She still looked wild, as though she had come through a long illness. But bit by bit, like a gazelle with golden eyes starting out of its head, she stepped nearer, slender hoof after slender hoof. We could laugh. She hadn't laughed since she left New York.

It wasn't *I* who made the difference. It was Alan, in his own way, interpreting me. She hadn't been finding things funny. Alan was the wizard who mentioned that.

Maggie is someone who finds her own life tragic and turns it into laughter. 'It's a comedy, darling,' he said. 'It's just up your street.'

This is a man who looks glum in rehearsal, makes his small difficulties, grumbles away, and ends up by making an audience laugh if he says and but or if. It's a risible tickle of genius. It's a timing of such a quality that he holds you in his hand. Some of this he communicated to Maggie.

We had two weeks in Boston. The same reviewer was asked to come again in the second week. He reversed his judgment – openly – in his newspaper. This was an enormous help between Maggie and me in the matter of 'trust'.

So then New York.

For the Opening in New York I asked Tucker to fly out and be with me. He said he would. I wonder if he can ever know the extreme of delight it gave me. He knew of my terrible wish to succeed and had said to me once in the greenhouse here when he was showing me what one could do with plant-solution: 'Can't you be *plainer*, Mummie?' 'No, I can't,' I said. 'I can only hint.'

'But when you talk you say things so directly!'

Which made me think of Alfred Lunt's remark: 'What the devil comes between you and the white paper!'

I went to meet him and the plane was very late. ('He's been killed, and I've killed him.') But he wasn't. He was only late.

It was New Year's Eve in Times Square and our heads were tickled with ticker tape. The buses didn't run and after a late supper we walked from Sardi's to 58th Street, (the last four blocks without my shoes). Next evening he was to see my Preview. In the afternoon I got him tickets for *Who's Afraid of Virginia Woolf?* and regretted it instantly when he had gone. After *that* play what was he going to think of mine?

That night Maggie was flat, down on the ground. She has this way of being a miracle, or a nervous tall woman fiddling with words. I had a terrible cough. I couldn't stifle it. Maggie could hear it. For the next night I bought some cough mixture.

'Don't shake it!' I said hurriedly to the drug-store man. I could see as it stood on the shelf it had sediment in it, I knew it was chlorodine. Carrying the bottle like a new-born baby I poured off the top in the street when I got outside.

✳ 262 ✳

The Library at Rottingdean

Up the stairs from Old Hall into New Hall, North End House
(*photographs by Richard*)

Roderick about 1951

Roderick in the courtyard, with
Zoë and Edward, 1952
(*photograph by Richard*)

The next night was *the* night, newspaper night. Maggie walked into the play with her magic; that thing she owns and that so terrifies her because she can't count on it. She had it that night; she glittered. She made the play glitter. Tucker and I had been as nervous as cats. He had failed to convince me that he 'adored' the Preview. I drank my cough-sediment but I didn't really need it. The whole play hung on Maggie's shoulders, and the slender shoulders lifted it till it soared. It wasn't even spoilt by Tucker's scrambling out of the third row of the stalls to be sick in the Men's Room. He had eaten shark at luncheon. Someone said it was navel-string trouble: but it wasn't, it was shark.

Afterwards there was a supper party in a top room at Sardi's, and we waited passionately for what the papers would say. Unlike earlier times the reviews are now telephoned through about eleven-thirty.

There was a stir at the far end of the supper-room. Tucker went to see. He came back towards me scribbling on a pad the words that he remembered from the telephone. They were glorious words for me. And glorious for Maggie. When I read the reviews in full, Walter Kerr and Howard Taubman had crowned with blessed agreement all that I had tried for in the long isolation of writing. No happiness higher.

If I quote – (in my own autobiography) – it is because the praise given had been striven for so long and denied me so often. That praise is part of my life. I remember it as a medal won for courage. And when I returned to London the medal was taken off.

Walter Kerr wrote in the *Herald Tribune*:

I find myself touched by *The Chinese Prime Minister* ... because there is not a single careless line. It shimmers on the stage – like a vast insubstantial spider's web, strung with bits of real rain. The lines are thoughts, not echoes, not borrowings.

– and –

Enid Bagnold, as must be obvious, is a playwright who is beyond caring for her box-office future or her literary past ... She sees [life] and writes the wild thing down without a misplaced or echoed word. ...

Margaret Leighton plays with the shimmering composure of a fine piece of crystal.

New York Telegram and Sun (Norman Nadel):
Chinese Wit and Acting light up Broadway Season.
Enid Bagnold wears intelligence like a jewel . . . This jewel of a mind last night lit up our theatre season with *The Chinese Prime Minister* at the Royale.

So Maggie and I were through.
We went on to a second supper in her apartment. It was there that the Company was given white china rosebuds from our director. Mine had a small card tied to it, 'To a Monster'.
A joke? – No joke? I put it aside.
Lyn Austen, Roger Stevens's deputy manager, asked me to farewell drinks at Sardi's the night before I was to sail. A snowstorm with a hurricane blew up all in a moment. It was like white sheets waving in the streets. At my little hotel on Fifty-Eighth the commissionaire said (so that he himself might stay in the warm) 'Walk a bit down Seventh Avenue. You're sure find a cab.'
I started down the Avenue, hissed at and blinded. I had no hat, no gloves, and as I went on and on (no cab) the pain in my ears, my forehead, my hands, was like different kinds of toothache. I set my teeth and walked the whole freezing way to Sardi's. It was practically empty. Even the Cloaks Girl hadn't come.
There was Lyn Austen. But she was sitting with two other people.
'Oh. . . .' (It was my director's wife.) 'Your poor hands!' She took them and rubbed and rubbed till life came back into them. He was standing there waiting. He wore a curious pullover against the cold, that had large blue lozenges on it.
When my hand came alive I put it out to him. He refused it.
'*When did you first mistrust me?*' (He. To me.) I sat down, his wife on my left, Lyn Austen on my right, both silent. He remained standing. I spoke direct into the blue lozenges.
'At the first day's Reading when you spoke to the actors.'
'*And then?*'
Staring at the lozenges the dreadful words came easily.

'When you weren't man enough to stand up to Ina Claire.'

The interchange was bitter and horrible. Words came like flashes from a rifle.

'You've ruined my life,' he said.

'For a man of fifty-three with a beautiful wife and two brilliant children your life's easily ruined.' I said.

He walked round to me.

'Lyn asked us to stay and eat with you. Shall we do that? Or would you rather we eat at another table?'

I thought.

Then quite gently (the storm was over): 'After what we've been saying to each other I honestly don't think we could either of us bear it.' So they went to another table.

I hadn't meant to add the Sardi story to this chapter. I could hardly bear to.

But I showed the chapter to Laurian and she said: 'But it doesn't make sense unless you tell it *all*.' So I noted that she noted the omission. So I've told it. He has never forgiven me. I don't think he has.

Chapter Fifteen

✻

AND now for London. How will I fare? – I seldom fare in London. The words, from *The Chinese Prime Minister*, seem to have been invented by Dame Edith, so like are they to those silver arcs of speech that she threw out as she paced her drawing-room in *The Chalk Garden*. It is Edith who speaks out of *The Chinese Prime Minister* as the script lies on your knee.

Even the theme was exclaimed by her, one night at Stratford years before when she had played so brilliantly and gallantly with a broken arm. 'Oh, write me a play about age! The *pleasures* of age!'

But I did not write it for her. I wrote it for myself. The play (I quote) is about 'the fascination and disaster of growing old'. No, I didn't write it for her, but her voice blew over the typewriter, her cadences, her 'lassoes' like ribbons in a wind.

Dame Edith Evans has her place for sure. She stands in the line of great actresses. She has – that beautiful and hackneyed word – Star-Quality; which, as Sickert said long ago, can shine, on peacock days, like a plume of luck above your genius. It has its nervous side, too. It's not capturable at will.

She is a lone dog in the theatre: not really entering that warm, if shallow, mateyness. She has no one to chide her and to tell her how to behave; and often she doesn't behave. In talk she can't tap common coin (no change in her purse); but a ten-pound note can fall out.

How marvellously she approached her part in *The Chalk Garden*. 'I shall pull on garment after garment till I get the right one. Don't *speak* to me while I'm pulling them on!'

And I didn't. I watched her. Tireless, determined, she was morose with the difficulty of putting truth into the character I had drawn (in words she didn't, by ordinary standards, understand). I'd rather say she understood bottom upwards. She gets her genius out of her boots.

We achieved lunching together with never a word about the play. But a moment came when she exclaimed at last: '*Now!* – You can give me one criticism! – Just one.'

I hesitated. The temptation was great. There was one – oh so small – suggestion. It was when, if a pause were put in the middle of a line, a finer point could be made at the end. I said it.

'*THERE!*' she cried out with extreme vexation. 'Now you've caused a block! I shall dry up when I get to that line!' She didn't dry up but I took in the desperate need not to be tampered with. I got out of it when she asked me again.

When she had completed the job she stood miles high – impregnable. She never had the gay, comedic timing of Gladys but she had a sweep and a grandeur unmatched.

I laid the gun cotton. She lit it. I thought she would be the same for ever. Oh alas.

The Chinese Prime Minister, begun in 1961, worked on through '62 and '63, had opened in New York in January '64. And now that I had come back to London with my handful of triumphant personal reviews, Binkie said she still wouldn't play it as it was. She wanted changes.

'What changes? – Why?'

'Well dear . . .' Binkie never explains: he's too wise.

But he came down and talked to me in the garden here – of how, vaguely, the changes might go. Nobody mentioned emotion. Binkie, that guarded marvel, held it back.

When one has finished a play, then in conceit and loneliness one thinks one can rewrite it, and better. One can't. It's not at all that it's perfect, but to 'develop' changes the tune.

I listened. It all seemed possible.

I set out on a new voyage – to capture Edith. Should one do this? But what is a dramatist to do?

You can't write a play without an actress. And such an actress – such a beauty of an actress – so variable, so without judgment, so triumphant. A stupid genius.

'I don't mind age! I don't recognize it!' she had boasted. She didn't know then what it would steal away.

I wrote and wrote and expanded and wrote. More than a year passed. To spend that time at my age is mad. But it was mad not to have Edith.

At last there was to be a meeting with Binkie at the Globe Theatre. Edith and I met in the foyer, both too early, and sat clumsily on a leather sofa; she thick-coated, tired, not happy. We said it was cold. So it was, in every sense.

Upstairs with Binkie she had her eyes unfavourably on me. Never very articulate, she spoke of still more changes. I felt like an elastic that wouldn't stretch any more. Would it be that fatal revolver of *The Last Joke* over again?

It was one of her bad days. She was lonely in the country. It was winter. She doesn't really garden, I think. Her flowers are only her adopted children. Catching hold of the tail-end of a sentence that might serve (but hardly served) (could we have been speaking of death?) she broke out petulantly: 'No one will go to *my* funeral!'

I laughed. 'They will if you behave!' (She would let me scold her if not on the stage.) She cheered up at my tease; it spelt intimacy. But it led on, with a sigh: 'If only you'd give up the social world...'

'What?' – Binkie looked astonished.

We were back at that old grudge (as it had been with Gladys) – that misconception that I lived in the 'great' world – the 'it' world, as Arnold Bennett called it, in that difficult and for me out-dated frivolity. I didn't: but they wouldn't believe it.

Where does it come from that old label? From my past? Which past? The Chelsea, the Catherine d'Erlanger, or the hard-working world of Lady Jones?

Long ago it had passed through Edith's mind that I might be a friend. She had mistaken my stage-worship.

But I on my side knew that a dramatist and a Star actress can rarely be friends. They are in a high sense enemies from the start. And this she had once, in talk, agreed. She had signed herself gaily in a letter to me 'your servant'... But as a king might say it to his country.

Who serves who? For it's not really collaboration. The arts are too different. *One* has to be master. It used to be the Star.

In Henry Irving's time it was the dramatist who was the vehicle. But for the last forty years the battle has been on. Ibsen had his deep troubles. Shaw was made of steel. For all they make use of his novels now, Henry James fled from the stalls to wander, broken, about London. So Ethel Sands told me – who went that night with him.

When a man goes through six years' training to be a doctor he will never be the same. He knows too much.

When a real actress spends her life in the theatre she talks their language and not mine. An Abyssinian to an Eskimo. She is changed by something that is thousands of years old. She is in a fortress behind a fortress behind a fortress. Knight them – Dame them – it will always be the same.

The meeting was neither this nor that. More work to be done. More time went by.

At last I was to lunch with her at her country home. 'Yes, she would probably do it.' (Binkie.) I was to meet her agent there.

We lunched; not a word about the play; went into another room for coffee (still no play).

'It's four o'clock,' I said. 'Are we going to speak of the play?'

'Yes,' Edith said. And went to sleep. Her agent and I looked at each other. Was it yes to the play? Or yes to speak about it?

She woke in a minute.

'Are you going to do the play?'

'Yes' (irritably). 'I'll have to! Everything costs so much.'

I was opening my mouth but she broke in crossly: 'I've had to buy another car!'

(To say something) – 'What kind?'

'Black,' she said shortly, and went to sleep again.

In spite of the total lack of pleasure, we got ourselves agreed and I drove back through Kent to Sussex.

Casting began (what a gamble). There was Alan, thank God. And I had Edith.

Binkie, very generous when he decides to spend, got the newest, most expensive young Set Designer. Out of my description, 'an old, once-fashionable house in London', he built me a castellated Set in Venice. Never mind, I had Edith. For some strange reason Binkie got a film star as 'husband' for Edith. He was the nicest man, and good-looking: but not rightly cast.

Vivian Matalon to direct. He had his work cut out. I think,

but shall never know, that he understood the play. I liked him from the start, but what was the good of that? He might have produced... Again we shall never know. For the play that came on the stage wasn't the one I had written nor the one he had wanted to direct.

He put out in his bark and ran into the *Queen Mary* stuck on a rock.

Oh what bad luck Edith and I had struck together! And at what a moment in our lives and after so much work.

If she had said: 'Enid, the speeches are too long for me,' though it would have been agony I could, I would have cast away the sailing ribbons I had written for her voice, for her wizardry.

Walter Kerr, in the *Herald Tribune*, had said in New York that this play 'was written with a steady, open, impish and boldly questioning gaze that will not take sentiment for an answer'. Would Edith play it that way? No. She found tears where she could. In the script there were none given her.

There are not many great subjects. Love (happy or unhappy, variations of jealousy, infidelity). Death. The dramatist tries to find a new way to serve them. But tradition on the boards has its old tricks. Watch out for them.

Take death, for instance.

Every writer who copes with death has to touch this terrible old nuisance with a new wand. Mine – in that play – was curiosity. The curiosity (about death) of the Living.

The old butler of a hundred (Alan Webb) pops lightly in and out of death. He dies twice. You can't weep over a man who dies twice. It must mean something else.

At his first death his Employer, his Mistress, observes him.

'So that's death,' she comments. 'No sound. No pain.'

Her Daughter-in-Law:
'You are thinking of yourself!'

Edith's answer:
'Everyone's death is a sample of the medicine we'll soon be taking.'

These are cool words. For a long time she wouldn't say them.

She leant over him, smothered his carefully-described appearance. Self-indulgently and delicately she wept.

Over this at rehearsals there was scene after scene. 'Am I not to weep for my old butler!...'

I was silent. Vivian got the works. When he protested she stood up and said, into the air, into the empty stalls: 'If this isn't a moment for emotion I simply don't understand this play!' She didn't: but she wouldn't listen.

Vivian said (like George Cukor years before): 'Ask Enid.'

'Oh it's no good asking Enid! She's too intellectual!' (*Me.*)

How could I be angry with her for being old? I am old myself. But I saw where we were going, what disaster I was in for. My play was written without pity. 'Savagely,' as Kerr said. Now she was going to milk it for sentiment; and no stopping her. Why do I write this? Because it's curious. In the books about the great actresses there is always something not said, not known. What happens between the dramatist and the interpreter? How is the 'coat' put on? Is it strained, pulled, or distorted? How much does the dramatist give in? How much does he resist? What do we know of Mrs Siddons, except that she was great, and a handful? They are all handfuls, the great ones. Even if the intention is distorted – the coat must be *made* to fit.

In May 1965 I went to the First Night in London with Terry and Cuthbert.* We sat in misery. She hadn't wanted to understand the play, and it had now become un-understandable.

Cuthbert murmured, 'You should never have let it come "in"...' I murmured back, 'Could I have stopped it?'

Are critics bemused by Stars? Going night after night, don't they get over that measles? Can't they isolate, in an offered production, the various collaborative components? I think no. I think they can't.

I was ready for compromise – but I wasn't ready to see my cool theme wrapped in butter. That 'sentiment', the absence of which Walter Kerr had admired, filled in the gaps and bound the play. Hung with feeling perhaps it worked better that way. I'd rather never have written it. I never saw it again, I never went back.

*　　*　　*

'I can't forget what happened as I could not forget it if I had been struck.' (Tchekov.)

* Terence Rattigan and T. C. Worsley.

NEW YORK

Walter Kerr: New York Herald Tribune:

The obvious word for a lofty, detached, unpredictably witty play of this sort is 'civilized'. But I think we should do Miss Bagnold the justice of trying to avoid obvious words. 'The Chinese Prime Minister' might more nearly, more properly be called humanely barbaric.

* * *

T. C. Worsley: The Financial Times, London:

... a comedy of manners depending for its success on style and speed. .... The protagonist is acted by a famous player who has cultivated an idiosyncratic manner to the point of art. What this player has specially seen in the script is the chance to exploit this idiosyncratic manner to the delight of many admirers. The player's style and the play's style are now at odds: we are heading for disaster. But the famous player is too set to adapt the famous style to the play's style. Lines which ought to be dry, thrown away, lightly dropped, are milked for their 'warmth', soppified, sentimentalized.

Of course it does not work. The author's intention is fatally distorted. And then what will be the verdict? Of course Shoot the Author, while the famous player receives handsome bouquets for a characteristic display which has in fact ruined the play.

LONDON SHOWCASE FOR THE DAME

The Chinese Prime Minister at the Globe

'... humanely barbaric ...'

(Photograph by Angus McBean)

Chapter Sixteen

※

So (not forgetting) I began another play. It took me two years.

Binkie read the first act but as there were two more to come he was non-committal. He didn't seem pleased. Whoever reads the first act – on paper – (*Call Me Jacky*) ought to laugh. It didn't work like that on the stage.

Frank Hauser wanted it. The Hampstead Theatre Club wanted it. Donald Albery, a man never certain, backed it in some cautious way to bring it to London. Elek Books has now printed it as one of the four plays of the year. There must have been something lying on those pages. Let us not go through this again. Failure becomes boring.

Frank Hauser directed. He had difficulties. He treated me beautifully. Albery attended the casting. A repetitive man – very hot on the right vintages. There was haste over the rehearsals. It needed more time and more intimacy to discover the barely-indicated, shrugged-off knowledge hidden in remarks and responses.

Once more I was in hell and near heaven and battling with ambition (not to say the compromise with art that is the bloody heart of the theatre).

We Opened.

I felt like a Japanese painter who had reduced his scenery to a single line and mislaid it.

The critics loathed it at Guildford, loathed it in Brighton, and doubled the loathing at Oxford.

Albery came up, took a look, and went back to London to wait for the Sunday papers.

The *Observer* critic (a nice man, I hear) wrote as though he had seen vomit on the stage. In his review he said he couldn't listen, so it wasn't odd that he got the theme the wrong way round. I was so astonished to read that I had written what I hadn't written that I asked him if I might send him the script. He wrote to say that he *had* got it wrong. A nice letter. But too late.

The play stopped short as though it had had a stroke. Later than was polite we got a cease-fire from Albery.

The director took me through the pass-door to the wings. The assistant-stage-manager was operating the final Curtain. His finger, on a knob, brought it up, down, up – and finally down. We slipped through on to the stage.

There stood my Group, my imagined creatures, unmoving, silent, facing the hidden, receding audience. Disciplined, historical, in motley, they heard the masses shuffle to the doors. The noise died away. The director said (and they turned back out of stone): 'I am very sorry to tell you that we end on Saturday.'

I felt like a ship that has put to sea and drowned its passengers. But they wouldn't have that. No, they crowded round me. 'We knew the risks! We knew what we took on when we became actors.'

Then, softly, someone said: '. . . but a long run would have been nice.'

Oh God so it would.

I said goodbye next morning. It was a most lovely day. I was pretty old and driving myself home from another failure, but a most peculiar song was singing in my breast. Of certainty. I was sure of my talent but not yet sure I had found the key.

As I drove my mind glittered. I felt a radiance and a shower of words. But the horns of the cars behind blew me forward and I couldn't stop. I wanted to tell of this glorious heart-breaking and little-known adventure – the horror, haste, hope and compromise of putting on a play.

And of its failure, when one bows, riddled with arrows like Saint Sebastian, before a condemning public.

No blood from the arrows falls on the blue sash (kept private from the days of Uncle Lexy). I draw the arrows out and drop them in the dustbin and nothing at all has happened to me. I am not in pain.

And I don't know why. Except that I think I am right and that they are wrong.

At the end of the week I lay on the sofa listening to my play dying. I knew by the clock where they were and what they were saying. I hope it died well.

I felt dull (and I like to feel drunk with expectation), dull with the play's loss – not all the time, never unbearable, never in the morning. And dull too with the loss of that surrounding belief of the twelve people most close to me on the play's small run. Its death made me think of my own. But I don't think I shall die. I think I shall escape.

That night Richard put Mozart on his gramophone. The room filled with a light, mathematical, repeating pattern, chilly and exquisite as a blackbird. Once again I thought with jealousy of that musical art which can preserve its shape through nearly two hundred years. And I, who can't even throw my pattern from my head on to the boards of the stage: and not because I can't but because they won't let me try. I should like not only to direct my plays but to *conduct them with a baton*.

How many years have I been writing plays, the hours so happy as the pages come together. To me it's an ascent of hard and grinding joy till I reach the peak and come out into the open. Then comes the destruction!

There are as many ways of writing a play or a book (or one's life) as there are flowers in the field. But only one tickles your fancy. The first and the lightest decision is the only originality. Forsake that and the governess-intellect begins sorting again.

I get sick of how well I write (like one's face in the glass). I get sick of those two voices – the one that speaks first and the one that (instantaneous, overlapping) suggests the improvement. Fling him out! He's the devil! What a vigil!

After this sort of battle, conducted alone, I approach the theatre. It is as though one had to stoop to go in at a doorway.

Half dazed at first by the gaiety and welcome, relieved, ready to be espoused and assisted, yet once again, as I have said before, what I have done isn't understood *in time*. I explain, but it is not words that are needed, but a more Chinese approach as though the talk were a ritual, and quite other than the essence. My extravagances of language should be taken as the common air of the Characters, allowed to float by unnoticed. They are not meant to be played to be applauded. All I expect is a little hum which though not quite catching the meaning yet catches it backwards. If I hear that, I know how unselfishly the players have played.

But instead hints are blown up. Talks open with the awkwardness of a beginning: no one behaves as though they had known each other well.

Things don't work out that way. But how *how* to work in double harness?

I would be prepared now to print and never be played. Perhaps I cannot bear again the non-communication. What hard and vigilant work!

* * *

Laurian, crossing over to tea, tots up my successes to comfort me. Yes, I have had successes. Is it cowardice that a failure blots them out? But it is the NOW that counts. That woman who printed and gave out in other books and plays has melted away.

'You ought to feel triumphant,' I think she urged. When she had gone I scribbled on a piece of paper:

I am *not* triumphant!
If I wear the habit of triumph it's only like my face-powder.
I wear triumph as one who hasn't seen the rags she wears for
    years.
It's only the hard, furious disregarded armour I wear because
    I have fought so hard.
But oh dear me it's not triumph.

* * *

I am not defeated but let's let up for the moment.
I have never been ill.

There is the strange newness of having something the matter with me. My legs give a little under me: I assume the ridiculous posture of age. I find, as I did at twenty (unequipped and fat) that it makes no difference. I forget myself and my appearance immediately I meet someone I love.

I use a stick. I try crutches. No good. Sticks and crutches

(discarded) are all over the place, slipping with crashes off shiny walls. Now that my eyes are opened to the impudent outrages of arthritis I see that half the village uses sticks.

When they ask me to swallow twenty-one pills a day I throw the lot away. It can't be like that. And now that I have come up against the top dogs in medicine I see they have changed. They are nearer scientists and I am less inclined to trust them. They are all for discoveries and less for me.

I made friends with one of them and he called me 'bizarre'. Why bizarre? I can't be other than I am. It is he who is bizarre. But later I find I am mistaken. It's the old trouble that puts on such broken faces. He was shy.

Now I am to come up against the surgeon who may slip his hand into my pocket and pull out my hip. (I see them do it so often with the knuckle-bone of the gammon. Does the gammon think it easy?)

I have written to him to make a date and at the end of eighteen days he hasn't answered. Is it an escape?

There are other (flighty) solutions. Faith-healing, aquapuncture, an Arab family at Hammamet who cure by signs on the sand. Each friend whose advice I don't take becomes faintly an enemy.

Tucker has a comforting attitude to large illnesses.

'You think you have cancer? Don't worry. You may be run over.'

('Did she have that hip-operation?'
'No. She died of a nose-bleed.')

Meanwhile, hesitating between the correct and the incorrect, the Learned and the wild surmises, I cook with pain, but not with great pain. Oddly enough I am not unhappy.

I am begged to get a woman companion.

What class? What kind? What salary? What rooms? How much with me? How little talk will keep her happy? *Will* she be happy? Shall I?

I am implored to get a woman companion.

I shall get a mastiff bitch.

When Henry died Timothy rang me up and said: 'Put me at the top of the queue to get you a dog.' But no, no, no I wouldn't let him. Now that I wanted a mastiff I knew how high the price would be.

When Ralph Hodgson wanted a dog it had to be a Staffordshire bull terrier, the murdering kind. He would be away a month on a hunting or wooing expedition. He looked at dogs, discarded, travelled, went north, thought it over, sat in pubs, talked it over, got in touch. Finally he knew whether or not he was to pass the next ten years with this or that one; finally came home with what was to make him happy.

I too get in touch, write letters, advertise. (But no one will sell a grown mastiff bitch through a newspaper.) I wriggle out of semi-engagements with other dogs; as I wriggled out of those near-marriages I might have made before I met Roderick.

In the end it's done. I have found her though never seen her. This wouldn't have suited Hodgson but I am at my wit's end. There are no mastiff bitches, fully grown, that anyone will part with. This is the only one. She is coming on Saturday. She is already called Lucy. She is fifteen months. I am preparing as one did before a baby. She is to eat fourteen pounds of bullock's paunch a week – which is untreated tripe. But there is a law against untreated tripe; I can't get it. I order fourteen pounds of treated tripe.

I order garlic pills and leaf plasma because she has been brought up a herbalist. I met a taxi-driver last week (on my way back from three specialists) who cured his wife from arthritis with cloves of garlic. Do we perhaps forget things that might be handy?

Through letters I hear that Lucy is not quite house-trained. Also that she dribbles. Could I use belladonna?

She is a brindle. That is rare. That is how it was four thousand years ago among the Assyrians. And the Romans found them (brindle) among the Saxons. And in the Bayeux tapestry brindle.

While waiting for her, my mind turns on the animal kingdom. The incommunication fascinates me. All over the world there is the most extraordinary secondary life – secondary to humans.

There are animals that I know – dogs, cats, horses. There are animals that I see in herds and flocks, that I eat.

But there are also live things that I look at and that look back at me, from behind a barrier, with incomprehension. The only thing between me and the stickleback is that we are both alive. I look in my pond (my canal) and see a reddish water-lizard with

Charles Laughton (*photograph by Richard*)

Alan Webb and Margaret Leighton in *The Chinese Prime Minister* (*Friedman-Abeles*)

Are Lucy and I cut out for each other?
 (*photographs by Richard*)

terrible eyes. I never put him there. Out of some law he has arrived. I am mesmerized by that eye, small as an eye, big as the sun. The wildest conjectures wave, bodiless, undirected, tendrils trying to find a hook of sense.

'Is it possible to understand? Do we know each other?'

'No,' says the eye, and over it he pulls down a green cover. Like a jewel thrown up from Ali Baba's cave, and which falls, he is gone again.

'The language of birds,' wrote a curate in 1760, 'is very ancient and like other ancient modes of speech, very elliptical; little is said but much is meant and understood.'

But by me nothing is understood. I hear that waking before dawn, that sentinel cry; and in thicket and thorn up comes the music. I hear it in the pillow; it intoxicates me. Why do they do it? I have never been taught about birds. Is it the triumph-shout – 'We have got through *another* night!' It may be. I too heard the owl and his murders. And I smelt the fox.

A vixen has cubs every year in my top field. Why does she come down my garden, deck by deck, at night to the courtyard? Do all foxes lay nightly claims round a house with their urine? Wolves do. A wolf will walk round his acreage spilling a drop on each bush like a surveyor.

These sorts of things I should like to have known.

Till yesterday I didn't know where the moon set. I had rather thought she crossed the sun. But at seven-fifteen in the morning darkness she sank at the side of the windmill. So it was the west. Of course I have looked at her a thousand thousand times but she never mentioned her direction.

I had thought I was unique.

But . . . .

'Does the moon set in the east or the west? *Quick!*' I asked Cuthbert.

'In the east.'

'Diana?'

'I've seen her in the afternoon. . . .'

'*Quick!*'

'In the west.' But she didn't sound certain.

There are flowers I have never seen, extraordinary fringes hanging from petal-blades deep in the Himalayas, more complicated than the Taj Mahal.

Now on the sofa, tired of reading (all those pages I have walked through – unremembered marvels of literature) I look up by accident and from a vase, hanging down, there is the bottom bell on the stalk of the eremurus. It was as structural as a cathedral, not meant to be seen, about to die. Would I dare write down that I *took part* in it? That I became for a second the bell of the eremurus?

Such things don't last; they are flashes and signals.

I turned and took up a book and the page opened by itself: 'If a Sparrow come before my window I *take part* in it for a second and pick about the gravel.' It was Keats who spoke.

'I wish you would believe in God,' wrote Georgina (who is mad about God). To answer her I wrote in pencil: 'I wish it were so I wish it were so I wish it were so' – idly to be thrown into the waste-paper basket. But as it was the pencil (so intimate) and not the typewriter I plunged into verse.

If I had Him I would be kinder, I would sleep better, I would last longer.
If I had God I would not worry my daughter: I would not cry to be remembered.
Yes I know each daffodil is a miracle.
I have lain on the sofa reading when a lily dripping over me from
A high vase tore my eyes from the page.
I looked up in her striped wild cup, past the yellow antlers,
Fascinated, frightened, and after a silence whispered 'Who are you?'
And the lily said – 'After centuries of beauty born every morning
No one knows how it is done.'
I have my hallucinations – as strange as the lily. He who made the lily made me.
They arrived dressed. They arrived in words unalterable because not mine.
I can pick them out of plays I have written. Words threaded together
And shaped curiously that no actress has asked to alter.
As though they had pollen on them.

My mind runs all day long like a television screen gone wild, running upwards.

But suddenly, suddenly, like Kennedy's death, there appears in white a message, unalterable, not mine.

(And yet I cannot include God.)

* * *

(People who push their poems into their autobiographies are perhaps doubtful whether they can publish them any other way.)

* * *

It's true I've never thought about God. I have thought about this incandescence – in me.

My French – and Catholic – son-in-law,* as he goes to Mass must be saying: 'What do these Protestants do with their religion? What, for instance, does my mother-in-law do – so near God?' Well I don't know either. But I trust Him not to be careless. I am good material.

* * *

I contemplate what I have written. How shall I stop? If one doesn't die it doesn't seem finished. Gibbon died.

He pretended at first that he wanted his coming autobiography 'secreted from the public eye till the author shall be removed beyond the reach of criticism or ridicule'. He found as it went on that it was better than he thought and was eager to live to see it printed. But he missed the boat and died.

It fascinated me that he didn't know how to begin. He was so afraid of not capturing 'the image of my character' (after having 'employed words as my servants for so long'). It was Lord Sheffield who chose, from the various beginnings left in a blotter, the one which opens the *Memoirs*.

* * *

Still the surgeon hasn't answered. Still the chance of escape.

* * *

* Comte Pierre d'Harcourt, author of *The Real Enemy*, who spent three years in Buchenwald.

I am unable to garden. One must do something with one's hands; not this eternal reading. I have read the whole (every word) of Henry James, and I know where he keeps his fine dramatic moments far apart by too much handling, and I know where he throws in three similes that are similar, all beautiful but he should have done with one. Towards the end he loved the page too much and slipped up in discipline. I have read half Joseph Conrad and deplore he came under the influence of Henry James. I have read all Trollope for the second time. For a moment I felt, 'Oh if we lived like that now . . . the cartwheels, cocks crowing, gigs bowling, earnest, deferential young men, women like honest gentle lilacs. . . .'

And then 'No! What frustrations and limits and hypocrisy too; and fathers to be obeyed and mothers obeying them, and dark-eyed, resolute clergymen . . . *no*. Better far what we've got. But who could have supposed that in eighty years those cartwheels etc. could change to bombs (the big ones, no use to name them, they will change their names), jungle warfare, hideous flight, the moon, and with the moon strange ambitions, possible ambitions, telepathy, L.S.D., and a blink at God. Not their God, not Trollope's.'

I have crashed through a hundred and forty-three Simenons. I have read Kilvert's *Diary** and wonder what Freud would have thought about his passion for bottoms, so innocently said, little passions like fires dropped in among the black mountains.

* * *

I learn to crochet. With a grimace I take to the opium of the twitching hook.

* * *

She has come. Lucy has come.

She has a sooty mask, an enormous head, and tiger stripes. About the size of a Shetland pony.

She is grave. I was so afraid of a joyous dog.

Timothy has sent me a pure gold disc worked with a wreath and my address on it for her chain-collar. It was designed by his daughter (and my granddaughter) Annabel. So, very elegantly, he has equalled the price of the dog.

* Robert Francis Kilvert, 1840–79

We have spent our first night. She wept. Hour after hour in my bathroom she wept. I slept from six-thirty till seven.
We have spent our third and fourth nights. We start on our fifth. She is still weeping. She accepts midnight chocolate from my hand and weeps on. On this fifth night – desperate – I have taken a slipper to her. All is quiet.
It is true Lucy is not quite house-trained.
Why did I write of the freedom of the very early morning, of my attempts at non-responsibility so that I might 'perceive' that desired landscape? Now I tremble in my bed before the alarm clock goes at what I shall find in my bathroom.
The troubles of the nursery begin again. The child won't eat.
Of the fourteen pounds of dressed tripe not one bite has been taken. Ox heart, ox cheek, pig's kidney, pig's liver, the sack full of vitaminized meal with which she arrived – nothing.
Nothing but chocolate crunchies. After six days she is staggering. I get the vet. He says it's psychological. (The couch again.)
I stick a long piece of cooked bacon in my mouth to show her that she and I have eating in common. It works. She leans forward and the black velvet drapes accept it. She wants more. . . . So it is *cooked* food! Against all the raw-food-laws I hurriedly fry up everything. She eats.
Why doesn't she follow me out of rooms? What second neurosis is this? I say 'Come'. At that she leans back against a wall, knowing her weight, and extending without moving. I pull and she recedes inside her skin.
How can she roll her eyes and look at me with total adoration and behave like a rusted-up tank? All the arts of rulership (of dog and man) that I have learnt are set at naught. When I am gentle with her she never gives in. If I make my voice rough she shuts her mind for the day. The smallest rebuke makes her lose her head. One has to find a special tone mixed with humour. It has to sound like a joke. I can't use chocolate all the time: it's degrading.
Is it self-indulgent to write about one's dog? Or is it comic that after all the people I have known one has arrived at this intense companion?
There is nothing cosmic. Think of tiny things, dew on ivy, small surprises, particles of living. It's by the tiny-personal that

we make what can be universally understood. (*Make* something of your dog, your age. They're usable.)

Two months have gone by. Lucy loves me but she would not defend me.

Thus spake AHURA MAZDA the Creator:

> I have made the dog self-clothed and self-shod, watchful, wakeful and sharp-toothed, born to take his food from man and to watch over man's goods. And whosoever shall wake at his voice, neither shall the thief nor the wolf steal anything from his house without being warned; the wolf shall be smitten and torn to pieces.... For no house could subsist on the earth made by AHURA but for these two dogs of mine, the shepherd's dog and the house dog. (Zoroaster 300 BC.)*

The wolf would not be torn to pieces by Lucy.

This curious sombre dog believes in the devil.

From the moment she arrived she would not go into a room that she had not first read with her nose. Floor, rugs, legs of chairs, soft corners of sofas, everything was carefully smelt. Then she settled, sure there was no devil.

She was wrong. There was a devil.

Last night she caught her chain-collar in the leg of a small chair. Tossing her head in terror the chair leapt like a jockey on her back. She jumped the gramophone, broke two legs off a stool, smashed a dome of glass so that the bride's bouquet of camellias, airtight within for a hundred years, evaporated in dust. This morning she came down and turned the room upside down, searching with her hard nose under rugs, throwing them over, for a sign of the devil.

And now in my writing-room it has happened again.

She caught her foot in the telephone lead and threw the room in an uproar, screaming like a baby. The telephone was smashed to pieces and the other extensions put out of action; the small notes in my files flew about like pigeons. I can see that she is beginning to connect me with the furniture-attack. Have I got to live with a neurotic coward? But now that I love her what can I do?

Does she love me? At least she loves no one else.

It's not a doglike love. No welcomings. On returning home

* P. M. Sykes' *History of Persia*. Page 113.

not a sound in the empty house. A listening silence. She is buried beneath fears and decisions. 'Might it be the devil and not Lady J? I will hide in my bed and Lady J will come to me.' She names me as Gladys Cooper once did because she hasn't got under my skin.

'Don't you ever talk to him?' Tucker asked once (of Henry). He knew I didn't. Henry got rather mute and perhaps too early deaf because he didn't hear my voice enough. But it didn't spoil the love. Dogs make shift with anything for love.

I must do better with Lucy. In the long hours of writing I forget her. But when I call her she takes so long to move. She is filled with long lumbering thoughts about which end should get up first. It's like calling Henry James.

* * *

I have been inquisitive about growing old long before I was old, i.e. at sixty. At that time Roderick was living and I had yet to put on a successful play on Broadway, yes and I had yet to fall in love with Charles Laughton.

Above all, I was agog to describe my decline. Each time I looked in the glass and saw the curiosities of another bit of writing on my face they seemed to be leading somewhere. Like the Rosetta Stone. A sort of clue.

And as for death one gets used to it, even if it's only other people's death you get used to. The grave digger doesn't speak the same language as the man he puts in. (And there is that cynical alleviation to unanswered letters. I remember when Sybil Colefax died I owed her a letter.)

I don't know what evaporates in age. Movement and speed, of course. But one adapts oneself. Appearance? Well yes: but one should look new in age. There should be a sirensuit of exquisite comfort; zipped, so that one single movement frees you from the melancholy of a hundred thousand dressings and undressings. The thing I feared to lose is not gone. The tactile suprises, the sensual love of the garden. Bare feet on grass, the heat of the cobbles after shade, the cold pool behind the fuchsia hedge where I bathe naked. I have more time. I am not pushed and hurried off a sensation. Last summer I wrote: 'Here today the magic is standing over me like a rainbow. The day is kneeling on the earth, the white buddleia never moves. Only the birds thread this extraordinary immobility. I got into our pool last night and the water all but fizzled. I waded about among dead moths with wings outspread and felt translated with happiness like being sixteen.' – I was about to be seventy-nine. (Oh, Desmond, why did you make yourself so unhappy?)

I once asked a very old gentleman (and he was deaf) across a luncheon table what it was like to be very old.

'Routine,' he twinkled, 'Just as good as love.'

But only a man can install routine. Much alone and independent – very slowly I may become a man.

One is afraid of no one. I wouldn't be afraid of Harold Macmillan. (Perhaps of Churchill.) A flicker, out of habit, of Cyril Connolly. Why Cyril? Because in that strange ugly mug I descry genius. I have always known it. And there is something uncertain, like a collie, about genius. I fear the whip that flicks out in his talk because he too knows it. But it is better, though a thousand times more painful, to be a genius manqué than a talented man.

I went to London on Friday. . . .

These last pages become a diary. I have pulled up the past and now we are in the Now.

I went to London on Friday for the Duff Cooper Memorial party, still (for the thirteenth year) held at my house. The tables are still there in the drawing-room where I made such a wail over the Japanese princes. I accepted the past as covered with dust.

At that moment the house was trembling in the grip of its sale. No one knew what I knew – that this must be the last party, the last sight of the house.

The party was as each year. Diana's face as beautiful; lightly touched with sadness. Cecil Day Lewis gave Roy Fuller the Duff Cooper prize for his poetry. I wished I had been brought up (in the country) with Cecil Day Lewis.

I told Cyril that I had spoken of him in my autobiography.

'I don't mind,' he said, speaking kindly.

'I said I was afraid of you.'

'There's nothing to be afraid of,' he said. (But he is wrong.) 'You should say you knew me when I was very young and had no money and was a sponge.'

'You were young and had no money, not even the fare to

London to end your visit with us at Rottingdean. But you sent back the three pounds I lent you two days later.'

It's not middle age that has mellowed Cyril but because he has a child he loves. The most barbed and rebellious young men make this reversal. I should have loved to have seen him get the Duff Cooper prize in my drawing-room; but he wrote *The Unquiet Grave* at the wrong time.

* * *

Violet dead*.

And how marvellous that televised, that week-old immortality, as though a bird had shaken off her body and returned. She was a plain and brilliant girl when I first knew her (at Antoine's) and now how blossoming and glorious that last lovely flutter of her strong wings. How moving the power with which she held the stage. How moving when the power went in fatigue, roundabout where she said: 'And what about Shakespeare?'

* * *

In all these pages I have hardly mentioned my children; I haven't spoken of the gaiety and anxiety, the long thoughts in the night, the worry and the fun. I haven't said that three of them had each two marriages, scrambling out of one and getting into another; or that one of them had special difficulties and with steadfastness and gallantry overcame them. To speak of them – to speak of me and them – would need another book.

Nor have I mentioned, or barely, my seven grandchildren, Annabel, Alexander, Romily, Harriet, Thierry, Victoria, Rebecca. Don't imagine they are unobserved, but they too would need another book.

I began all this to write about myself. It was meant to stop at thirty. Then I was led on, fascinated, into marriage.

If I don't write of the four 'children' who are all my world it is delicacy. They will excuse me.

Their kindness to me was unexpected. Why? Because in the adolescent battles and irritations (for them) it was difficult to distinguish the young, hard, unalterable, unmeltable love they felt. *Family* love. This is something everyone now is prepared to throw away. They are asses.

I now value *only* their opinion. All the travellers of my life go

* Violet Bonham Carter.

past me, deeply occupied with themselves. But I have this one woman and these three men who can't forget me. 'Can't because it's impossible. My experience is that I shall return to them as they grow old, as my father and mother have returned to me. It matters from whom you are ejected. No envelope so close. It's not the bringing up, it's not even the love, it's the womb and the penis which lock you into the line where you belong.

There is a rope of continuity not to be disregarded. It seems to move both ways. When waking suddenly I have sometimes mistaken Laurian, in thought, for my mother. I hardly know as we grow older which way the parenthood lies.

Should one say these things? Yet everything is precious, anything may be a discovery. It is an extraordinary literary liberation to be old. You have not got to decide.

I have also a curious tenderness for my unknown forefathers. The sense of the family group pacifies me in this overfilled world.

'. . . We fill up the silent vacancy that precedes our birth.' Gibbon again.

There used to be an uppish expression – 'my people'. You find it in Harold Nicolson. But I mean it more as in Arthur Grimble, in *A Pattern of Islands*. I could envy the consanguineous club of his savages, not excluding the annointed skulls.

'He pointed to a rectangle of coral slabs planted edgewise beside his dwelling. "See there!" he said. "That was the shrine of my ancestors. My father's skull was buried there, and his father's, and his father's fathers for five generations. I saw them near me as I lay down to sleep; every evening I went down and annointed them with oil; and I spoke to them, and they answered me and I was happy with them. Thus it was until those men came and took them away from me."'

* * *

This morning the surgeon has replied and made a date. How horrible and yet it's like being engaged.

Index

Albery, Donald, 273, 274
Alger, grandfather, 6-8, 11
Alger, grandmother, 3, 5-11, 13, 18, 26, 55, 102, 154, 157
Amery, Rt. Hon. Leopold, P.C., C.H., 176
Ashcroft, Dame Peggy, D.B.E., 257
Asquith, General the Honble Arthur, D.S.O., 165, 169
Asquith, the Honble Mrs (Betty), 165, 169
Asquith, the Lady Cynthia, 37, 120, 169
Asquith, Elizabeth, 125, 126, 201
Asquith, Herbert, H. (1st Earl of Oxford and Asquith), 127, 197
Asquith, Margot, The Countess of Oxford and Asquith, 156, 197, 202, 211, 227
Asquith, Michael and Simon, 169
Asquith, the Lady Violet, Baroness Asquith of Yarnbury, 120, 168, 185, 187, 207, 287
Austin, Lyn, 264, 265

Bagnold, Alexis (Uncle Lexy), 46, 47, 48, 91, 274
Bagnold, Alice (aunt), 46, 47
Bagnold, Col. Arthur Henry, C.B., C.M.G., 1-6, 10-13, 15-21, 23, 24, 26, 27, 29, 35-42, 45-48, 50, 52, 54-59, 63-65, 75, 77, 86, 91, 92, 96, 100-5, 112, 115-17, 121, 123, 124, 135, 137, 193, 247
Bagnold, Clara (aunt), 46, 47, 48, 91

Bagnold, Mrs Ethel, 2-9, 11, 12, 13, 16-21, 23-27, 29, 34-38, 40, 46, 47, 48, 50, 51, 52, 54-57, 62-65, 91, 92, 104-6, 112, 117, 121, 137, 222
Bagnold, grandmother, 46
Bagnold, John (great-uncle), 42
Bagnold, General Michael Edward (grandfather), 40-3, 45, 46
Bagnold, Brig. Ralph Alger, O.B.E., F.R.S., 8, 11, 13, 15, 19, 21, 29, 40, 54, 110, 112
Bagnold, Thomasin (great-grandmother), 42-43
Bagnold, Thomas (great-uncle), 40-42, quoted, 43, 44, 45; 46
Baring, the Honble Maurice, 28, 163, 167, 168, 209, 210-14
Beaton, Cecil, 212, 227, 228, 231, 232
Beaumont, Hugh (Binkie), 119, 219, 220, 231, 235, 243, 244, 246, 255, 267, 268, 269, 273
Beaverbrook, Lord, P.C., 156
Beerbohm, Sir Max, 88, 95, 96, 97, 98
Bellingham-Smith, Hugh, 83, 85
Belloc, Hilaire, 167, 211
Bernstorff, Count Albrecht, 180, 181, 184, 185-90
Besant, Mrs Annie, 89
Bibesco, Prince Antoine, 104, 114-28, 137, 181, 185, 200-7, 242, 253
Bibesco, Prince Emmanuel, 118-26, 143, 202, 204, 205, 206, 211
Bibesco, Princesse Marthe, 119, 206, 207, 208
Bibesco, Priscilla, 126, 204
Bismarck, Prince Otto von, 188, 190

Bismarck, Princess Otto von, 190
Blanche (maid to Princesse Marthe Bibesco), 207, 208
Bland, Hubert, 55
Bonham-Carter, Sir Maurice, K.C.B., K.C.V.O., 207
Bonham-Carter, the Lady Violet, D.B.E., *see* Asquith, the Lady Violet
Boris, Georges, 104, 115, 122
Botha, General the Rt. Honble Louis, 176
Bottomley, Horatio, 91
Boyd, Phyllis, 104
Brandt, Carol (of Brandt and Brandt), 232
Brome, Vincent, quoted 88, 92
Budberg, the Baroness (Moura), 132, 134
Budge, Sir Ernest Alfred Wallis, 54
Burne-Jones, Sir Edward, 163, 164
Burne-Jones, Lady, 164
Burnham, Olive, Viscountess, 139, 161
Byam-Shaw, Glen, C.B.E., 242–5

Caledon, Eric, 5th Earl of, 105
Camrose, the Viscountess, 161
Capote, Truman, 234
Carmi, Maria, 104
Carson, Sir Edward, 165
Casati, the Marchesa, 104
Casson, Sir Lewis, M.C., 144
Chamberlain, J. Austen, 189
Charpiot, Mademoiselle Ruth, 36
Charteris, Vere, 83–5
Claire, Ina, 256, 257, 264
Cold Spring House, Jamaica, 15–18, 21
Colefax, Lady, 195, 285
Conan Doyle, Mary, 28
Connolly, Cyril, 91, 108, 286–7
Cooper, Sir Alfred Duff (1st Viscount Norwich), P.C., K.C.M.G., D.S.O., 104, 105, 163, 214, 215
Cooper, the Lady Diana, 104, 113, 114, 132, 152, 153, 163, 173, 190, 202, 203, 212, 213, 214, 215, 217, 231, 232, 257, 279, 286
Cooper, Dame Gladys, D.B.E., 227, 229, 230–34, 267, 268, 285
Coquelin, 35
Coward, Noël, 214, 234, 245
Cravath, Paul, 178
Cukor, George, 228–30, 232, 271

Cunard, Lady, 215
Cunard, Nancy, 104
Cust, Harry, 151–3
Cust, Nina, 151–3
Cutmore, F. B., 146, 147, 149, 150, 157, 198

Davies, W. H., 79, quoted 80, 81
Day-Lewis, Cecil, C.B.E., 286
Deakin, Miss, 34
Degas, quoted 49, 108
d'Erlanger, the Baroness Catherine, 102–13, 118, 206, 268
d'Erlanger, the Baron Emile, 103, 104, 105, 112
de Vilmorin, Louise, 215
d'Harcourt, Comte Anne-Pierre, 281
d'Harcourt, Harriet, 287
d'Harcourt, Thierry, 287
Dogs, the,
    Edward, toy Manchester terrier, 195, 196
    Henry, toy Manchester terrier, 195, 196, 285
    Jacob, fox terrier, 193
    Lucy, brindle mastiff, 279, 282–5
    Mary, bulldog bitch, 193, 194
    Nell, Welsh terrier, 12
    Togo, fox terrier, 12
    Zoë, bull mastiff, 195, 196
Donaldson, Sir Frederick and Lady, 57, 58, 61, 62
Douglas, Lord Alfred, 88
Drogheda, Kathleen, Countess of, C.B.E., 104
Duff, the Lady Juliet, 212
Duleep Singh, Princess Pauline, 162
du Paty de Clam, Colonel, 54
Durant, Susan, 49

Eastman, Miss (of Villa Léona, Neuilly), 35, 36
Eastwood, Geoffrey, 181
Ede, James Chuter, quoted 66, 67, 68, 69, 70, 86
Elliott, Mrs, 164
Epps, Daisy, 23
Epstein, Sir Jacob, K.B.E., 70, 155
Evans, Dame Edith, D.B.E., 235, 257, 266–72
Evans, Miss (governess), 13, 19

Faulker, Mrs ('Tanta'), 176
Finney, Albert, 240
Fleming, Evelyn, 135
Fontanne, Lynn, 144, 246, 247, 253-6
Foord-Kelsey, Kitty, 59
Freedman, Harold, 218-20, 234, 246, 252
Freedman, May, 244
Fuller, Roy, 286

Gattey, Mademoiselle, 19
Gaudier-Brzeska, Henry (Pik), 65-70, 87, 131
Gaudier-Brzeska, Sophie (Zosik), 65-70
Ghyka, Prince Matila, 104, 120
Gibb, William, 176
Gielgud, Sir John, 235, 240, 243, 244, 245, 257
Gilman, Harold, 73
Gladstone, the Viscountess, 137
Gosse, Silvia, 73
Great-Aunts: Bertha Snell, 9, 10
Lizzie, 9, 10
Mary Grace, 9, 10
Guest, Capt. the Honble Frederick, C.B.E., D.S.O., 107

Harris, Frank, 87-100, 109, 120, 131, 239
Hauser, Frank, 274
Hayes, Cecil, 96
Heinemann, William, 128
Hemming, Lady (wife of Governor of Jamaica), 20
Henson, Mrs Violet, *see* Dolly Tylden
Hewlett, Pia, 28
Hill, Lieutenant, 56
Hobson, Thayer, 171
Hodgson, Amelia, 79
Hodgson, Ralph, 72, 77, 79, 82, 83, 84, 85, 88, 96, 102, 108, 128, 150, 156, 278
Hoesch, Herr von, 180, 188-91
Horner, Lady, 152, 198
Horridge, Mr Justice, 94
Hudson, Lady, 161
Hudson, Sir Robert, G.B.E., 161
Hulton, Sir Edward and Lady, 70
Huxley, Aldous, 24, 29
Huxley, Sir Julian, F.R.S., M.A., 24, 29

Huxley, Mrs Leonard, 24, 25, 29, 30, 31, 32
Huxley, Leonard, 29, 32
Huxley, Trev., 24

James, Henry, 199, 207, 209, 269, 282, 286
James, Julia, 104
Jameson, Sir Leander Starr, 176
Jekyll, Lady, 31
Jekyll, Pamela and Barbara, 31
Joel, Wolfie, 91
John, Augustus, O.M., R.A., 104
Johns, Glynis, 217
Johnson, Jules, 254
Jones, Alexander, 288
Jones, Annabel, 195, 196, 239, 282, 287
Jones, Dominick (Tucker), 148, 168, 211, 245, 250, 262, 263, 277, 285
Jones, Laurian, 117, 143, 147, 148, 159, 170, 193, 194, 199, 211, 217, 245, 265, 276, 288
Jones, Rebecca, 287
Jones, Richard, 145, 148, 171, 245, 275
Jones, Romily, 287
Jones, Sir Roderick, K.B.E., 1, 9, 28, 39, 99, 109, 126, 132, 135-47, 149, 150, 151, 153, 154, 156-65, 168-70, 172-9, 181, 182, 184-7, 189, 190, 191, 194, 197, 203, 211, 216, 217, 224, 225, 232-5, 245-50, 285
Jones, Timothy, 114, 148, 170, 174, 175, 182, 192, 194, 199, 211, 239, 240, 245, 277, 282
Jones, Victoria, 287
Jordan, Edith, 36

Kelly, Felix, 243
Kemsley, the Viscountess, 161
Keppel, Violet (now Violet Trefusis), 136
Kerr, Walter, quoted 263, 270-2
King, Cecil (Harmsworth), 246
Kingsmill, Hugh (Lunn), 67, 90, 91, 94
Kipling, Rudyard, 163, 168, 193, 194, 195, 197
Kipling, Carrie, 194
Kitchener of Khartoum, Field-Marshal Earl, K.G., K.P., G.C.B., O.M., 61, 87
Korda, Sir Alexander, 87
Krishnamurtri, Jiddu, 89-90
Kruger, Paul, 176

Lahovary, Marguerite, 121, 122, 126
Lanchester, Elsa, 239, 241
Laughton, Charles, 238–41, 285
Lehmann, Rosamond, 108, 119
Leighton, Margaret, 257–64
Lemoine, 91
Lessore, Thérèse, 73, 75
Lewis, Elizabeth, 164–8
Lewis, Sir George, 109, 163–6
Lewis, Georgie, 164, 166
Lewis, Lady (Marie), 163–8
Lewis, Peggy, 164
Lovat Fraser, Claud, 64–6, 68–73, 75, 76, 79, 83, 85–88, 101, 102, 107, 131, 156, 201
Lovat, Lady (Laura), 209, 213, 214
Low, David, 132
Lunt, Alfred, 246, 253–6, 262
Lunt, Mrs, see Lynn Fontanne
Lutyens, Sir Edwin Landseer, O.M., 151, 153–6
Lynn, Olga, 212

MacCarthy, Sir Desmond, F.R.S.I., Hon. D.Litt, Hon. LL.D., 46, 109, 111, 125, 126, 128–30, 135, 150, 156, 181, 185, 187, 196–201, 209, 214, 222, 285
MacCarthy, Molly, 196, 197
McEvoy, Ambrose, 73
Macfall, Haldane, 65, 67–8, 69, 86, 95
McHardy, 147–9, 193
McIndoe, Sir Archibald, C.B.E., 57, 236–8
McKenna, Siobhan, 227, 230, 231
Main, Molly, 4
Manners, Lady Diana, see Cooper, the Lady Diana
Mansfield, Katherine, 66, 86–9
Marre, Albert, 232, 233
Marsh, Rupert, 119, 244
Matalon, Vivian, 269–70, 271
Maugham, Fredk. Herbert, 1st Viscount Maugham of Hartfield, 155
Maugham, Robin, 2nd Viscount, 155
Maupassant, Guy de, 90
Maurois, André, K.B.E., 168
Mayer, Louis B., 218
Miles, Eustace, Vegetarian Restaurant, 77, 79, 82, 88, 131
Mimi (ex-valet-housemaid to Herr von Hoesch), 190, 191
Mitford, the Honble Nancy, 203

Montagu, Cardie, 134, 183
Moore, Henry, O.M., 154, 239
Morand, Paul, 104, 115
Morrell, the Lady Ottoline, 104, 106 111
Mounet-Sully, 35
Mount Edgcumbe, Earl of, 10
Murat, the Princess Marie, 104
Murray, Prof, Gilbert, O.M., D.Litt., D.C.L., LL.D., 28, 31
Murray, the Lady Mary, 31
Murray, Rosalind, 28, 89
Murry, John Middleton, 67, 86–8

Napier, the Honble Mark, 177
Nesbit, E., 55
Nesbitt, Cathleen, 253
Neurach, Herr von, 180
Neurotsos, Emma, 31
Nicholson, Sir William, 164
Nicolson, the Honble Sir Harold, K.C.V.O., C.M.G., 157, 158, 181, 188, 289
Northcliffe, Viscount, 138, 156, 159–61, 246
Northcliffe, Viscountess, see Lady Hudson
Noyes, Frank, 175

Olivier, Sir Laurence, 240, 241
Olivier, Sir Sydney and Lady, 22
their daughters, 22, 23

Painter, George, 121, 204
Pankhurst, Emmeline, 32
Peto, Ruby, 104
Playfair, Nigel, 71
Preece, Sir William, K.C.B., F.R.S., 115, 116
Pritchett, V. S., 52
Proust, Marcel, 121, 127, 204
Pryde, James, 72, 95, 96

Queenie, the donkey, 20, 22

Rattigan, Terence, 271
Reading, 1st Marquis of (Viceroy of India), 164
Reith, Lord, 216
Reuter, Baron Herbert de, 177
Reuter, Baron Oliver de, 162
Reuters, 140, 142, 143, 147, 158, 159, 175, 177, 216

Reveille's, 135, 136, 138
Ribbentrop, Joachim von, 188, 189
Richardson, Sir Ralph, 243-5
Riddell, Lord, 156
Rider, Dan, 86
Roberts, Field Marshal Earl, 103
Rogers, Claude M., O.B.E., 75
Rosebery, 6th Earl of, 213
Ross, Robert, 128, 129
Rumbold, Hugo, 104-7, 112
Russell, Bertrand, 3rd Earl, O.M., F.R.S., 109, 112
Russell, the Honble Conrad, 212
Rutherston, Albert, 72, 73
Rutherston, Sir John, 70

Sackville, Victoria, Lady, 135, 136
Sackville-West, The Honble Victoria (Vita), C.H., 156, 181
Sands, Ethel, 29, 269
Selznick, David, 218
Selznick, Irene Mayer, 218, 220-36
Shaw, George Bernard, 55, 61, 189, 269, quoted 95, 96
Shumlin, Herman, 217, 261
Sickert, Walter, 64, 65, 72-5, 77, 78, 80, 104, 156, 266
Sidgwick, Ethel, 31
Sieff, Israel Moses, Baron, 170
Siemens, Frances, 29
Simpson, Joseph, 95, 96
Slattery, 82
Smuts, Field-Marshal Rt. Hon. Jan Christian, O.M., C.H., K.C., 9, 176, 182
Smyth, Dame Ethel, 211
Stevens, Roger, 256, 259, 264
Strathcona and Mount Royal (Donald), Baron, 180, 181
Stuyvesant Fish, Carola, 36
Suggia, cellist, 129

Tait, Archibald Campbell (Archbishop of Canterbury from 1868-82), 176
Tarver, Captain, 14
Taubman, Howard, 263
Taylor, Elizabeth, 170
Thesiger, Ernest, 244

Thomas, Edward, 79
Thorndike, Dame Sybil, D.B.E., 144, 212
Todd, Ann, 212
Tonks, Professor (Head of Slade School of Art), 75
Townsend, Major, 22
Tree, Sir Herbert Beerbohm, 163
Tylden, Dolly, 60, 61-3, 65-8, 87, 88, 101, 107
Tylden, General, 60, 63
Tynan, Kenneth, quoted 235, 236

Usher, Lieutenant, 21
Ustinov (Klop), father of Peter, 181

Verey, the Rev. Lewis, 167
Vernon-Harcourts, the, 29
Voysey, Charles Francis Annesley (architect), 30
Vuillard, Edouard, 118, 127

Waley, Arthur, 157
Walton, Alan, 153, 154
Ward, Georgina, 154, 254, 280
Ward, Mrs Humphry, 29, 30
Webb, Alan, 258, 260, 261, 262, 269-71
Weinthal, Leo, 176
Wellington, the Duke of, 154
Wells, H. G., quoted 130; 131-4, 188
Marjorie, his daughter-in-law, 134
West, Dame Rebecca, D.B.E., C.B.E., 131, 187
Wetzlar-Coit, Margie, 25
Wills, great-grandparents, 9, 10
Wilson, Sir Matthew ('Scatters'), 182-4
Wimborne, Ivor Churchill Guest, 1st Viscount, 107, 138, 171
Woolf, Leonard and Virginia, 182, 184
Worsley, T. C., 59, 210, 271, 279, quoted 272

Zuckerman, Sir Solly, K.C.B., F.R.S., 239